THE
ENDLESS
HARVEST

JOHN SABURO YAMAMOTO

ISBNs:
Hardcover: 978-1-64184-833-6
Paperback: 978-1-64184-834-3
Ebook: 978-1-64184-835-0

Conversion Publishing LLC

XMAS 2022

CONTENTS

NOTE TO READER

Welcome!

My name is John Yamamoto, and I have written this book specifically for *you*.

This book is for working men and women, business owners, retirees, and anyone looking to have their money work for them instead of working for their money. If this is you, you are interested in growing a bountiful harvest that never ends.

The tactics and strategies mentioned in this book are cultivated from decades of real-life experience with clients and endless years of personal development. I say *"we" in this book* because this is a journey you and I will be taking together. Think of me as your knowledgeable and friendly guide who will walk shoulder-to-shoulder with you as you learn how to grow an endless financial harvest.

"The secret to financial freedom is to become a cash flow millionaire." All businesses survive or die based on cash flow. The business fails if more cash flow is going out than coming in. Therefore, the lifeblood is cash flow.

All of the stories inside are about real people. For their privacy, I have changed details like their names. These case studies show you real-life scenarios and profits/losses from their investment and life decisions.

Together, we will help you plant and maintain an Endless Harvest of financial freedom. Let's begin!

"It is not cash that makes you financially free. It's cash flow."

– John Yamamoto

Special thanks to my wife, Yvonne, and daughter, Jillian, for their support while writing this book.

Also, thanks and appreciation to Andrew Izumi for his work on making this book exceptional.

PREFACE

BECOMING A CASH FLOW MILLIONAIRE

"Run your investments like a business. Maximize the cash flow."
– John Yamamoto

Why are we talking about money? Money is one of the most critical topics in our lives. It is highly influential and drives many of our emotions.

If we can successfully manage our money, it allows us to control our emotions. We are constantly trying to control our finances to control our emotions.

This book will tell you exactly how to finally gain complete control over your finances. As mathematical and straightforward as money can be, it also seems driven by our ups and downs. That is why *The Endless Harvest* will tell you the mathematical and emotional way to grow your wealth. You will be a better investor if you can control your cash flow. One of the most significant hazards to wealth is the desire for more. The desire for more leads to impatience. Impatience leads to mistakes. I wrote this book to guide you towards permanent and endless wealth and to help you avoid traps and pitfalls along the way.

I want to begin by giving you a short scenario:

A parent is dropping off their daughter at a university out of town. Their child is living away from home for the first time. They make sure to leave a city map for their daughter to navigate around town. They do not want her to get lost. Their daughter is constantly getting lost for the next week and cannot find her way around the city.

Looking closely, she sees the problem. The map is from 1974. Her parents gave her a map from when they went to university. How often do we give our children incorrect maps of the financial world? We teach them the ways we learned to manage money. We often learn about our money management methods or financial map from our parents.

A financial plan is like a map of our financial future. It provides valuable insight into our future. Like a map, it has to be based on current reality. Changes have made financial maps of the past obsolete. We need to update our financial maps constantly.

Consider 1993, interest rates on bonds were paying 9%, while today they are paying 2%. People in the 1950s lived much shorter lives than in 2020 and beyond. The cost of living is much higher in dollar terms than ten or twenty years ago. It makes sense that your financial map should be adjusted every year to be current.

An important lesson is unlearning outdated investment ideas that you may be following. Unlearning in the 21st century is as important as learning.

The Endless Harvest is your 21st-century map to get from someone who works hard for a living every day (not that there is any shame in this) to someone who is on the right path to financial freedom provided by investment cash flow or passive income. This book will give you the four steps to grow your money tree and harvest it for life.

In today's day and age, it seems like we are all working hard towards retirement. The reality is that many of us have to keep working long after we want to. The truth is that many of us see life as a never-ending hamster wheel.

The Endless Harvest is your guide to:

1. Maximizing cash flow
2. Gaining wealth
3. Maintaining wealth
4. Growing wealth

You've likely noticed there are many types of finance books available. You may see books on:

- Cryptocurrency and how to make $100,000 in 10 days.
- Following the technology boom and cashing in on data mining.
- The oil industry and its volatile past, present, and future.
- Building a portfolio and day trading.

I'm writing to you saying, *This is not that kind of book.* In the pages ahead, you will learn my simple three-step process to acquiring the type of wealth you want in your current economy and passively maintaining your income throughout retirement. I do not promise to make you $1 million, $10 million, or $1 billion. (Although many of you will get to these numbers.) I promise to help you define your realistic goals and map out a concrete way to get there.

This method has worked for so many of my clients and continues to be successful today. I'll even show you real-life case studies of different situations. Although everyone has different circumstances, you can use this method to achieve a prosperous lifestyle.

To give you an idea, this has worked for:

- Clients who have hundreds of thousands of dollars and want to multiply their income.
- Clients nearing bankruptcy and needed to dig themselves out of a hole.
- Clients who were hit hard by some unforeseen circumstances and got back on track.
- Clients who lost all of their income and came out the other side better than before.
- Clients who lost their spouse and needed help keeping up their living standards.

The list goes on as I've been working with people for decades. The reason I am writing this book is for *you*. I know I can't help everyone one-on-one, so I've written this book to give you the tools to succeed. In the last section, I'll even teach you how to hire your financial team to help you achieve success.

Many investment books and even advisors create additional stress in your life. New numbers to evaluate, different strategies to implement, and confusing terminology you don't understand. We are doing the opposite here. Whether you have a prestigious University degree or have only graduated high school, that will be enough to understand the principles ahead.

Investing is when your money works for you, not you working for your money. This is the foundation of *The Endless Harvest*. Money should run itself. We are going to learn to work smarter, not harder.

INTRODUCTION

The Endless Harvest is written from what I have learned from decades of experience in the finance world. Mathematically, finance may seem easy, but the reality is that finances are one of the hardest things in life to manage. Additionally, finances are one of the most important things to manage. That's why we are talking about finance.

In this book, I will describe the experiences and lessons I have passed along to clients. These are real-life examples I have learned and then taught. Finance and money are a part of everyone's life. This is true whether you have millions in the bank or live paycheck-to-paycheck.

The first thing we'll do is describe precisely who *The Endless Harvest* is for. This method is not for everyone. This method is for people who want to be comfortable and stable with their finances. That being said, you don't have to be passionate about finance like me. You only have to understand the importance of money.

You are the RIGHT person to read this book if you:

- Understand that money is an essential part of life to achieve what you want.
- Desire to retire with passive income and not have to work an active job till the end.
- Want to live life comfortably rather than live in financial debt.
- Are willing to set up a system enabling you to remove risk and enhance savings.
- Feel like a hamster running on an endless wheel and want to use financial momentum to get ahead.

Alternatively, you may need to read this book if you:

- Want to spend all your money and have no financial safety cushion.
- Don't care about how much things cost and spend uncontrollably.
- Cannot control your emotions and let them control your actions.

- Won't take advantage of the most powerful mathematical formula, compounding.
- Are looking to get rich quickly by taking huge risks, like gambling in Las Vegas.

The lessons applied throughout this book are not limited to the amount of money you have in your bank account. These lessons are limited to your mindset and what you are willing to commit to. If you are set in your ways and are not open to new advice, you can close this book now. But if you want to grow your wealth, apply proven principles, and be more financially healthy than ever, keep reading.

Most people I speak to are in one of two categories. Either they have had an urgent or unexpected circumstance that has put them at a considerable financial disadvantage, or they are very financially stable and want to ensure their wealth continues to grow throughout their retirement.

Although these two situations seem like opposites, the same principles are applied to grow wealth. The rate at which your wealth grows is only limited by your initial investment or principal dollar figure. There is one common trait I find with my clients. They are all either burnt out or stressed from the endless hours of active working. Active working can also be a 9-5 job, with endless hours of consulting or punching the clock every day.

The Endless Harvest will grant you the desire for freedom. Why invest money? To become free from the prison of debt and poverty. Although money is a desired asset for almost everyone, debts can be a prison for most. The need to have more money, pay our bills, and put food on the table can be stressful for anyone. Money is the source of both happiness and worry.

No matter which emotion you are feeling, it's not your fault. Even in my previous years of education, I never learned the importance of money and how it worked. All I knew was that money existed as a finite resource. But this is where we have been misled. Money does not have to be a limited resource. Abundance does apply to the concept of money, and I am here to teach you how to see it as endless.

Through gaining, maintaining, and growing your wealth, you can grow your very own money tree. And, even if you don't want to grow it yourself, we'll talk about how to hire a team to grow your tree for you. Don't skip ahead to this later section in the book, though, as you must understand the fundamentals. You don't have to perform all the actions of growing a tree, but you do have to know the fundamentals of how it grows.

There is one huge reason I have written this specific book, which applies no matter where you are in your lifespan. This reason is the real danger of outliving your money. Nobody thinks of this when they have a job or the cash is rolling in. But the danger is here and present.

I have seen too many people work hard their entire life yet retire without the cash to live in style. After a lifetime of work, people should be free to do what they desire in retirement.

Traveling, owning a new car, or going out for a tasty meal should be well within the budget of a well-financed retirement plan.

A few years ago, I was reading the Sunday paper. There was an exciting story about a local woman who had won the lottery two years ago. Social Services turned her down after applying for welfare. She was declined because she had won the $2.2 million lottery just twenty-four months before applying for welfare.

Where had that money gone? She explained that she had spent much of it on friends, family, bad investments, expensive food, and clothes. Because she was living on government assistance before she won the lottery, she did not believe it was possible to spend $2.2 million. After receiving conflicting advice from relatives, friends, and some financial salesmen, she was confused. As a financial novice, she felt these ideas were better than hers. Her broker recommended some very speculative penny shares that unfortunately declined to zero.

Some money also went to help a friend starting a new restaurant. This deal also went badly when her friend closed the restaurant due to poor business traits. She had many expensive parties and felt rich amongst her friends. They ran up substantial liquor bills, which all went unpaid.

She had also purchased some costly clothes. Then her creditors started to demand payments. The credit card bills were so large that she almost went bankrupt since no money was left to cover them. After settling with all her creditors, she had no job, no savings, and had to apply to the government for assistance.

This story is important because it is a common occurrence. Many rock stars, movie actors, and professional athletes have similar stories. After making millions of dollars, these people often retire broke.

Similarly, many entrepreneurs who start and sell successful businesses can lose their money and retire poorly. How can people earn millions of dollars and still retire broke?

This book is the basis for what causes this to occur and how to prevent it. Many of us have not won the lottery, recorded a platinum record, or won a professional sports championship. That is ok. The lessons that apply to them, apply to the everyday working man and woman.

Having money and being financially secure are two very different things. Before you are financially secure, you must correctly convert this money to permanent wealth. This is The Endless Harvest three-step method.

Before we move on, I feel that it is my responsibility to tell you a little about myself. This way, you will understand whom you are listening to.

I have been an investment advisor since 1988. I'm practical since I manage millions of dollars of clients' hard-earned cash daily. I focus on building income-generating investment plans and retirement planning.

Since 1988 I've been a financial investment advisor managing millions of dollars. Some of my other books include *Retirement Income for Life*, *The Complete Chicken's Guide to Risk*, and *How to Avoid the Retirement Gap*. Regarding my education, I've earned both a Bachelor of Commerce and a Master's Degree in Business Administration from the University of Alberta in Canada. I've also completed one of The Canadian Securities Institute's highest levels of education. The Institute has granted me the designation of Canadian Investment Manager (CIM) and the prestigious Fellow of the Canadian Securities Institute (FCSI) for my investment, commodities, and options training.

I also have earned the Professional Financial Planning Designation (PFP), a designation in Divorce Financial Planning, and have experience with Life Insurance, Disability, and Estate Planning training. If you want to read about my other accomplishments, feel free to flip to the end of this book in the About The Author section. But this introduction is not about me. It is about you.

I only want to let you know that my mission is to help people become financially successful. I focus on the investment strategies of busy people who want investment income.

This book will educate you to getting on the right path and taking the proper steps to organize your finances. Financial planning is exciting because it is like a time machine. We can look to the future and identify your future based on what you are doing today and the projected savings and returns you are receiving.

Most investment books are written on how to become rich from the stock market, mutual funds, bond market, real estate market, and the commodity market. Many of these books work great for a classroom but are impractical for any benefit in real-life trading. PhDs in mathematics have even written some books. I've read these books, but they do not apply to most readers. *The Endless Harvest* is different.

This book is different because it combines the investment theories of many books described in layman's terms. It is more comprehensive since it combines economic, human psychology, and financial planning. By the time you are done with this book, you will learn how to have your money set up in a way where it works for you, rather than you working for your money.

Retirement is a finite goal—a goal with a set date or age. Investing is an infinite goal with no beginning and no uncertain end date. In his book, The Infinite Game, Simon Sinek describes that success or failure depends on whether the game is finite (set goals), such as losing 10 pounds or infinite to be healthy for life. Short investing with an infinite timeline, such as your lifetime or your children's. The result will be better decisions and strategies.

INVESTING BASICS YOU DID NOT LEARN IN SCHOOL

I am often asked, *What is investing?* To most, this is a broad verb that has many different meanings. Before diving deeper into this book, let's review a few basic definitions many people do not understand investing.

We need to understand what investing means before acting. You wouldn't drive a car without having a driver's license. You wouldn't bake a cake without looking at a recipe. So let's get grounded before we get into the finer details.

Today, we are all busy with our day-to-day tasks and responsibilities. As busy as we are, we often neglect our finances. Chaos can reign over our investments, so one of the critical objectives of this book is to help create a simple, easy, and well-designed method for aligning your investments with the forces of compound interest.

Here are a few foundational definitions from The American Heritage® Science Dictionary and Investopedia I want to give you:

Momentum (for investment purposes): The property or tendency of a moving object to continue moving.

Wealth: An abundance of valuable material possessions or resources; riches.

Investing: Converting cash to capital. (In this book, I define capital as anything that generates a stream of cash flow or money paid to you.)

1. The purchase of a financial product or another value item with an expectation of favorable future returns. In general terms, investment means the use of money in the hope of making more money.
2. In business, the purchase by a producer of a physical good, such as durable equipment or inventory, in the hope of improving future business.

I have used the method described throughout the book for over two decades. Using this will help you build your wealth with minimum effort. Also, by utilizing the power of compound interest, your wealth will build much quicker and easier.

**"Money does not make you wealthy. Capital makes you wealthy.
Do not mistake having money with being financially independent.
They are two different things."**

– John Yamamoto

We all have read about someone who won the lottery and was broke because they spent all their money in a few years. We have seen movie actors or rock stars who earned millions and then filed for bankruptcy. Don't let this be you! These people confuse having money with being financially independent.

Being financially independent is when you set up your investments, so the return on your investments pays for your needs. If you can live off the return on your investments, your principle will last forever. Ideally, the growth of your money should be greater than your withdrawals. The additional growth can help your investments keep pace with inflation.

To become financially independent, you must set up your investment portfolio correctly to generate income to cover expenses without depleting the principal. Beware of the danger of outliving your money. We will touch on this in a later chapter. Before we do this, let's dive deeper into the word *investing*.

WHAT IS INVESTING?

Investing is the reason you are reading this book. So what exactly is investing? Let's define it. Investing is simply converting your cash to capital. The rules for building, cultivating, harvesting, and eventually expanding your wealth are pretty simple. They follow the rules of agriculture.

Financial gardening is the concept behind this book. I want to help provide you with a reliable and time-tested way of investing and building your wealth. Some of my most outstanding teachers have been my clients and students in my thirty-plus years of building, managing, researching, and teaching about investing. These lessons are learned from real-life situations. There is no theory here. The fruit tree is capital, and the fruit is the return on capital.

To invest appropriately, we have to start at the very beginning. It is knowing where you are currently before understanding what needs to be done.

Foundation number one of investing your wealth is appropriately spending. One of the biggest wastes of time is not understanding that appropriately spending is the foundation of wealth creation.

There are four ways to spend your money. Spend money on:

1. Assets = Things you need to live.
2. Capital = Anything that pays you money.
3. Liabilities (Negative Capital) = Things that cost you money to own.
4. Stuff = Things you buy but did not need.

I will define these concepts throughout this book in more detail. In short, assets are anything you need to live your life. This can be a house or condo, a car, clothes, food, and other life necessities. The big mistake most people make is focusing too much time and money on gathering assets. Assets do not make you rich.

The second way to spend your money is on capital. Capital is the key to wealth creation. Capital is anything that generates a positive cash flow in dollars, yen, pounds, pesos, rupees, etc. To become wealthy, you must get

1

a return on your assets (ROA). Return is anytime you receive a payment in cash from your investments.

The third way to spend your money is a bit harder to understand. Most people, even companies, do not understand or are conscious of negative capital. Negative capital is the opposite of capital. Negative capital causes you to pay out dollars. The most common negative capital forms are interest on loans, credit cards, mortgages, taxation, and inflation. Negative capital is much more expensive than people realize.

The fourth way we spend our money is on stuff. Stuff is defined as anything you spend money on that is unnecessary to living a full life. If your closet, basement, or garage is full of stuff, you may suffer from an addiction to shopping. Stuff will sink your financial dreams if you do not control your spending. Today, most of us are drowning in stuff. A negative symptom of this may be high debt levels.

In the book, *The Millionaire Next Door* by Thomas Stanley and William Danko, the key to self-created millionaires is focusing on capital and not on stuff. The millionaires spent mainly on capital, while non-millionaires primarily spent on stuff and assets. Millionaires did not waste money. They lived within their means. If they earned a dollar, they spent less than the dollar. That's simple math, right? If you spend even a penny more than you make, you will be in financial trouble.

The trouble with assets is that they cost money to own and can depreciate over time. Depreciation is the decline in the value of an asset due to wear and tear. A car must be insured, fueled, maintained, and depreciates in value over time. As it gets older, it becomes worth less and less.

For example, let's consider Frank, age 51. Let's determine precisely where he is at:

- *He owns two sports cars, a cabin, a large house, a boat, a motorcycle, and a closet full of designer clothes.*
- *He is single and has saved $200,000 in his retirement plan.*
- *He has no pension plan.*
- *He earns $120,000 a year as a sales manager.*
- *His company is restructuring, and Frank is worried that he may be out of a job due to downsizing.*
- *He currently has a total debt of $200,000.*
- *He is confident that he has a garage full of assets.*
- *He continues to add more toys, like a new truck in the next year.*

Frank's biggest mistake is that he does not understand that assets are unimportant if he loses his job. From here, you can understand Frank's current state. We know what he has, but Frank needs to find out what investments he will possess to secure his future.

Both assets and investments are dynamic items. They can increase or decrease in value. So let's talk about how to run your investments. From the last chapter, we know the definition of an investment, but what do we do with them? How are they managed? Here are the basics of those investments.

RUN YOUR INVESTMENTS LIKE A BUSINESS. Your investments, or business, must pay you a positive cash flow:

- It must be managed to seek higher cash flows when the opportunities arise.
- It must be managed to control risks to your wealth.
- It must optimize returns. WHAT ABOUT CAP GAINS

You must also fire unprofitable investments. No cash or minimal cash must be kept in the portfolio. No low-quality or speculative investment gambles will remain in your portfolio. Active management is required for sound investing.

Here is a quick list of things you should do to manage or balance your portfolio properly:

- Get rid of any investment that is not paying you anything.
- Get rid of investments where you have made mistakes and lost most of their value.
- Stop treating your investment portfolio like a casino.
- Fire any advisor who is helping you speculate and gamble with your money.
- Cancel any newsletters which are constantly full of doom and gloom. (These newsletters make it hard to think long-term. They sell fear and anxiety.)

Only after getting rid of these "investment balls and chains" can you build an effective investment portfolio.

In the next chapter, we'll dive even deeper into the things that make you rich and the things that make you poor. We just spoke about the four things you can spend your money on, capital, assets, liabilities, and stuff. We all have these in our lives, and we must understand their differences.

CAPITAL, ASSETS, LIABILITIES, AND STUFF

There are four main types of "things" you can acquire in life:

- Capital – anything that pays you a return or cash flow from ownership
- Assets – things you need for your lifestyle but don't pay you anything
- Liabilities – anything that costs you money to own
- Stuff – something you buy but don't need

Knowing the difference between them is essential because they are not equal. They each serve a different purpose and have a different effect on your life. So we will take a look and understand what we are dealing with.

Let's start by talking about what is going to make us wealthy. This is capital, and even better yet, it is permanent capital. But what is permanent capital? Let's dive in.

THE ENDLESS HARVEST RULE:

To become wealthy for life, you need to create a permanent pool of capital. The capital must generate enough cash flow to fund your lifestyle.

To become wealthy for life, you must first separate your money into two piles. The piles of cash are temporary wealth and permanent wealth.

Money cannot make you rich since money is temporary wealth. To become wealthy for life, you must convert your temporary wealth to permanent wealth. This occurs when temporary wealth is invested into assets that generate long-term growth. Assets that create long-term growth are called capital assets.

The principle is the seed money we accumulate from savings, business sales, etc. Gains are the earnings our principle makes us.

Here is a short case study to consider:

Two sons inherit their parent's farm. One son follows the principles of perma-nent capital. He collects 120 eggs each day. He eats 6, sells 100, and reinvests 14 eggs for additional chickens. He also collects 100 liters of milk every day. He drinks 1 liter and sells 99 liters. He also does the same for his wheat. He eats about 5% of the wheat yearly as flour, sells 50%, feeds his cows 25%, and replants the remaining 20% for next year's harvest. He has a permanently growing capital base. His chicken operation is producing more eggs than ever. His milk herd is growing. His wheat operation is stable.

The second son did not understand the difference between money, assets, and capital. Each day he killed and ate one chicken. He also ate and sold all of the eggs. He sold or ate his cows for steak. He sold and ate all of his wheat. He spent all his money on toys, such as a new snowmobile and a powerboat. At the end of the second year, the second son had to sell the first son his farm. If he didn't, the bank would take it for non-payment of loans. He then had to work for the first son so he could survive.

They both started with the same assets. One saw the assets as capital, the other as money. Having money never leads to financial independence. Having money is finite or limited. It is like the second son eating a chicken a day. You may have 365 chickens, but you will run out of chickens and have no assets next year. The wise son preserved his capital (the chickens) by living off the eggs (return from assets). By smart investing using the principle of compounding, in which you reinvest some of the gains, you will live well. You also increase the number of chickens or revenue from selling some eggs. This is the principle of permanent capital.

This is not to say the price of assets such as cows and chickens will not fluctuate in value. The price of each chicken or cow is not very important since you do not intend to sell the principal assets. You are simply collect-ing the revenue. (The eggs, milk, and wheat earned off the principle from your chickens, cows, and wheat seeds.)

This is why the prices of dividend-paying stocks, bonds, and mutual funds are less important than the investment income generated from these assets. Since these are permanent wealth assets, we need to be con-cerned about the long-term appreciation and income rather than the daily or monthly fluctuations in value.

Make sure you reap from what you sow. Only by maintaining the long-term value of the principle can you create endless wealth. You will be on the path to financial independence only when you invest in income-producing assets and intend to spend the income generated from these assets. You can live permanently off a smaller asset base by not spending or killing your principal.

TYPES OF CAPITAL

Capital is anything that generates positive cash flow in dollars and cents. The primary forms of capital are:

1. Human Capital or Wages and Salary

Human capital needs some effort before cash is paid out. Human capital requires time and effort to generate positive cash flow. An hourly wage is the basis of human capital. The problem with human capital is that you can lose a job due to illness, downsizing, or business closure. As people age, they can grow tired and may not continue to work. Normal aging, illness, or accidents can reduce or end a salary. Human capital is finite and unreliable.

2. Business Capital

This is cash flow from the ownership of a farm or business. It is the positive cash flow generated from participation and ownership of a business. Examples are if you own a restaurant, law practice, farm, or other types of business. The downside of business capital is it can take your time and energy. Business owners can get tired from the constant grind.

Often, a business is sold at some point, and the owner needs to take this cash and invest it into the following form of capital: financial capital.

3. Financial Capital

Financial capital is the ownership of shares, mutual funds, exchange-traded funds (ETFs), bonds, GICs, or Real Estate Investment Trusts. The primary key to financial capital is generating positive cash flow without the owner spending energy. A property portfolio of financial capital can earn money while the owner sits on a beach in Hawaii sipping a Mai Tai.

4. Real Estate

Real estate can be separated into physical real estate, which tends to involve management companies, renters, insurance, property taxes, and upkeep. A more manageable form of real estate is high-quality real estate investment trusts (REITs). These are diversified real estate holdings such as apartment buildings, shopping centers, and office towers that provide rental income to the owners of the REIT.

The REIT is traded like a share on the stock exchange and can be sold and bought quite easily. Also, they can be set up to reinvest the rental income to buy more shares automatically, so your property holdings and income grow. You must be careful of REITs since they tend to rise and fall with property prices. If real estate falls, then REITs will fall in value.

The positive is that single property rental income can remain the same even if the shares fall. Stay clear of high yield REITs, which are in higher risk and speculative pieces of property. Use Real Estate ETFs or real estate mutual funds to (which have multiple partners) mitigate the risks of single property ownership. These will have a dozen or more properties and be more diversified and safer than owning individual REITs. Real estate should be part of your overall portfolio.

STUFF, ASSETS, CAPITAL, AND LIABILITIES HOW DO THEY RELATE, AND WHAT'S THE DIFFERENCE?

Now that we understand what capital can do for you, we will group stuff and assets. Possessions and stuff have precisely the same meaning. I called it "stuff" because I want you to understand that this has a negative connotation. I will refer to stuff as possessions for the remainder of this chapter. It is not uncommon for people to confuse possessions and assets since people can easily view them as one or the other. Let me further explain.

The financially unsuccessful always focus on possessions like a designer purse, fancy watch, or luxury jewelry. They confuse owning something with being wealthy. This is a big mistake. Possessions drain your financial resources and leave you poorer in the long term. Since possessions depreciate or fall in value over time, you become poorer each time you buy a possession.

Possessions have a shiny characteristic or illusion to them. Since you can touch, see, and feel possessions, they seem to increase your wealth. Be careful of this illusion. Cars, furniture, boats, clothes, and other possessions often offer financing plans. Going into debt to buy possessions is the opposite of wealth building. Financing your car is spending money; you do not have to buy something that falls in value over time. When you pay off the car loan, your car is worth far less than the amount you paid. This may be a big eye-opener unless you use your car to make money as a cab, Uber, or delivery person.

Assets are often intangible, while possessions are tangible. Consider a million-dollar house and swimming pool. They are often seen as a sign of a person's wealth. It is not an asset but is a possession. Your real assets are intangibles such as stocks, bonds, and mutual funds. These you cannot touch and feel. These exist in the intangible world of finance and capital. Because assets are often intangible, they are often less appealing to spend your hard-earned money on. You may feel that a shiny new sports car is much sexier than a high-quality mutual fund. Be careful about overspending to appear wealthy while not having money in the bank.

A simple tip is that clutter is a byproduct of purchasing stuff. If you have a garage or basement full of stuff, you may be overspending on stuff.

THE ENDLESS HARVEST RULE:

Assets are improperly defined as physical possessions such as your car, house, or stamp collection. These are possessions, not assets. The wealthy know that true assets are anything that generates a return on investment or cash flow.

In recent times our houses have risen in value. Be careful as house value can suddenly drop as in 2007-2009. Borrowing against your house can be risky. Since your house does not make you any money, it is an expense. Unless it is a rental property, your house is an expense, not an asset.

When you invest your money wisely, you are looking at putting your money into assets that will generate cash flow without working for that money. Wealth can be defined as getting significant results with little effort. With a well-planned wealth asset strategy, you can grow your income by investing each $1 into assets that will generate revenue for you.

Take, for instance, this real case:

Susan and Robert sold their business recently. They came to me for help setting up an asset strategy to generate an income stream to fund their retirement. I set up the following program for them.

Assuming a 5% dividend yield:

- *$200,000 in dividend mutual funds generating income (at 5%) of $10,000 a year in dividends = $10,000*
- *$100,000 in income mutual funds generating income (at 5%) of $5,000 a year in interest income = $5,000*
- *$200,000 in global mutual funds where they redeem the income of approximately $15,000 a year = $15,000*
- *$100,000 in dividend and capital growing stocks where they redeem and receive $6,000 a year = $6,000*

  = $36,000 / year

The total income also is supplemented by their government pension plans for another $12,000 a year, totaling $48,000 a year.

Other possessions include a house, two cars, and a recreational vehicle (RV). Because these need to be insured, upkept, and have property taxes, these expenses must be covered by Susan and Robert's cash flow.

It is essential to constantly invest in assets using the true definition of wealth. This defines capital as anything that generates cash flow or capital gain. The biggest mistake is using your house as your biggest asset. It is an asset. Even though your house might have risen in value, it is still a possession, not an investment. If you sell your house and invest in income-generating mutual funds, you have converted a possession into capital.

Being asset-rich and capital-poor results in a difficult retirement. Capital is anything that generates a return in cash for you. In the case of a rental property or real estate trust, you receive a return from real estate. This is not the case for your home. We do have to live somewhere, so having a home is essential. But it still does not generate any income. Making homeownership, your only strategy is not a wise one.

We have all heard stories about professional athletes, movie stars, and lottery winners who declare bankruptcy after earning millions. If money is spent only on possessions and stuff, you will become poor when the money runs out. Money or savings also does not make you rich. Money is only the raw material of wealth. Money itself is an asset. Money only becomes powerful if you properly convert this asset to income-paying investments or capital. The conversion of cash or money to capital is called investing.

I know it can seem like I've been very repetitive with examples and explanations. But can you see how there is a fundamental difference in assets and capital? This is VERY IMPORTANT to understand. Even though they are both considered positive, you should treat each differently.

Don't get me wrong. Both are very important in life. You can't live your life without any assets. We all have basic needs that need to be met. A roof over our head, a mode of transportation, a phone for communication, and more are necessities for the 21st century. This book is focused on getting you to an easy, comfortable, and enjoyable life. We are talking about ensuring you have the capital to live out your life and achieve your goals.

I want to give you another example to consider. Let's call it, How To Get Rich On 5% a Year. The key to wealth is getting a nickel or more a year. You can become wealthy if every dollar you invest gets you a nickel. The key is to have many nickels. The more dollars you have in income-generating investments, the greater the absolute return on your investments.

The Formula for Wealth is: Your Total Capital multiplied by Your Return on Capital in % multiplied by Time Periods.

"The most powerful formula in the universe is compound interest, called the 6th Wonder of the World."

– Albert Einstein

Consider Jim:

He saved $100,000. He invests this at a 5% return. In his first year, Jim receives $100,000 x 5% or $5,000 return on capital. Next year, Jim has

$105,000 x 5% and receives $5,250. He gets an additional $250 this year from compounding the return from last year.

The most powerful way to become wealthy is to gain capital from capital. This is called "compound interest." More income from doing nothing. It is just investing in last year's return. Pretty cool, right?

Return on capital is called residual income. This is income received without having to exert energy to earn it. This is the power of an income-generating investment strategy. The detachment of your energy and time to earn income. This is different from "linear income," which is income you expend time and energy to earn, such as an hourly wage from a job.

In his book, *Multiple Streams of Income*, Robert Allen makes a critical point that you can retire only when your residual income is high enough to cover your expenses. When your investments generate enough passive investment income to cover your living expenses, you are financially independent of work.

I want to give you one more example of capital versus an asset because this is a fundamental mistake many people make. Let's take gold, for instance. Gold is not capital. It is an asset. Anything that does not generate cash flow or returns in dollars and cents may be an asset but may not necessarily be capital. Stocks that do not pay you dividends may be assets or negative capital if they decline or go bankrupt. Any mutual fund or Exchange Traded Fund (ETF) that does not generate any interest, dividends, or rental income is not capital.

Here is something interesting. Chasing the illusion of capital gains is one cause of investment failures. Capital gains are created when you sell something higher than you paid. If you bought a stock for $10 and sold it for $18, the $8 gain is a capital gain. The problem with capital gains is that a stock, house, commodity, or gold bar can also fall in value or stay the same price for years.

THE LAW OF COMPOUND INTEREST

The law of compound interest is one of the most outstanding achievements in investing. This is what can make your initial investment multiply. Compound interest is also a reason to start investing as early as possible. Many clients have often told me, "What would have happened if I invested ten years ago?" My response is, "Let's figure out what will happen in ten years when you start investing now!"

Don't think about what you could have made when you should focus on the rewards in front of you. Simply said, *the glass is half full. It's not half empty.* Even though this simple phrase can be applied to many different aspects of life, it also applies to investing and the law of compound interest.

Take our apple tree, for example. What happens when you produce one apple and then plant the seeds from that apple? You end up with multiple apple trees producing more and more apples. This is just like our other example of the chicken and the egg. You can eat all the chickens or eat all the apples. Or you can harvest more eggs into chickens or plant more seeds to produce more apple trees.

"The most powerful formula in the galaxy is compound interest."

– Albert Einstein

The law of compound interest is kind of like using apple seeds from your new apples to grow more apple trees that produce even more apples.

Let's listen to one of history's brightest men, Albert Einstein. He tells us about harnessing the financial genie of compound interest.

Albert Einstein (1879 - 1955) was once asked what the most powerful formula in the universe was. His answer surprised everyone. Most people expected him to say the theory of relativity or $E=MC^2$. Instead, he said the compound interest formula or $FV= PV (1+i)^n$. Einstein referred to compound interest as the 8th wonder of the world. It can work for you or even against you. When you invest, it works for you. When you borrow (or accrue debt), it works against you.

When it comes to investing, compounding means you can earn interest on your principal, as well as on any other interest you may have accumulated. Compound interest is beyond the human brain's grasp. This situation can simply explain the true power of compound interest. If you have a choice between a check for $1,000,000 or starting with a penny and having that penny double every day for one month? Which would you take?

The power of compound interest is astonishing. If you start with a penny on day 1, you will have:

Day 1 = $ .01
Day 2 = $.02
Day 3 = $.04
Day 4 = $.08
Day 5 = $.16
Day 6 = $ .32
Day 7 = $.64
Day 8 = $1.28
Day 9 = $2.56
Day 10 = $5.12
Day 11 = $10.24
Day 12 = $20.48
Day 13 = $40.96
Day 14 = $81.92
Day 15 = $163.84
Day 16 = $327.68
Day 17= $655.36
Day 18 =1,310.72
Day 19 = $2,621.44
Day 20 = $5,242.88
Day 21 = $10,485.76
Day 22 = $20,971.52
Day 23 = $41,943.04
Day 24 = $83,886.08
Day 25 = $167,772.16
Day 26 = $335,544.32
Day 27 = $671,088.64
Day 28 = $1,342,177.28
Day 29 = $2,684,354.56
Day 30 = $5,368,709.12

Day 31 = $10,737,418.24

$$FV = PV(1+i)^n$$

The principles of physics must apply to building wealth. Why fight the forces of nature. We can use the power of the physical universe to build our wealth. Albert Einstein was one of the most intelligent humans ever to walk the earth. He was asked, "What is the most powerful force in the universe?"

If you haven't heard of Albert Einstein, let me list some of his Achievements listed by Thinkexist.com:

(He's done a lot, so this is a large list that isn't even complete.)

- Einstein showed that absolute time had to be replaced by a new absolute: the speed of light.
- He asserted the equivalence of mass and energy, which would lead to the famous formula $E=mc^2$
- Einstein challenged the wave theory of light, suggesting that light could also be regarded as a collection of particles.
- Einstein later published a paper in 1915 called "General Relativity."
- In 1917, Einstein published a paper that used general relativity to model the behavior of an entire universe.
- Between 1905 and 1925, Einstein transformed humankind's understanding of nature on every scale, from the smallest to that of the cosmos.
- Einstein and de Sitter, in 1932, proposed a simple solution to the field equations of general relativity for an expanding universe. They argued that large amounts of matter might not emit light or be detected. Now called 'dark matter,' this matter has been shown to exist by observing its gravitational effects.

There are more accomplishments of Albert Einstein, but we are here to talk about money and compound interest. Compound interest means that interest earns interest.

Here is an example of Positive Compound Interest:

David invests $10,000 into a 5 year bond earning 5% compounded annually. David would have the following:

- *End of year 1 he would have $10,000 (Principal) + $500 (Interest received) = $10,500*
- *End of year 2 he would have $10,500 (Principal) + $520.50 (Interest received) = $10,520.50*

- *End of year 3 he would have $11,020.50 (Principal) + $550.12 (Interest received) = $11,570.62*
- *End of year 4 he would have $11,570.63 (Principal) + $570.88 (Interest received) = $12,150.51*
- *End of year 5 he would have $12,150.51 (Principal) + $600.78 (Interest received) = $12,760.30*

An easy gain of $2,760.30 without having to spend any extra hours at work, at the plant, or the office.

Now, here is an example of Negative Compound Interest:

Jack takes out a car loan for $25,000 at 5%. He would have paid $3,272 of interest on the car. The total payment would be $28,272. Avoid negative compound interest on items that generate no cash flow, like personal vehicles. Instead, consider only borrowing to buy items that go up in value or create a cash flow. Avoid consumer debt on depreciating items at all costs.

I want to give you some fundamental rules of compound interest:

- Compound interest is the most powerful force in the world.
- Compound interest can work for you or work against you.
- Align your investments to maximize positive compound interest and minimize negative compound interest.
- The longer the term, the greater the impact of compound interest.
- Time can work miracles if you use compound interest strategies.

A guide once wrote: "Buying gold is for other reasons such as alcohol, crises, wars, etc."

Detach your investment choices from chasing capital gains. If you rely on capital gains, you will experience a very unreliable return on your wealth. Instead, focus on earning a solid return on your investments from interest, dividends, and rental income. Capital gains will become a bi-product of a solid investment strategy. If you can compound or live off the revenue generated from your investments, you will have a much more reliable and consistent return.

Let's quickly talk about a negative you will encounter, liabilities. Liabilities are also considered negative capital. Negative capital is a major cause of financial poverty, bankruptcies, and financial hardship. Most people, even highly educated people, do not understand or are even aware of negative capital. Negative capital is a cost to you in dollars and cents. This is the worst type of cost to your financial future.

i. Inflation or the increase in costs is not as firm as negative capital. It is when your money buys less and less over time—E.g. Gasoline, food, etc.

ii. The most common form of negative capital is interest on loans, credit cards, mortgages, or debts.

This is a huge problem since it is easy to get into debt but much harder to pay off debt. The interest charges and other fees make the total amount paid back much larger than the amount received. Have you ever heard people complaining that their paychecks always go to paying off credit cards or they can never get their bank account balance in the green? This is primarily due to liabilities.

Negative compound interest accumulates against you. You have to earn extra money to pay back the loans. In addition, most credit cards have an annual fee and high-interest rates. The interest on loans is higher than the income paid out on investments. A credit card can charge 18% interest, while a bond may pay 4% to the owner. The interest cost of negative capital can be much more costly than the return from positive capital. Please watch out for negative capital. Simply put, if someone lends you $100 and wants you to pay them back $118, doesn't that seem lopsided?

iii. Depreciation is another form of negative capital when something declines in value based on wear and tear, such as your car.

That last "thing" I want to refer back to is the term "stuff." I will refer back to "stuff" rather than "possessions" to conclude this chapter. It is one of the easiest pieces to visualize and control. Yes, this is a very broad term. Stuff is anything you buy that can be considered clutter. (Due to stuff, you have no room in your garage or basement.)

- It is the health club membership you pay monthly even though you rarely go.
- It is the new cast iron skillet you wanted to use but never went camping.
- It is the third car you purchased, just cause your friends had one too.
- It is the $800 guitar you bought, thinking you would learn to play for your spouse, but it sits in the corner collecting dust.
- It is the red velvet blouse that was 30% on sale, so you "had to buy it" but never wore it.

- It is the vacation package you purchased but had expired because you were too busy at work to notice.
- It is even that extra box of Cheerios you bought because you wanted to be healthier during breakfast, but you always just drink a cup of coffee.

As you can see, the list goes on and on. We won't talk about this too much because everyone (even me) will purchase stuff occasionally. We are human, and we do make purchasing mistakes. We fall for great marketing advertisements, have urges and cravings, and change our minds. This is a fact, and it is a part of life.

What I want you to realize is what stuff really is. The more you realize you are purchasing things you don't need, the more you will pay attention to your spending and the less money you will waste. It's almost like taking the money out of your wallet and putting it directly in the trash can. When it comes to stuff, you would be better off just putting money in the garbage can rather than spending it. Just think of the gas wasted to get to the store, the hours are taken out of your day, or even the aggravation you may cause yourself when you realize you didn't use the item.

It's okay. We all buy stuff, but you will waste less money on stuff when you know exactly what it is. Next, we are going to talk about building a bigger future. We've almost gone through all the basics before getting to the three-step process, The Endless Harvest, to building financial wealth.

Rich (Do These Daily)

1. Invest in capital
2. Pay off debts
3. Assess costs
4. Buy stuff/shopping

Not Rich (Do These Daily)

1. ~~Buy stuff/shopping~~
2. Assess costs
3. Pay off debts
4. Invest in capital

A tip is to live a life of ease. If you are in debt, you will worry about bills, and the future becomes scary. It is like riding a bike. Downhill is easy riding and enjoyable, but going back uphill is three times as difficult. Getting into debt is like riding a bike downhill. Riding a bike uphill afterward is difficult and painful! Paying off the debts you accumulate is like riding uphill. Try to avoid getting into debt by not buying things you do not need

WHERE IS THE RULE OF 72?

BUILDING A BIGGER FUTURE

W e've discussed some investment basics and defined the foundational terms you will need to secure your financial future. So you might be thinking, *Okay, I'm ready to start the plan and take action. Tell me what to do next.*

I'm glad you are ready to take action because I often see people who love to only talk about financial strategies, their favorite mutual funds, or the latest industry trends. This is all good and fun, but it's only that. Talking about starting your investment plan or what will happen is only talk. This does you no financial good until you get out of procrastination and into action.

Even though you may think it's safe to stay in this "limbo" state, it is pretty dangerous. Yes, not making any decisions means you will not fail. But not making any decisions means you will never succeed as well. You are reading this book because we all want to secure our financial future for ourselves and our loved ones. To do this, you need to take action. It won't happen on its own. (By the way, don't forget opportunity cost and the cost of inflation. The more time passes, the more wins you will lose out on, and inflation will continue to hit you below the belt year after year.)

Let's start with a short parable. I like to call this:

The Ant and the Grasshopper

In a field one summer's day, a grasshopper was hopping about, chirping to its heart's content. An ant passed by, bearing an ear of corn he was taking to the nest.

"Come and chat with me," said the grasshopper, "instead of toiling and moiling."

"I am helping to lay up food for the winter," said the ant, "and I recommend you to do the same."

"Why bother about winter?" said the grasshopper, "We have plenty of food at present."

21

But the ant went on its way, and the grasshopper had no food when the winter came and found itself dying of hunger. The ant lived well off the corn and grain from the stores it had collected during the summer. The grasshopper learned that:

It is best to prepare for the days of necessity in times of plenty for when times are bad.

— Aesop Fables

THE ENDLESS HARVEST RULE:

It is dangerous to your financial future to put off saving and investing until later. The best time is now. You will always have bills to pay. Start investing. Even pocket change is a great place to start.

WHO
- WHEN

Procrastination or putting off doing something is not caused by laziness. It is caused by a lack of knowledge, advice, or direction. If you are putting off reorganizing your investment portfolio, you either need to learn more about investing or need to shop around for a solid accountant, lawyer, and investment advisor. Find the right who(s) for your financial life. Consider reading the book, *Who Not How* by Dan Sullivan and Benjamin Hardy.

Even for myself, last year I bought a computer and scanner. I set up the computer system and scanner myself to save money. I could not get the scanner to work correctly for weeks, so I put off using it. Finally, I called a computer person who quickly set up the computer system and scanner.

The short lesson here is to start using more specialists to help provide services with the complexity of today's world. If you are putting off setting up your investment plan, try interviewing some investment advisors and financial planners who can help you get started. Stop doing all your investments, taxes, and legal work by yourself!

Also, saving during the good times for the bad ones is imperative. There will always be recessions and economic downswings. When times are good, it is easy to forget the bad times. Remember to save for those bad times. Start now. Every cent you invest can grow for the future. Determine ways you can find money to start investing. Can you cut down on your smoking and invest the difference? Take a bag lunch more often? Return your bottles and pop cans to a bottle depot? Every bit helps.

There are and will always be reasons for not starting an investment program. Action is the key to starting an investment plan. Even one dollar a day adds up to $18,045 at 8% growth in twenty years! That's some mind-blowing math, isn't it? Almost everyone can afford to invest one dollar a day. Even tiny drops of water from a dripping tap can become gallons and fill up an entire house in time.

Many people have the misconception that only the rich can afford to have an investment program. The truth is quite contrary—you become rich by starting small and building an investment program.

This brings us to the last part of this chapter. Once you have decided to take action and start investing, it's imperative to keep the investing momentum going. Sometimes you will do extraordinary in the first five years and think you now have extra money for a new house renovation or even splurging on a gambling trip to Las Vegas.

Instead of losing momentum and stopping your investing streak, I encourage you to continue growing your fortune. The moment you stop, your investments will cease to grow, and they will become much harder to start again. I want you to take out what you need from your financial growth, but not more than necessary. Don't spend your hard-earned money carelessly; please remember to save for the downtimes. Sir Isaac Newton said it best, "What goes up must come down."

Do you remember the example with the two sons from the last chapter?

If not, I'll give you another very similar case study for reference:

There were two brothers, Stephen and Wilber. Each brother inherited the same assets. Each brother received 100 chickens, 3 cows, and 10 acres of land filled with apple trees and wheat.

Steven knew and applied the principles of momentum. He lived off the milk, eggs, and apples. He sold the excess produce to buy more land and upgrade the farm. He added 6 more chickens each month and stored extra wheat for hard times.

Wilber did not apply the principles of momentum investing. He ate the cows for steaks and ate most of the chickens. Two years later, he had to sell his farm and work for his brother Steven. Wilbur ate up his capital.

How many of us do the same as Wilber? I think most people live like Wilber. We can spend all of our capital and invest very little in cash-generating investments.

To become wealthy, we need to turn active income into passive income. Multiple streams of income are essential to becoming and staying wealthy. Let your hard work start working for you, and your life will become easier.

As we wrap up this chapter, I want to touch base on the big picture of multiple income streams. They are divided into two parts: Active Income and Passive Income.

Types of Active Income

Stream 1: Your job
Stream 2: Your business
Stream 3: Real estate you manage

The problem with active income is that you must put in time and energy to create this wealth.

Your longer-term focus should be passive wealth. Passive wealth creates wealth without much time or effort on your part. This is your hard work working for you.

Types of Passive Income

- Interest income earned from bonds, savings accounts, money market, term deposits, retirement plans, and GICs.
- Dividend income comes from ownership of stocks, preferred shares, dividend ETFs, and dividend mutual funds.
- Capital gains come from the growth of your original investments. If you paid $10 a share for a stock, it is now worth $15. The $5 gain is called a capital gain.
- Real Estate Investment Trusts (REIT), royalty trust ETFs, or REIT mutual funds.
- Passive real estate ownership or a business where you get cash payments without managing the property or business.
- Pension plan at work.

This book will focus on passive income from interest and dividend income rather than active capital gains.

Momentum investments pay you income without you expending time and energy. It is referred to as "passive income" or "multiple income streams."

Here are a few types of momentum investments:

- Dividend-paying stocks
- Dividend-paying ETFs
- Dividend-paying mutual funds
- REIT (Real Estate Without the Hassles)
- Trusts
- Bonds
- Bond Funds
- Bond ETFs
- GICs/Term Deposits
- Retirement Plans

Now that we have our bearings set on how to build our bigger future let's look at what you are doing right now as you read this book. You are going to learn about the power of planning. I applaud you for taking this big step toward securing your financial future. The majority of people never take this step. Let's jump right in.

Summary

Active investments are: your job, your business, and the property you own, plus collect rent.

Passive investments are: your retirement plans, investment portfolio, pension plans at work, government pension plans

THE POWER OF PLANNING

"The best way to predict your future is to create it."

– Abraham Lincoln

"If you do not plan your future, it may happen in a way
that makes you miserable."

– John Yamamoto

No good investing strategy gets into action without a great plan.
So what exactly is a financial plan? *No To Complied*

A financial plan, defined by Investopedia, is a comprehensive
evaluation of an investor's current and future financial state using currently
known variables to predict future cash flows, asset values, and withdrawal
plans. Most individuals work with a financial planner and use current
net worth, tax liabilities, three asset allocation, and future retirement and
estate plans in developing financial plans. These metrics are used along
with estimates of asset growth to determine if a person's financial goals
can be met or what steps need to be taken to ensure that they are.

That was a bit of text, but let's simplify it with a short metaphor.

Think about an apple tree for a moment. The blossoms and fruit are
pretty to look at, but the most critical thing for the apple tree is the roots.
Think of the roots in the ground as your financial plan. The fruit is like
the returns from your portfolio. The fruit comes from the proper care
of the roots, not the other way around. Too many people come to me
wanting to talk about the fruit. The truth is that they should focus on the
roots, their financial plan, and their portfolio.

When you take care of and water the roots, the fruit or harvest will be
bountiful. Instead of asking for a good return, the question(s) should be,
*How do I get a good return? What do I have to own to get a good return on
my capital?* A good return is a result or by-product of a proper financial

plan. A tree without roots is like an investment portfolio without a plan. It's not set correctly and can be easily knocked over with the slightest wind or rain. Everyone wants to talk about what is in their portfolio—the fruits and flowers—not realizing that the actual health of the tree is underground. It is always a problem when I see a portfolio without a plan.

The plan is the start. You need to do the plan first. Think of your financial plan as your goal and ask yourself these questions:

- What do you want to achieve by when?
- How much are you starting with now?
- What is your expected rate of return?
- When do you want to retire, and where are you now?

"Don't be a prisoner of your past. Be an architect of your future."
– Anonymous

The plan is the foundation, and your risks are overlaid onto the plan. We identify the risks from the plan. Then we determine what investments are suitable for you based on the plan. At the end is the return from the portfolio. Find out if the return is adequate to achieve your objectives. I cannot emphasize how important it is to plan first. Financial plans make your future less anxious and scary. By estimating your cash flow in the future, you will learn whether you will outlive your money or not.

START BY BUILDING AN EMERGENCY FUND

We will take a little time in the rest of this chapter to dive into two extensive details you will not want to miss. Later in the book, we'll get into planning details, but right now, I want to talk about these two pieces. The first is making sure you build an emergency fund. It's the necessary step you need to take before looking at your profitable long-term future. Make sure you are on steady ground, and when your foundation is laid, you can move to focus on growth.

On a recent episode of 20/20 or Nightline, I watched a TV special on America's homeless. The shocking conclusion was that many of the homeless were ordinary people. They were not abnormal at all. Their main problem was that none had an emergency or "rainy day" fund. There was no surplus money over and above general expenses.

The first financial shock they experienced turned their lives upside down. They were always just six paychecks from being homeless. One person had lost his factory job and could not make ends meet with a wife at home and three children. They missed mortgage payments and lost their home. They lived in their car without family support and joined the homeless.

Another couple earned very good money over their lifetimes, yet when downsizing at 51, they were forced to sell their big home and live in an apartment. They also could not afford to keep their cars and were forced to sell them. The husband took a labor job to make ends meet since the money they earned from their registered retirement savings plans only added up to $450 per month. They are now forced into financial survival for the rest of their lives.

Peter, age 43, was a successful lawyer. He was physically and mentally exhausted. He needed to take one year off from his law practice. Because he had one year of expenses saved in his emergency fund, he could afford to take one year off to re-educate and refresh his health.

This is why your emergency fund is so critical. When the good times are good, it is human nature to think they can only get better. In reality, good and bad times are a part of everyone's life. Remember, what goes up must come down. Don't live your life paycheck-to-paycheck because there may be a time when your paycheck disappears.

Tip: Use your tax-free savings plans and retirement plans, and have a personal line of credit as your everyday fund.

ENDLESS HARVEST RULE:

Start by setting up a reserve fund of three months to one year of expenses. This will give you financial freedom from short-term stresses or financial disasters such as a job loss or unexpected financial expenses.

The best investment choice for a rainy day fund are things such as dividend mutual funds, bank shares, utilities, or strip bonds. If there is a real danger of job loss or layoffs, you should only use money market funds for your rainy day fund.

FINANCIAL PLANNING RISKS AND TIPS TO SUCCEED

This is a short section. Below you will find a list of risks of having a poor financial plan. Sometimes we make mistakes, and this book is written to prevent you from making them.

Here is a list of some financial planning risks to your wealth:

1. **Debt**
2. **Not saving enough money**
3. **No investment goals**
4. **Having unrealistic expectations**
5. **Little estate planning**
6. **Lack of a financial advisory network**
7. **Lack of proper diversification**
8. **Listening to the wrong people**
9. **Fraud**

Now that we've identified those let's talk about some wealth-building financial planning tips.

"Your investment portfolio needs to be systematically organized and designed. Most people would never build a $15,000 garage without a plan, yet they have a $350,000 portfolio with no planning."

– John Yamamoto

My research has shown that devastating risks stem from the less noticeable risk of improper investment planning.

First, do not invest a cent until you have a risk strategy in place.

Many risks are caused by the lack of consideration or planning for risks. Some examination of the risks involved could have prevented the losses. The risk you forget will be the one that causes you pain.

There are many risks to consider. Let's look at **#1, debt**.

Credit cards are like financial cocaine, very addictive. With record bankruptcies happening today, debt is one of the most prominent threats to your financial security. Since it is easy to get into debt but very hard to get out of debt, you should pay close attention to some of the dangers of debt.

Some key dangers of financial debt are:

- With debt, the power of compound interest works against you.
- (Since the unpaid debt keeps accumulating 24 hours a day, 7 days a week, compound interest is a powerful opponent to fight. It is relentless, does not rest, and does not have mercy.)
- Debt is negative wealth since it makes you poorer since the interest charges accumulate against you.
- Debt decreases your ability to save money.
- Debt causes you to defer savings.
- Debt makes you work for money instead of having your money work for you.
- Debt can take away your peace of mind by causing you to worry about how you will pay next month's bills.
- Debt can make you vulnerable to job loss or unexpected cash needs.

#2, #3, and #4 risks are:

2. **Not saving enough money – no money to retire on**
3. **No investment goals – no focus = no results**
4. **Having unrealistic expectations – results that are too high to achieve**

"It is better to be approximately right than precisely wrong."

– George Hartman

Investing is not an exact science since events such as 9/11 (World Trade Center attack), Desert Storm 1 and 2, SARs virus, Covid-19 pandemic, and other sudden and unexpected global shocks can change the direction of the stock market. *2008/09 — No Exec's to JAIL*

A portfolio is always a work in progress. You will never have the perfect portfolio. A portfolio is like a garden. In a garden, we expect weeds to grow. We are constantly on guard to pick the weeds out. Similarly, a successful portfolio needs to be "weeded" as well. Sometimes circumstances outside our control force us to change certain stocks or bonds within our portfolio.

Plan to be wrong and don't have unrealistic goals. Forget perfectionism. Investing is an inexact science. It does not exist in the investment world.

This brings us to financial planning risks **#5, #6, and #7:**

5. **Little estate planning – no will, personal directive, or power of attorney**
6. **Lack of a financial advisory network – trying to do it all yourself**
7. **Lack of proper diversification**

Diversification is critical, so I'm going to include a case study. We've all heard of diversification, but even the best of us can get shortsighted from time to time:

Sam, age 56, now runs a successful dental practice. But just ten years earlier, Sam was close to early retirement. He put all his money into a joint venture with two other dentists.

He was set to own a third of a large apartment building. The building was built, and things seemed to go very well. Sam and his partners were confident that the apartment building income would fund their retirement. So Sam sold all of his stocks, term deposits, and mutual funds to buy this apartment building. In order words, "He went all in."

They fully rented the building, and things seemed to be perfect. But within six months, things started to fall apart, literally. The apartment walls began to crack. Sam met with the developer and found that he poorly planned the foundation. The soil underneath the apartment was too soft to support the weight of the apartment. It started to sink. The city inspectors shut the building down and rated it unsuitable for tenants.

Sam and his partners sued the engineer and the developer. Both declared bankruptcy. Sam's other two partners, who were much younger than Sam, also declared bankruptcy. Sam was left with the choice of trying to keep the building going or declaring bankruptcy himself. He eventually declared bankruptcy and is now working at age 56, when he would have already retired.

The moral of this story is never to have all of your money in a single asset. Have your money set up so that any single failure will not completely wipe you out. It is very tempting to "go all-in" because the potential upside can be enormous. You need always to remember the risks, however. Don't put yourself in a position where one loss will make you lose everything. Those types of decisions can negatively be life-altering and force you to start all over.

That sums up our chapter on the power of planning and the risks you need to watch out for. Next, we are going to talk about the retirement gap. Everyone wants to retire. Even many Millennials want to retire well before their 50's. Let's discuss the retirement gap, so we finish setting the stage for your simple three-step process to financial freedom.

AVOIDING THE RETIREMENT GAP

The retirement gap is critical to discuss before we take any detailed steps toward wealth generation. So what exactly is the retirement gap, and why does it matter? This is what everyone who is going to retire needs to know. I mean everyone. We think about the good times, how much money we can make, and how to spend our fortunes. But not everyone thinks about how they can be safe to retire.

Don't be the person who believes they are retired, only to find themselves back at work in a year or two. Don't be the person who is "retired" but still is stressed about their finances and lives on a strict budget.

Let me give you an example of what I mean. These are fictional names, but let's call this couple Len and Debbie, who are both age 60:

This year, they retire and have $420,000 saved in their retirement plan. They expect a 4% return from their investments going forward. At age 60, they start to take $4,000 after tax each month out of their retirement plans.

What is their retirement gap? Do they have one?

Now consider yourself:

- Will you outlive your money?
- Will you be able to maintain your current lifestyle without working?

The question I ask Len and Debbie is, "Do you have a retirement gap?" Most people in this situation would answer no. What's the real answer in this case? The real answer mathematically is that Len and Debbie will run out of money in the next 10 years. By age 70, they will be dead broke.

The critical thing for Len and Debbie is to know when they will run out of money. Do they take out less income each month? Do they need $4,000 a month? Can they work longer, or can they work part-time? Can they get a higher return on their investments?

The vital point for Len and Debbie today is that by having a financial plan, they will identify that their retirement gap will appear in 10 years, and they will be dead broke at 70. Financial planning is probably the most vital part of investing. Remember to include a 2%+ rise every year in the cost of living.

Most people spend much time deciding whether they should own stock A or B or purchase mutual fund A or B. The real question is, "Are we saving enough?" and "Will we run out of money at retirement?" Start with a plan and determine if your financial goals are realistic today rather than in 10 years when you run out of money.

So why would Len and Debbie run out of money so quickly? They would spend more of their principle than their investments would make. This is fundamental in financial planning. Realistically, Len and Debbie could take out $3,000 a month and not go broke. They could not take out $4,000. By taking out an extra $1,000 every month, they would run out of money in 10 years. Also, add your taxes that will have to be paid out at retirement. This can add an extra 20% to your retirement burdens.

> **"If you want to succeed at my level in business.**
> **In finance, you have to deal with risk."**
>
> **– Tony Robbins**

What needs to be done is to find a realistic capital they will need by retirement. At a conservative 4% return, practical in today's market, the capital will be enough income to generate money for the rest of their lives. A million dollars with a 4% return will generate a $40,000 a year income if you think about it. Len and Debbie are taking that out with only $420,000. Therefore, they will run out of money.

So now that we have defined the retirement gap, let's talk about how to avoid having a retirement gap. Consider these questions:

- Do you worry that you may not have enough money to last your retirement?
- Are you set up for your financial future, or are there things you are unsure about?
- Have you factored inflation, taxes, and future health care costs into your plan?

- Do you know if you will end up with a financial gap when you retire? (A financial gap would be the difference between what will financially happen to you versus what you want to happen.)
- Have you included income taxes in your budget? (Include an extra 2% increase in your cost of living budget each year.)

The truth is, most people do not sit down and do a formal financial plan. But when they do, they can see on paper that "Yes! You can retire!" It is a feeling that provides great relief. Or, if you find there is a gap, you can make the necessary adjustments now when it makes a difference.

You have the power to alter the future. Think of your future like wet cement. Wet cement is malleable. The future is like cement in that as the future unfolds, the cement hardens. It is almost impossible to change it at a certain point, so the earlier you plan, the easier time you will have to create the future you desire. Do not wait too long and let the cement harden over.

A financial plan consists of:

- A risk plan = potential for losses
- An asset allocation plan = where to invest
- Projections of your future assets = how does my future look 5-20 years from now
- A gap analysis = will I run out of money?

This book contains the strategies necessary to ensure you do not face a financial gap. Later in this book, we'll talk more in-depth about your financial plan. It is like both a map and a time machine. It provides you with a map linking today with your future. What happens in-between is what you will need to adjust over time. This means you will make new maps and new time machines every few years.

The message is simple, do a financial plan regularly at least once every two years. Do this while preventing and locating any gaps between where you are going and where you want to be in the future. It will help guide your actions to achieve your goals better.

BUILDING A NEEDS ACCOUNT VS WANTS

Needs: Thing you require for basic survival.
Wants: Thing you desire.

In the last chapter, we created an emergency or survival fund. After doing this, you will want to build your needs account to cover your survival needs at retirement. Here you will focus on your long-term survival needs (see diagram).

PERMANENT WEALTH HIERARCHY OF FINANCIAL DEFENSE

Step 1 Survival Fund

Step 2 Needs Fund=Long-term Survival

Step 3 Luxury Fund=Long-term Wants

Step 4 Estate Planning Needs

Step 5 Debt Reduction

This step will build up your financial strength so you do not end up working forever. This fund will provide your day-to-day living expenses at retirement. This fund consists of your:

- Work pension plan (if applicable)
- Government pension plans (if appropriate)
- Registered retirement savings plans

Interestingly, many Baby Boomers don't have income for life when they retire. During this boomer era, many workers had good pensions backed by blue-chip companies providing income when they reached retirement age. The flip side is that many people end up having to work until the day they die. The real issue here is that we are now living longer and longer.

Unlike the 19th century generation, who may have been old at 60, people are jogging and camping and are much more active than before. 80 is the new 60, and it's not uncommon to see people living to be 90. Science is excellent, but who will pay for the remaining 20 or more years we live as we live longer? This is a newer problem that will get even bigger as more people live even longer.

Also, those boomers are very active people in their retirement. This isn't a generation of people who will just retire and never be heard from again. Baby boomers have a much higher lifestyle expectation than their parents did. I'm a boomer and know I'd like to travel when I retire. I want to stay active by skiing and riding my mountain bike. However, the truth is it will take more money to do all those things.

Boomers typically don't understand that the real risk to their money is not stock market crashes. It's spending more than they are earning. Can you see why having a needs fund is so important now?

RETIREMENT DEFINED
NEVER RETIRE FROM LIFE

"Retirement is not a goal but a journey."
– John Yamamoto

We are moving into a new mindset focused on avoiding the retirement gap and keeping you alive and well. After counseling hundreds of clients over the years, I find the biggest mistake is planning retirement without considering what life will be like after retiring. Retirement is an abused and misunderstood concept. This wrong vision of retirement has led to unnecessary depression, poor health, and early death. (See diagram)

The wrong vision of retirement is leaving work because you have the money or feel too old to work. I also want to replace the word "retirement " with the word "lifestyle liberty" or "freedom." The word retirement is loaded with negative connotations such as being useless, non-productive, or "being sent out to pasture." The stereotype of a retiree is a poor one. The retiree is sitting on a lawn chair, watching the world go by.

Many people also tell me they want to retire at age 50 or 55. When I ask them what they plan to do with their free time, they often blank out and are unsure what they will do.

The solution is not simple. Defining what to do with your life has more to do with replacing retirement with a "lifetime focus" on enjoying each day of your life. This is rather than the dichotomy of working for a living, retiring, and doing what you enjoy. This traditional definition of retirement is very unhealthy. It is unhealthy because it defers doing what you want to do with your life until you quit working.

I encourage people to travel while they are working. Why defer traveling until you retire. This makes no sense. I have put a big purchase account for items such as traveling in my savings system. By doing the things you enjoy while working, you can enjoy the years before you leave your job. These are and will truly become the best years of your life.

I've got two actual retirement cases for you to consider:

Retirement Case 1

When I met Martin and Edith, age 58, they were both working. They had put off traveling until after retirement. After doing the numbers, I found they could afford to travel two months a year. Having some confidence, Martin approached his boss and asked for two things. He asked for every Friday and two months off each February and March to travel for golf in Arizona. He was granted both and enjoyed his new lifestyle for the next four years until he permanently retired.

Retirement Case 2

Daryl, age 69, is an oil rig inspector. Although he can retire, he still enjoys working six months a year. He loves the oil business and enjoys seeing the boys on the rigs. He looks 15 years younger than his 69 years of age. Although he is constantly told he is too old to work, he loves his consulting job and continues to do rig inspections. The critical point is that it is his choice to work. We have set up his finances to retire anytime he wants, yet Daryl has the option of working.

This is the difference between financial failure and financial success in both cases. Financial failure is when you have no control over your life. You have to work. You cannot travel. Or you have to spend less than you desire just to survive. Here, you cannot do what you want in your life. You do not have financial liberty or freedom. Financial success is when you have control over your life.

The solution again is to have a plan. Plan your finances so you have choices at retirement. Also, plan to enjoy each year of your life by traveling, taking adventures, and developing yourself. Gear your life to spend your time doing things you enjoy doing. No one has a job where everything is enjoyable. Make sure to plan a lifetime of enjoyment. The chapters to come will outline a simple three-step plan for finding this freedom.

As we wrap up this section, I want to reinstate the importance of not separating non-retirement and retirement years. Instead, have a continuous lifetime balance of fun activities, such as traveling, with goal-oriented activities like working at a job or for a cause you believe in. An example of a goal-oriented task is a 72-year-old man who loves being a doctor.

Another is Roy, an 86-year-old client. He looks and acts twenty years younger than he is when he volunteers at two different charities. Roy has a healthy view of retirement. This is an example of his view:

HEALTHY VIEW OF RETIREMENT

Learn to balance the two objectives for your life. The first objective is to have a lifetime of positive activity and liberty. The second objective is to have a solid financial basis to achieve lifetime investment income. This will provide you with money to fund your first objective of having the freedom to do what you want.

We've spent some time learning about the financial basics you will need to succeed in investing and enjoy your financially free life. I would like to introduce you to my three-step method of accessing your financial freedom. It is called The Endless Harvest.

THE ENDLESS HARVEST

T he Endless Harvest is the three-step method to secure your present and future wealth. Throughout this book, you will continue to see the metaphor between harvesting an apple tree and growing your wealth. It's just as essential to building our wealth as it is to maintain and keep it growing. Just think, you've put time and effort into planting an apple seed. You made sure you fertilized the soil, the environment was sunny, and it had the proper water to grow. Getting that tiny seed to start sprouting into a tree is much effort. Then what would happen if you got distracted and went on a month-long vacation? Would your young apple tree still be alive when you get back?

I think we all know the answer to that question. Unfortunately, it wouldn't survive, and that's precisely what happens to people growing their money. So many of us focus on how to get rich quickly but then forget about maintaining our wealth and continuing to grow it. Those people will find that riches do not last forever and will be at "square one" when funds run out. This is planting the seed all over and restarting the cycle.

This is figuratively growing your "money tree" or apple tree. We want to set ourselves up with an Endless Harvest. It is not just getting the growth started and letting it die, not ignoring all the other forces that may endanger our healthy tree, and not seeing the apples grow but letting them fall to the ground.

The Endless Harvest is about growing your money tree, keeping it healthy, and continually harvesting it season-after-season as it gets bigger and bigger. Your money tree is something you will work hard to grow and then pick the bounty year after year. Take care of your money tree just like you would an apple tree.

The Endless Harvest has three main steps we will discuss in this book.

Step 1: Becoming a Cash Flow Millionaire

This is kind of like planting a seed and watching it grow.

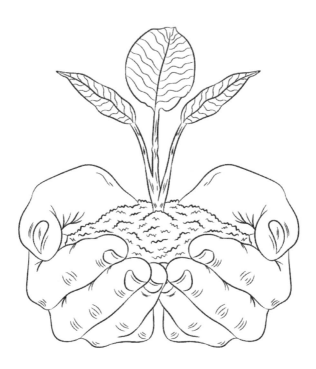

Wealth has to start from somewhere. Here, we will get down to the roots of your finances and find out where money comes from. There are multiple avenues for cash flow, and you should be using multiple methods. I cannot understate the importance of this part because you will never be able to harvest your money tree without it.

Step 2: Staying Rich

This is kind of like watering a tree and keeping it alive and healthy.

"What you appreciate, appreciates."
– Lynne Twist

Your hard-earned money is useless if you waste it or let it die. An apple tree needs water, sunlight, protection against the elements, and many other things to stay alive. With your finances, many different factors may harm it. Tax risks, unplanned global events, and even personal emotions can be hazardous to the health of your money tree.

Step 3: Managing Millions

This is kind of like picking the delicious fruit off your tree. Take care of the roots to maximize your fruit.

After planting the seed and taking care of your growing tree, you will want to harvest the fruit. Make sure you utilize the fruit to its fullest potential. It is also essential to keep your money tree producing profit and know what to do with the continued supply of funds. You will learn what to do with your harvest and even how to expand your money tree.

This is why I call it The Endless Harvest. Lifelong finances take the proper steps to set up. Once you do, you can enjoy the comfortable benefits of a monetary harvest yearly. This book will give you all the steps to grow, maintain, and harvest your money tree for life. Don't worry if this sounds like many steps. It's not as complicated as it might sound.

Even if you don't want to manage your funds, I will talk in detail about how to find the right financial advisor who has your long-term interests in mind. Finances and money are often the root of many life's problems and enjoyments. Everyone works for money during their lifetime. I will teach you how to protect it and keep it growing.

I've been a successful and happy financial advisor for decades. I am very passionate about what I do, but I know not everyone is "head over heels" in conversations concerning finance. I want to end this chapter by telling you why it is so important to follow The Endless Harvest. Your money may not last forever, so protect yourself until the end. I've seen this with multiple acquaintances throughout my life.

THE DANGER OF OUTLIVING YOUR MONEY

**"You will spend as much time in retirement as you have worked…
20-30 years is common."**

– John Yamamoto

With medical breakthroughs, people are living longer lives. This is both good and bad. It is good because naturally, we all want to live long lives. It is bad if you do not financially plan for a long retirement. You may find that you outlive your money. If you retire at age 60, you may need to fund 25+ years of retirement.

People are being downsized across the world. At age 50, many employees find that their company wants them to take an early retirement package. Some packages offer one to two years' salary as an incentive to leave the company early. Sometimes, this works out very well for the person who has saved and accumulated a large pension plan to retire.

In other cases, it works out very poorly when employees find out they were not in the pension plan long enough to get their full benefits. Even more, pensions are now very hard to come by. People often spend their severance package in the first years on essential expenses and survival needs such as food, taxes, and home maintenance.

Many companies are now in the process of laying off more senior employees. No jobs with the same salary are available. These situations often lead people to worry about outliving their money.

Being downsized earlier and living much longer makes it critical to financially plan for a lengthy retirement. A big mistake happens to people is spending too much of their retirement principal when they are younger.

The common argument is that when you are older, you need less money since you will not physically be able to travel or be active. Remember that medical bills, nursing homes, and physical assistance are costly. These are everyday needs of people in their older age. Not to mention, medical insurance will be at a high premium price at an older age.

The need for permanent and endless wealth is because your needs vary throughout your retirement. Inflation can drive up the costs of food, taxes, and transportation. Although your earlier retirement needs will be on travel and golf memberships, your expenses will not necessarily be cheaper later. You should expect the costs of nursing homes and other medical products to rise in price.

NEGATIVE CASH FLOW = INCOME LESS THAN EXPENSES

= BAD SITUATION OF OUTLIVING YOUR MONEY

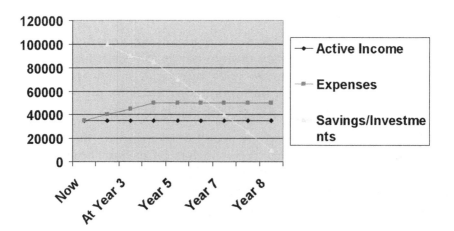

There is a real danger of outliving your money, which is why The Endless Harvest is essential. With earlier retirements and longer life spans forced upon us, we must have a permanent wealth strategy in place throughout our lives. With inflation and rising medical bills, you could find you cannot pay for the quality of medical services you desire. You may outlive your money and need to depend on the Government, your children, or relatives to survive. Follow The Endless Harvest, and don't let this happen to you.

This situation may be all too familiar to someone you know. That's why I am so passionate about the topic of finance. This even stems from my father and what he taught me about money. This is not only something that I have learned, but I have also experienced firsthand. In the next chapter, I will reveal a little about my journey with money while growing up.

"The biggest risk I see in retirement is not market crashes but outliving your money."

– John Yamamoto

MY JOURNEY WITH INVESTMENTS AND FINANCE

B efore we get into The Endless Harvest method, I want to tell you about my humble beginnings. Although my passion for finance has been with me since I was a child, success was not something that came quickly. The knowledge presented in this book comes from over 32 years of hard work, hard lessons, and education.

Let's go back to when I was young. I grew up in a family of six, and we were not rich. We had the bare essentials, but by no means were we considered wealthy. This, in turn, ingrained in my mind the value of a dollar. Money was always a topic of conversation, and it was an important one. Sometimes I felt like life revolved around money. Does this sound familiar to you?

My father was a businessman and had an entrepreneurial spirit. He always spoke to me about stocks and money. He was interested in finance topics, and I followed in his footsteps. We loved the subject of money, and my father hired multiple financial advisors. I remember him being very optimistic about the new advisors, as they seemed to give him advice we had never come across.

Although we were hopeful, these financial advisors did not succeed in helping. One after another failed with our finances. They recommended highly risky stocks, which disappeared one by one. One of these advisors even hurt my father's potential for retirement. This was extremely disturbing. At that time, I was a 24-year-old adult. Right then, I realized how critical money is to everyone's lives.

I had two choices. One was to run away from finance and go in a different direction. I could leave behind the investment I put into my education and pursue another path. Maybe pursue something that wasn't so stressful. The other was to embrace the situation and see if I could learn more about money and help my parents manage theirs. Since finance was in our family and still got me excited daily, I chose to dive in deeper and learn as much as possible.

The first thing I observed was that a lack of patience was harmful. My family was pulled into the "make money fast" advisor trick. Sometimes when talking to an advisor, it seems like everything will go up daily. The more you put in, the more you will reap the rewards. Although this is true in some cases, it is not always the case. This was my first real-life lesson. I learned that not managing risk was harmful. In my father's case, it had cost him an earlier retirement.

"Rewards follow risk management."

– John Yamamoto

At this point in my life, I was all in with finance, but I had a difficult situation. I had just graduated from University. Debt was building from school, my car, and the remaining everyday living expenses. So, I sought out advice from anyone that would give it. Any advice, even free advice, seemed like it would help me get closer to the finish line.

Interestingly, when listening to and studying the advice I received, not all of it made sense. Much of the advice was contradicting. One said to sell, and the other said to buy. This didn't make any sense to me and was highly confusing. It was almost like the advice I received was based purely on emotion. Person A felt like we were in a bad situation. Person B felt like we were in a good situation.

Everyone is different. Each person has different feelings and emotions. This is true not only for investing but for life in general. I now understood why I had contradictory advice. These so-called "advisors" were investing based on emotion. And at that time, so was I.

I learned that the most expensive advice is often free advice. Yes, some free advice can be great, but you will have to run through quite a bit to get what you need. The question is, *Will you have any funds left when you get the right advice you need?*

There is a Do-It-Yourself (DIY) movement in today's day and age in the investing world. People are trading on apps like Robinhood, learning from YouTube videos, and reading blogs about trading. Again, I am not against this. This book gives you everything you need to do it yourself. The problem is that most of the advice is not intended for your long-term benefit. Additionally, most advice is designed to pull at your "emotional strings."

The advice we hear about for free comes in the form of "How to make $100,000 from Bitcoin in the next 30 days." It can also look like, "Take the money from selling your car and 10X it before the year's end." I understand how captivating and exciting these opportunities are.

I realized these "make money quick" schemes do not always work. Yes, there are finite instances where this reality does play out, but the stars have to align for it to work perfectly. In the majority of cases, they fail. This could be considered the same as playing the lottery or gambling in Las Vegas. People do win the lottery, and people win millions in Vegas. But what is the actual ratio of success to loss?

Right here, I learned that the biggest obstacles in finance and investing are ourselves and our desire for more. It is human nature to want things quicker and better, but you must play smart when investing. Play for your long-term success and ensure a comfortable and enjoyable retirement.

When I realized this, I was finally pointed in the right direction. Unfortunately, time was not on my side as this was a very low point in my life. Here was my situation. I had achieved a bachelor of commerce and an MBA. But even with those, I had built up a ton of debt, and had received poor financial advice, and I knew I needed to make a change.

I remember going to the ATM to take out cash for necessities. The machine must have been broken because it wouldn't even give me $20. No, the machine was not broken. I was. My bank account didn't even have twenty dollars in it!

So, let's recap my situation. I just went to school for seven years. I knew I didn't learn anything about cash flow management, and my bank account was empty. Here's what I did about it. I took the hard road of having four jobs for four years to pay off all my debt. It was tough, but I was smart about the jobs I had.

At one job, I taught finance at a college. Although I already had an MBA, I learned more about stocks, bonds, and mutual funds to teach the students. I would not give them useless information, as this had hurt me earlier. I wanted my students to receive the best information hidden from me.

It was the year 1987. Many of you remember this as the infamous year of the stock market crash, Black Monday. Everything was plummeting, and the world was in a financial crisis. Next year, 1988, a job as a financial advisor came up. Many advisors had quit the industry, so spaces were now available. Right then, I walked in 100% to the finance industry.

"Debt is like riding a bicycle uphill. It is easy to coast downhill (get into debt), but is much more difficult to ride uphill."

– John Yamamoto

"Debt is easy to get into, but difficult to get out of due to compound interest."

– John Yamamoto

After four years of working four jobs, I had paid off all my debt. This is something I never wanted to do ever again. It was incredibly hard to come out of this challenging situation, but I landed back on my own two feet and was not going into debt again. I learned the lesson on debt for life, so I literally cut up all my credit cards.

As a financial advisor, I knew I needed to plan for long-term success. This was not only for myself but also for the clients I had. Everyone experienced the big crash of 1987 and needed protection from something like this ever happening again.

One of my first clients allowed me to design a long-term plan. The client had two young children; unfortunately, her husband had just passed away in a car crash. She collected insurance money from the incident and came to me to invest it. The task at hand was simple. Use the insurance money to raise two young boys until they finished university and living independently.

It was my second year as a professional advisor, and I knew exactly what she needed. She needed a plan to create a steady stream of cash flow year after year. It would be designed for long-term wealth. Not for one year, two years, or even five years. This new plan would have to be prepared to last her 20-30 years and not run dry.

During my brief experience in investing, I saw what my competitors were doing up close. Most advisors were showing clients how to chase growth. The situation presented itself very nicely, as many clients had significant losses from the crash of 1987 and were extremely eager to offset their losses. My competitor's strategy was to help their clients get rich quickly. This was not the objective I was tasked with for the single mother.

Instead of chasing growth, I needed to pursue cash flow. During this time, I met a man named Tiff. He said something to me that has stuck with me for life. Tiff said, "Chasing growth is silly." That is a simple statement, valid for the long-term game. Chasing growth may work for you if you want high risk and high reward. But if you are trying to last 20-30 years into the future, you are betting your life on too many high-risk gambles.

"Investing is an infinite game and therefore must be viewed in the context of a lifetime."

– Simon Sinek, author of *The Infinite Game* (a brilliant book)

I learned that you must treat your investments like a pension fund or business. All pensions and successful businesses are created with one thing in mind, cash flow. Business owners start because they want to grow a money tree that keeps producing yearly. Most do not create a business because they want to sell it. They want a money machine to support them, their family, and their employees for many years. If I treated my investments as a business, cash flow would be the primary objective. The main objective would not be a big one-time payout.

This was the one realization that made my whole career in investing. It has allowed my clients, myself, and many others to live a healthy and stress-free life through retirement. And taking into consideration the single mother with two young children. Those children have grown up to be very successful, and their mother still has money left over for her retirement. This was made possible from the initial insurance money she received many decades ago.

This strategy is cash flow based investing. This is what The Endless Harvest method is all about. We are all in the finance game for the long haul. We have beautiful lives, and we want to live them out fully. The Endless Harvest is how we can use cash flow based investing to achieve this goal. Focus on the yield of our investments and not on the growth or worth of the company.

It was refreshing to finally have a long-term strategy that worked for my clients and myself. This could have and should have been used for my father's finances. He would have retired at a much earlier age with this strategy.

I used this successfully with many clients for about a decade. Things were going superb, but then the year 1997 hit, and there was a dramatic change in the market. This was the age when digital electronic companies were booming. It wasn't just a little. It was a lot. Companies were growing exponentially, and financial advisors playing the short game were winning. Their high-risk, high-reward investments were paying off big time.

Things went from my strategy looking like it was the only one to use to my method looking like it was the only one not to use. The digital tech boom lasted more than a month or even a year. It took up the three years of 1997, 1998, and 1999. This was extremely hard because I looked like I didn't know what I was doing for three years in a row. It would have been one thing if it was just a month or two, but three years is a long time.

My strategy was still working for long-term planning, but many investment strategies raced past mine in those three years. I fought "tooth and nail" to stick with my method because I knew it worked for the long haul. We will mostly live past the next three years, won't we? I didn't want to give into growth-based stocks. (I will discuss taking advantage of these situations later in the book.)

Then something interesting happened in the year 2001. Those digital tech companies that saw exponential growth beyond imagination started to crash and crash hard. Companies experienced upwards of 80% loss in their market value, and others went bankrupt.

My cash flow strategy was now back on top, and long-term investing continued to be profitable. Many investors who made millions of dollars in the past years were now losing it all in the blink of an eye. Many of them lost much more than they had made.

This period was very stressful for me. I had considered altering my course from cash flow based investing to growth-based investing more than once during those three years. But I am happy I stuck it out, and my clients were delighted.

Sometimes if you do the right thing, it looks wrong. If something goes up, it doesn't always mean you are right. If something does go down, it doesn't always mean you are wrong. I learned three lessons from this short digital era that will stick with me forever.

One, In investing, you have to be disciplined to achieve long-term success. Every time you move away from your discipline, it will cost you money. This is why we are often our worst enemy in investing. Human beings make many decisions based on emotion. Don't give in to emotion, as it will lead to self-sabotage.

Two, go after cash flow and not growth. Income is a byproduct of cash flow.

After the big rollercoaster ride between Black Monday in 1987 and the digital tech boom in 1997, I had proven this.

The year was 2009 when I set this in stone for all my clients. It has worked successfully for those who choose long-term wealth and desire to have their Endless Harvest.

Three, the key to success when using this system is good tracking. That is how we define what success really is. Many of my past and even current new clients have no factual knowledge of how their investment portfolio is performing. All they know is they are investing. This means absolutely nothing if you don't track your progress. It's impossible to quantify if your investments succeed or fail over time.

This is how we are successful and always have happy clients living long and prosperous lives. They have worked to grow their money tree and have an Endless Harvest.

Today, chasing cash flow is more important than ever before. The world experiences many bubbles that can take any investor off track and get them in trouble. Just recently, we had the DotCom Bubble and Cryptocurrency Bubble. Bubbles are becoming more common now, so you have to watch out for these situations that may sway you off course.

One of the cornerstones of my method is the power of structure and discipline. For example, reporting, optimizing on return, and risk management are three key areas we always consider. In the remaining chapters of this book, I will lay out a step-by-step structure to follow.

Follow these three steps, and you will achieve your Endless Harvest:

- Becoming a cash flow millionaire
- Staying rich
- Managing millions

This simple structure is designed to prevent us from making mistakes. As humans, self-sabotage is our worst enemy. Following structure allows us to think of both the pros and cons. How often have you thought about how much money you could make but not considered the pains you might experience?

Things really seemed to fall in line after I set up my three-step process, The Endless Harvest. I'm not only talking about monetarily but personally as well.

It's interesting. If I went back to the beginning, I would want to know how to control my emotions. Mathematical formulas, algorithms, and other tools are all great, but they are useless if you can't control your emotions. The truth is, we spend too much time on mathematics when we should be learning how to manage our emotions.

This personal growth has benefited my financial life and personal relationships. Make sure you follow a structure and don't get too sidetracked. Veering off course is when you will get in trouble.

You may have heard the expression; We *are only human*. This is true without a doubt. We all make mistakes, and it is a part of life. What matters is what we do to get ourselves back on track. A very successful investor and founder of the company Vanguard always keeps in mind what is called "reversion to the mean." This can be explained as follows: If you have a winning strategy, or the stock market goes up over time, things may fluctuate up-and-down short term. We may have bubbles, crashes, and everything in between, but the long-term situation will always revert back to the mean.

Reversion to the mean applies just as much to stocks as it does to our lives. Take a look at stocks in the Dow Jones or S&P 500. They may go up and down monthly, but they have been trending upwards for multiple decades when you look at the long-term investment chart. Just make sure you are following the correct long-term strategy.

I've had many great coaches and attribute my success to them. Interestingly, the word "coach" is typically only associated with sports like basketball or baseball. We need coaches just as much for life successes as for sports.

I wanted to reveal my humble beginnings to show you that I am not a superhero. I learned these lessons the hard way, so you don't have to experience that pain. Make sure you take advantage of this information and use it to build your best future and Endless Harvest.

YOUR HARVEST OVERVIEW

LEARN HOW TO BECOME A CASH FLOW MILLIONAIRE

We are at the "meat and potatoes" of this book. This is where I will explain to you the three-step process of The Endless Harvest. Let me first tell you what The Endless Harvest will provide to you and who this is for:

- If you are looking for a way to invest your hard-earned money that will pay you dividends for the remainder of your life, this method is for you.
- If you have tried many different strategies before but none of them succeeded long-term, this method is for you.
- This method is for you if you want to live stress-free without worrying about where your finances will come from after you retire.

To be fair, The Endless Harvest is not for everyone. If you meet any of the criteria below, my three-step method is not for you, and I would urge you to soak up the information given but stop continuing to read. I respect your time, and my method is not for everyone. Don't continue if you identify with any of these below:

- If you want to gamble and take high risks to get rich, hopefully, this method is not for you.
- If you do not have self-control and will not follow a proven path to success, this method is not for you.
- If you have an urgent requirement to make two to three times your current net worth in the next year or less, this method is not for you.

If you are still reading, I know you associate with the first list rather than the second. You are precisely the type of person I am confident I can help. I am excited to walk you through the remainder of this book and give you the keys to success in three simple steps. We even have a bonus step if you want to turn up the fire afterward.

61

As you know, money can and will always be a high-stress point when considering retirement or life in general. You can let go of that stress when you realize you are in control of your finances. (And in control of your life.) The end goal we want to achieve in this book is to understand the three-step simple process of investing our money to live out a healthy, desirable, and stress-free retirement.

There is nothing more freeing than this experience. That is why it is called financial freedom. Financial freedom doesn't necessarily mean having millions or billions of dollars stored in the attic. This would be classified as nothing less than extremely rich. Financial freedom is the freedom you will experience when you know how to invest your finances, so you can stop worrying about how much will be left tomorrow.

> **"The main payout of money management and investing is simply freedom."**
> **– John Yamamoto**

Take the stress of money out of the equation and completely understand your wealth and control of your life. This doesn't mean spending money haphazardly or never considering a price tag. This financial freedom you will experience will be one of the best feelings in life. You will achieve the ability to shape your future financial destiny to fit the lifestyle you want to live.

You may now feel that you haven't read books like this before. Everyone wants to tell you how to make a million dollars in the next 30 days. You may feel a little lost in the finance world. Some of your finances work very well, while others might be struggling. I know finance can be confusing, but I will simplify it in three steps.

Of course, you may experience obstacles along the way, and your emotions might sometimes get the best of you. But if you stick to this process and always come back, you will be much better for your long-term wealth. This destination is different for all of us. Some people want to afford that private island in the Bahamas they've always dreamed of and have the initial capital to make it happen. Others want to have the ability to simply go out on date night and drink a glass of wine with their spouse every Friday night for the rest of their lives. Whichever is your goal, The Endless Harvest can be catered to you.

You might be thinking, *How can the same method work for someone with much money and someone with a bit of money?* The truth is that the same principles work no matter your current net worth. The only difference is the exponential results you will see.

So with that in mind, here are the three steps to The Endless Harvest:

Step 1: Becoming a cash flow millionaire

In this step, you will learn the essentials of focusing on cash flow instead of growth. You'll learn different methods to achieve multiple income streams and how they will compound over time.

Step 2: Staying rich

In this step, you will learn how to protect your finances from external and internal dangers to your wealth. You'll learn how to outlive your money and what to do when Black Swan events, like Covid-19, happen worldwide.

Step 3: Managing millions

In this step, you will learn why a finance report card is important and how to read one. You'll learn why organizing and planning your financial future is essential every year.

And then… there is a secret step after you have completed The Endless Harvest:

Step 4: Asking the right questions

In this step, you will learn how to hire the right financial advisors and assess your risk. You'll learn how to simplify your finances and get them quickly turning in high gear.

Throughout this book, you have already and will continue to see the analogy between planting an apple tree and harvesting your money tree. Financial advising and wealth generation are about growing and tending to your money tree. This process can be related exceptionally well to growing an apple tree.

I'll take you through the steps of planting the seed, protecting your tree, harvesting the fruit, and automating the process. You will see illustrations throughout this book for reference. So without further ado, let's get right into step one, Becoming a Cash Flow Millionaire.

BECOMING A CASH FLOW MILLIONAIRE

T he first part of The Endless Harvest is becoming a cash flow millionaire. This is where it all begins. Without this step, you can never reap any rewards from growing your financial money tree. It is a lot of work, and you will often not see results immediately.

Do this so you can:

Build a sturdy foundation for your financial future. This is your wealth base and where you need to start before harvesting any monetary reward.

Let's take the analogy we use throughout The Endless Harvest, planting and harvesting a money tree. In this step, you are putting in the hard work of planting your tree's seed in the ground. Apples, or money, don't appear right away. Even in the beginning, you won't see any green. The seed will be under the ground, just starting to sprout.

This means your tree will be starting to grow roots and sprout out of the seed, but you won't be able to see it. Becoming a cash flow millionaire doesn't mean you will immediately see dollar bills rain from the sky. It means you will work hard to start investing in capital focused on cash flow.

You'll have to pour water on your seed. Then give it fertilizer for it to flourish. (All in the meantime, allowing it to receive sunlight for photo-synthesis.) These, along with other activities, let your tiny seed begin its growth into a healthy and fruitful apple tree.

Cash Flow Millionaire	Returns	Net Worth Millionaire	Owns (value)
Retirement Fund at 5%	$500,000	Large Home (w/ $20k debt)	$200,000-800,000
Tax Free Plans at 5%	$100,000	Luxury Cars (w/ $5k debt)	$100,000
Stock Portfolio at 5%	$800,000	Recreational Vehicle	$50,000
Home (debt free)	$500,000	Cabin	$250,000
Cars	$50,000	Boat at Cabin	$20,000
		Retirement Fund at 5%	$300,000
		Stocks at 5%	$200,000
CASH FLOW	**$70,000 per year**	**CASH FLOW**	**$25,000**

This is kind of like planting a seed and watching it grow.

Do you remember us talking about cash flow during my journey to success? It started all the way back when I spoke to Tiff. He told me, *Chasing growth is silly,* and this stuck with me for life. Well, here is when we will put this into play. Let's focus on becoming a cash flow millionaire so you will be set up for life.

In this section, I will explain exactly how to do this for yourself. Together, we will review some of the main ways to gain your cash flow. But even before this, I want to tell you why having different sources of income is essential and what laws you need to follow to keep them alive.

This is the sturdy foundation we need to build to have an Endless Harvest. Before we get into the details, I want to give you a short real-life case study of why this is so important.

It is the case from my personal life journey you just read, but I want to explain it further in detail. I call this case:

Raising Two Boys and the Disappointment of Formal Education

In my third year in the business, I learned an important lesson. After teaching an investment workshop, I was approached by a man who requested a meeting to manage his investments. We arranged an appointment for next Monday morning. His wife showed up for the meeting a few days later, and her husband was absent. She explained that he was killed in an accident a few days ago and she had a problem. She has two children, two and five years old, present with her.

She needed me to develop a financial plan to help raise her two boys for the next 20 years on only the proceeds of her husband's life insurance payout. She could not work as her job did not cover the daycare costs and the boy's other needs. Her husband had a great job, a solid salary, and was only 32 years old. The plan was to stay home and raise her boys while he worked. His sudden passing changed everything.

That was a wake-up call to me. The wake-up call was that, up to that point, my Bachelor's and Master's Degree in business, plus my formal industry training and company training, did not provide me with a strategy for dealing with their long-term income needs. How could I develop a plan to provide a monthly income for this widow for the next 20 years without spending all of her capital? What is the best strategy to create a sustainable and predictable income stream for 12 months x 20 years = 240 monthly payments? I had no choice but to figure this out.

The answer was to create a maximum income strategy that maximized the income stream from her proceeds from his insurance money. I calculated the minimum % return had to be 5%+. I then set up a series of investments to generate predictable and reliable cash flow. We achieved this income stream for the next 240 months from 1993-2013. The capital continues to grow and is still providing income to this day into 2021 and onward, helping fund the mother's retirement. The boys, now men, have grown up and are leading productive and successful lives.

I have successfully used this method of maximizing cash flow for many other clients. I refer to it as the chicken and egg strategy. If you have 365 chickens and live off the eggs, you will have a sustainable plan. If you eat a chicken a day, in 1 year, you will have no chickens or eggs. Chickens represent capital. Eggs represent returns on capital, returns on investment, or yield. Another metaphor we use throughout this book is to plant financial gardens of wealth, such as apple trees. Apple trees are capital, and apples are the return on capital. Money is no different where stocks, bonds, and real estate are capital. Yield, or return on capital, can be dividends, interest, and rental income.

We should all learn from this story to focus on creating multiple streams of income from your investments. Live off the returns from your investment while keeping your principal or capital intact. Live off the eggs and don't eat the chickens. Grow your apple tree and eat the apples.

This section is step one of The Endless Harvest. By the time you are done with this section, you will learn how to become a cash flow millionaire.

In this section, we will talk about growing your multiple streams of income. We'll also review some of the rules and laws I follow based on this cash flow model. The last pieces we review in this section are four primary principles where cash flow comes from. There are many more places where cash flow originates, but I will discuss the top four that we concentrate on with our clients.

At the end of the section, I'll explain the law of compound interest. You can think of this as "the icing on the cake." It's super sweet and profitable. Get ready to have a ball as we get ready to plant the seed for your money tree!

GROWING GARDENS OF WEALTH

G rowing gardens of wealth are essential to your financial foundation. These are the elements that are required to feed your investment plan. Without these elements, it is impossible to perform any investing. You will need to have a systematic saving strategy. These savings are the fuel for your investment plan.

Here are some important reasons why you should save money for your retirement:

- Government pension plans are rare, poorly funded, and do not base your old age on these plans.
- Old-Age Social Security will probably be granted only to those in need, and people with other investment income may not qualify.
- Rising life expectancies mean you could live long past the age of 65.
- Rising costs for post-secondary education mean it is more expensive to provide for older children going to university or college.
- Over-dependence on low-paying term deposits and savings accounts means little real investment growth after consideration is made for inflation and taxes.

Let me tell you a short story of when this fact hit me. One night, I watched a television show about the street and working people in America. After interviewing the street people, the news reporter was surprised to find that they were just ordinary people caught in unfortunate circumstances due to unexpected job loss or the primary income earner's death. After interviewing working Americans and calculating their savings versus their debts, the reporter concluded that the average working person was just seven paychecks away from living on the street.

It was shocking to see how unexpected circumstances could lead to severe consequences. The show impressed upon me just how important it was to save a "nest egg" or "rainy day fund" for times of trouble.

I live in Canada, and Canadians are in a similar situation, just like the Americans in the news story. Over 40% of working Canadians have not made retirement preparations. Statistics Canada reported that almost half of all Canadian seniors qualify for the Guaranteed Income Supplement paid to seniors who live below the poverty line. (A yearly income of less than $10,000.) nearly 20% of men and 50% of women between 65 and 69 live at or below the poverty line.

To grow your gardens of wealth, you must learn to pay yourself first with a concrete savings plan. You must create a high-impact savings plan before you can ever become financially independent.

THE ENDLESS HARVEST RULE:

Most portfolios suffer from malnutrition. They are not fed enough cash to grow and provide for retirement.

It is crucial to think of money as life energy or life force. Money is valuable because it represents time and the effort needed to earn it. Since we have a finite amount of life and only live a short time, money is valuable because of the amount of time it replaces. Suppose a person earns $40,000 yearly for an after-tax income of $28,000. It would take one year of that person's life to make money to purchase a $28,000 car.

You can also think of it this way. If you earn $36,000 per year ($3,000 per month) and save $6,000 a year, you are banking two months for your retirement—you can retire two months earlier. The more money you save, the more time you are banking and the earlier you can retire.

If everyone lived to be 300 years old, we would all become wealthy because time would not be as finite. Financial fitness is the key to becoming wealthy in 20 to 25 years. The same principles apply to financial health as to physical health. You become financially fit through small efforts over time, not by going to the gym once a year or through fasting diets.

I want to tell you a fable of someone who understood this very well:

Hundreds of years ago, there lived a man named Eric. Eric was a simple man. He worked hard and was paid eight coppers a day for his work. He would take the coppers home and put one copper each day into a clay urn in his home. He determined that his family needed five coppers a day for living expenses, and unexpected expenses would take the other two coppers. Thus one copper a day was all he could save.

70

Eric also earned 35 coppers each summer from his small farm. At the end of each year, Eric would take his 400 coppers and exchange them for 40 pieces of silver. Due to his simple savings plan, Eric, his wife, and his children lived a very comfortable life long into his retirement. Eric understood the simple universal law of accumulation—small sacrifices become big rewards over time.

Remember, to become wealthy; you must pay yourself first and save money each month. This is the first step to becoming a cash flow millionaire.

THE LAW OF THE HARVEST

We have saved money to supply cash to support our gardens of wealth. Before getting into how we can generate cash flow, we need to lay down some ground rules. The law of the harvest is the most important law to understand before taking action.

You will generate cash if you plant a cash-generating investment in your portfolio. If you plant weeds in your portfolio, you will produce losses. I know this seems like common sense, but I want you to soak this in. You get exactly what you plant.

This applies to the "stuff" or assets you spend your money on. That multimillion-dollar house on the beach is very attractive but carries a substantial financial burden. Housekeeping, hefty annual taxes, robust security, and many other expenses will need to be paid to keep your asset in working condition. If you keep buying these assets or weeds, you can expect high costs that diminish your wealth yearly.

For example, a famous professional boxer, Mike, went bankrupt quickly by spending money on shiny assets. M.C., a rock star, who made $35 million in his career within the music industry, also ended up broke. $35 million quickly went to $0. To my knowledge, he owned three huge mansions in various high-dollar locations. The assets he owned turned into weeds that sucked up all of his cash. You can be classified as a millionaire by having many different assets, but you will become broke if you don't have cash flow.

This is my general rule of thumb. You should spend 20% of your after-tax income on income-generating investments. You reap what you sow. If you plant income-generating investments, you will harvest income. If you plant assets, like mansions, you will harvest property tax and other costly expenses. I'm not saying all assets are bad. I enjoy the comforts of a nice home just as much as the next man. You need to be aware of what you are planting in your financial life.

CREATING A MONEY TREE

This is a great time to tell you about different ways you can choose to plant your harvest. It all starts in the beginning by creating a money tree. The biggest mistake people make when building their portfolio is underestimating the amount of money they will need at retirement.

I use the money tree concept based on a chicken and egg concept. If you are forced to kill and eat a few chickens a month, you will reduce the number of eggs you receive, and your principal, or chicken base, will decline over time. If you can live off the eggs without killing any chickens, then your money should last for the rest of your life.

USEFUL DEFINITION:

A portfolio is simply a basket of wealth. It is a container of different investments. Like a garden, a portfolio is merely a garden where you have planted various investments. How financially successful you are depending on how well you have nurtured, weeded, and taken care of your investments in the garden.

The best way to design your portfolio is to use a money tree concept. A money tree is like an apple tree. Each year it produces apples. Each branch of the tree has apples growing from it.

A money tree is a tree that you create to produce passive or residual income forever without any effort on your part. Each branch becomes a different cash flow avenue. The key will be to take care of and nurture your money tree so you can generate income for your life's needs at retirement.

There are several ways to create passive or investment income. The easiest way is using investments. For your money tree, you can:

- Buy stocks that pay dividend income.
- Buy stocks that grow using capital gains.
- Buy mutual funds that pay dividends.
- Buy mutual funds that grow using capital gains.
- Buy mutual funds that pay interest income.
- Buy term deposits or GICs that pay interest income.
- Buy bonds that pay interest income.
- Contribute to your pension plan at work that pays an income at retirement in the form of pension income.

- Invest in a registered retirement plan which is converted to income at retirement.
- Buy real estate investment trusts (REITs) that pay income from a bundle of real estate investments.

CREATING YOUR OWN MONEY MACHINE

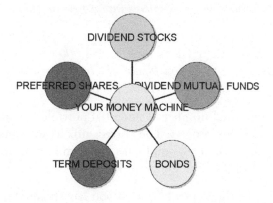

Here are some more difficult ways to earn passive residual income:

- Write a book and get royalties.
- Create and sell music to get royalties.
- Network marketing trailer income.
- Universal insurance or annuities that pay an income.
- Oil well royalties.
- Renting farmland to others to farm for a fee.
- Rental properties
- Etc.

I want to give you an example.

Marilyn's Travel Plan

Marilyn (not her real name) and I met at a charity speech I gave. She then opened an account, and we transferred her money to create a residual income portfolio. Five years ago, Marilyn retired after being a teacher for 30 years. At age 58, Marilyn is divorced with a grown-up daughter. Her teaching pension allows her to live without working, yet she does not earn enough to travel.

She can cash out some of her mutual funds and term deposits to travel, but she did not because she worries she might run out of money. I looked at her money and found she had term deposits in four banks. She also had money fragmented in other places.

In other words, she had many small-term deposits due at different times. Her mutual funds were in very aggressive emerging market funds. So we transferred and consolidated her investments into a new program. This is what it looked like:

In the end, Marilyn now receives a check for $4,000 every year. She has traveled to Hawaii, Costa Rica, and Japan. She has harnessed the power of her money into a permanent and perpetual income stream.

There are an unlimited number of potential portfolios. Finding the right portfolio is a complex process. The correct mix of investments depends on the client's circumstances, bond rates, economic conditions, goals, risk tolerance level, and the time the client has to invest.

Your return would also depend on what you have planted in your portfolio. Slower investments such as term deposits or bonds would have grown more steadily, but not as quickly as stocks, just as an oak tree would grow slower than a corn plant.

There are two types of money trees you can plant. The non-registered luxury account money tree and the registered or tax-assisted retirement money tree. What kind of tree you plant depends on your goals and time frame.

YOUR LUXURY PORTFOLIO OF UNREGISTERED ASSETS

We've talked much about being conservative, but humans desire luxurious assets. Precisely for these, I recommend setting up monthly or yearly investment plans. Without some money outside of your pension plans and retirement savings plans, you may not be able to afford luxury items. Travel, cruise ship holidays, or golfing in sunny places may not be in your budget. With a combination of stocks, bonds, and mutual funds, you can live off the dividends and interest or sell them to purchase the luxury items that make life enjoyable.

Your portfolio of unregistered assets should be your first line of financial defense. A rainy day or travel fund outside of regular retirement savings are critical for a prosperous and worry-free retirement.

The advantage of an investment or non-registered account is the freedom and lack of restrictions on the types of investments. Foreign content rules do not apply to non-registered assets, so you can buy shares of American, Japanese, European, and other global investments. There are no restrictions on the amount you can invest into non-registered investments. You could invest in a sudden windfall or inheritance at any time.

Why limit yourself to a few choices? To create an effective portfolio, you must access all the investment products and select the most suitable ones. What you invest in is what you will harvest. Next, we'll discuss one more rule concerning cash flow before getting into the different investment methods. I call this, The Rule of $20.

THE POWER OF CASH FLOW USING THE RULE OF $20

For every $20 you invest, you want a $1 return on investment, return on capital, or 5% return. I call this the power of cash flow using the rule of $20. If you spend $20, it will cost you that $1 every year. I'm not saying never to spend your money, but be aware of the opportunity cost associated with assets and stuff.

This is why the rule of $20 is an excellent standard to live by. Think about this example. If you invest $1M and it returns 5%, you gain $50k annually. In 20 years, you have made $1M. That is a pretty fantastic return on investment, right? And this isn't even considering compound interest.

The rule of $20 is not to spend more than $1 if you have $20. That will keep your investments and live rich for the long term. This gives you a rule of thumb on discipline.

"Cash flow" means saving enough for the future and controlling your debts. Achieving a complete financial plan balances spending money on necessities, spending money on wants, and determining where your money is going.

You can also think of this in terms of saving money. You have to save money from every dollar you earn daily and not just worry about putting money away to pay down debts. If you only spend money on paying down debts, you will retire with no debts and no money saved.

The second amount of cash should pay down debts by putting money into long-term or capital investments. The rest goes to fun and needs. Living off 70% or 80% of your wealth is the key to financial success. We must determine where our money is going and save enough to reach our goals.

So far, we have learned why cash flow is so important, where the cash flow should come from, and some simple rules based on savings and investment earnings. Let's get down to business now. It's time to talk about the different sources cash flow comes from. First, we will talk about cash flow from stocks.

CASH FLOW

FROM STOCKS

I n the following chapters ahead, things will get a little more technical. Even though there is much more terminology to explain, I am keeping it to the basics. As I said before, *I'm giving you everything you need within this book.* But I won't get you "too lost in the weeds." This can seem like much information, but the following are the basics you need to understand, even if you have your financial advisor.

Let's start with stocks. I have found that most people are afraid of stocks. This fear is somewhat justified. Many people have experienced stocks through the purchase of a speculative penny stock. Someone close to you may have lost money in a penny stock. Combine this experience with tales of the great crash of 1929 and 1987. Stories of the depression, told by parents and grandparents, often warn us about the dangers of stock ownership.

The truth is, it is hard to retire in style without stock ownership. In the long term, the best return of any asset group is from the stock market. The stock market is your most significant potential for gains and losses.

We are in section one, Becoming a Cash Flow Millionaire, which is like planting a seed and watching it grow. Cash flow from stocks is the fertilizer used to expedite the growth of your apple tree. Stocks can rapidly produce growth for your Endless Harvest.

Stocks are kind of like using fertilizer to expedite your tree's growth.

You should always treat the stock market should with respect. You should research before buying any stocks. This chapter will provide some good rules for managing your stock portfolio.

So why do people avoid stocks?

- They have not considered inflation to be a threat.
- They do not understand stocks.
- Stocks seem too risky.
- They have heard negative stories of stock ownership.
- They do not realize that stocks can pay an income.

One of the best ways to become wealthy in a capitalistic society is by owning a business directly or buying shares in businesses run by others. Stocks produce consistently superior long-term results compared to any other type of financial asset.

Consider a short case:

George and Marilyn's Stock Ownership

Although George and Marilyn work for the government, they are interested in owning shares of good businesses. They currently own shares in several companies.

100 Shares of Wal-Mart – a retail store
25 Shares of Coca-Cola - a soft drink company
115 Shares of McDonald's Restaurants – a fast-food chain
50 Shares of Hewlett Packard – producers of high-quality computer accessories
15 Shares of Sony – an entertainment company
25 Shares of Honda Motors – an automobile manufacturer
200 Shares of Royal Bank of Canada – Canada's largest bank

George and Marylin happily look forward to building their fortune by owning great high-quality companies. Although they have seen their stock prices go up and down, they are confident in the long-term benefits of owning companies that are well managed. I'm sure you recognize some brand names above, like McDonald's, Wal-Mart, and Honda Motors. They also reinvest their dividends and receive more shares in a dividend reinvestment program set up with their Investment Advisor.

Now, you have heard of the good. But what about the negative? Here are some common reasons people do not profit from stock ownership:

- They do not do any research.
- They do not sell bad shares.
- They buy companies they do not understand.
- They don't stick to a disciplined approach to investing.
- They buy stocks with the crowd and sell at the same time everyone sells. (AKA getting influenced by the crowd mentality and not thinking like business owners.)
- They view everything from a short-time perspective.
- They incorrectly view stock ownership as gambling, not as ownership in companies.

Equities or stock market investments represent ownership in a company or business. For your investment, you are rewarded with dividends and gains or penalized with a reduction in value or losses in the stock's value. There are two main equities or stocks: common and preferred stocks.

Common stocks (equities) are certificates that document ownership of part of a company's capital stock. I'll focus on publicly traded shares, mainly on New York and Toronto Stock Exchanges. Gains in the value of common stocks are treated as capital gains for tax purposes. Preferred stocks entitle the owner to fixed dividends payable before common stock dividends. They don't carry voting privileges. Dividends are given good tax treatment and qualify for dividend tax credits.

There are two ways to invest in stocks. You can either trade them or buy and hold them long-term. The low-maintenance way is to buy and hold dividend-paying stocks or growth stocks. The higher maintenance way is to be a short-term stock trader.

WHY BUY STOCKS?

If appropriately chosen and held over the long term, stocks will produce the greatest returns of any asset group. The growth of any single company can be infinite. They can grow many times from their initial startup. A stock can grow with the development of a company.

Stocks offer significant growth potential. For example, McDonald's stock history is an excellent case. Starting from a few restaurants, it branched out over the entire planet. Wal-Mart stores also started as a few stores. It also grows into hundreds of stores in many different countries.

Stocks also provide an excellent defense against inflation. Favorable tax treatment means that dividends and capital growth from stocks will result in lower taxes than bonds. Although stocks increase and decrease in value, their growth rate provides a good hedge against inflation. A stock portfolio or equity mutual fund will outperform safe investments like term deposits and bonds in the long term.

Remember the movie "Back to the Future," where Michael J. Fox was sent back to 1955 in a time machine. Imagine if you were given the same opportunity as Michael J. Fox and were allowed to use that time machine and go back to the 1950s, 1960s, and 1970s. If you invested in stocks of successful companies (McDonald's, Coca-Cola, Sony, IBM, Apple, Microsoft), you would have acquired a fortune. You can follow this strategy today and acquire a fortune by investing in profitable companies.

THE ENDLESS HARVEST RULE:

Buy stocks of companies that you admire.

There are many benefits to owning stocks. Stocks are as risky or as safe as the company you are buying. Stocks are an excellent way to receive the benefits of company ownership without all the hard work associated with running the company. Stocks can rapidly increase in value, and you can multiply your wealth many times over in a short period. That's pretty awesome, right?

Next, we will talk about purchasing bonds. Another type of fuel to grow your money tree.

CASH FLOW

FROM BONDS

Bonds, or fixed-income investments, are used to build a secure low-maintenance portfolio. Fixed Income investments are based on a set interest rate and provide the buyer with regular interest payments. Any interest earned is taxable and should be considered when evaluating the rate of return on the investment. Fixed income investments include bonds, strip bonds, government savings bonds, term deposits, and guaranteed investment certificates (GICs).

Bonds are like the sunlight needed to grow your plant. Sunlight is a necessity for growing your apple tree. It is strong and controlled, but not all days are sunny days. Sometimes the sun can be blocked by cloud cover or even other trees.

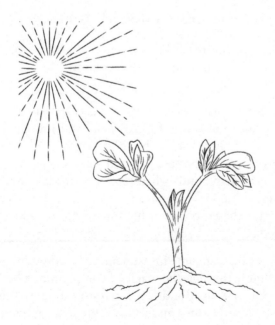

Bonds are kind of like the consistent sunlight plants need to grow.

Bonds are a certificate of debt issued by a government or company—the bondholder loans money to the bond issuer for a definite period at a specified interest rate. The borrower pledges assets as security for the loan, except in the cases of government bonds. Bonds reflect interest rate changes.

Term deposits and guaranteed investment certificates (GICs) are securities issued by financial institutions such as banks, trust companies, and credit unions. They earn interest at a fixed rate for a specific time and are locked in until their maturity date.

Two markets trade millions of dollars daily—the stock and bond markets. The bond market is very large and has booms and crashes like the stock market. People are familiar with the stock market because of the media's focus but often don't know that a bond market exists.

When you buy a bond or term deposit, you lend your money to a bank, government, or business. In return, you receive interest as a return on your investment. The interest rate directly corresponds with the risk level of the investment. The higher the interest rate, the higher the risk of not receiving your initial investment back.

THE ENDLESS HARVEST RULE:

Interest rates reflect the health of the economy—the higher the interest rate, the unhealthier the economy.

Bonds, especially government strip bonds, are an excellent way to plan for retirement because they allow for excellent and low-maintenance planning. Bonds provide investors with a high real rate of return plus a significant capital gain or an increase in bond value if sold before maturity. Buying long-term strip bonds when rates are high is one of the best returns at the lowest risk possible. I have witnessed investors receive 70% returns when they purchased bonds at high-interest rates and sold them when rates dropped.

The rate of return for fixed income investments is based on interest rates. These investments grow through the magic of compounding because you earn interest on your interest. Bonds are interest-bearing and mature in one year or more. Cash and money market investments are interest-bearing and mature in less than one year.

There are several ways to make money in the bond market. The primary method is to buy government-strip bonds when interest rates are high and sell them when rates are low. Another way is to buy bond mutual funds when rates are high and switch them to stock or equity funds when rates are low. By doing this, you can make capital gains from owning bonds.

Capital gains are simply the difference between what you paid for an investment and what you sell it for. There is a much more precise definition in the tax guides. However, for our purposes, simply subtracting your original cost from the sale price gets you either a capital gain, in a positive outcome, or a capital loss, if you sold the investment for less than you paid.

Owning bonds when rates are high is an excellent way to profit using the risk-reward tradeoff. You can make exceptional gains when you buy bonds when rates are high. It provides a worthy risk-reward tradeoff that is often better than buying only stocks.

When interest rates are high, you should purchase long-term bonds. When rates are low, buy short-term bonds, term deposits, or treasury bills. Then when interest rates go up, you can reinvest in longer-term investments.

Buy bonds rather than stocks during recessions and lock in during high-interest rates. The high rates hurt stocks, and bonds make a better reward for a low-risk level. Eventually, the high-interest rate breaks inflation, and the rate falls. Bonds, locked in at high-interest rates, benefit from their high rates by increasing in value as new bonds are issued at lower rates, creating a capital gain. When the economy turns around, you should buy stocks rather than bonds.

GUARANTEED INVESTMENT CERTIFICATES AND TERM DEPOSITS

Term deposits are guaranteed to a maximum of $100,000 by the CDIC (Canada Deposit Insurance Corporation). Interest rates directly correlate with the term of the investment. The longer the term, the higher the interest rate. Most common are the Guaranteed Investment Certificates (GICs) locked in for one to five years. When an investment is "locked in," it cannot be readily liquidated—you cannot receive your money back from the investment until it matures. So before investing in GICs, be sure you won't need the money before the maturity date.

Shop around for the best interest rate before you buy a term deposit. Just because an institution says it has the best interest rates doesn't mean it is true. Be cautious when you choose the term of the investment. Consider when you will need the investment and are interest rates stable or increasing? You want to lock into term deposits when interest rates are dropping, just the opposite of a mortgage strategy where you lock in when rates increase.

CORPORATE BONDS

A corporate bond is a promise a corporation makes to repay any money to the lenders at a predetermined interest rate and on a predetermined date. Corporate bonds do not have any guarantees. Because of the higher risk to the lender, corporate bonds usually pay a higher interest rate than a Government bond.

You have to be careful only to buy companies with solid finances. You may not receive any interest payments if the company has financial problems. You also might lose your money if the company goes bankrupt.

Most corporate bonds are issued at par, which generally is $1,000. More commonly, brokerage firms sell them with a minimum purchase of $5,000. They usually pay interest twice a year. The interest rate is called the Coupon Rate, and the amount of time the bond is outstanding is called the Term of the Bond.

THE ENDLESS HARVEST RULE:

It is essential only to buy bonds from quality issuers. This helps minimize the risk that the bondholder will not honor their interest payments or go bankrupt before maturity.

When purchasing corporate bonds, look for:

1. The credit rating of the issuer.
2. The term to maturity.
3. Level of interest rates.
4. Level of debt of the issuing company.
5. Cash flow of the issuing company.

BOND RISKS

There are some risks to consider before you buy bonds. Although they are conservative investments, the risks are:

Purchasing Power Risk

Since inflation erodes the purchasing power of fixed-income security, consider the prices of items and the possible cost of living when the bond matures. For example, at 6%, a bond will triple over 20 years. Will the cost of living also triple over the next 20 years?

Liquidity or Marketability Risk

Can you quickly sell the bond before maturity if you need the money? If it is not liquid, you might have to hold that bond until it matures. This could be five, ten, or twenty years from now.

Credit Risk

Non-government bonds could go bankrupt before maturity. How solid is the issuer? Foreign government bonds can default on their payments. How stable is that government or company that issues the bonds? Make sure to purchase top-quality bonds to help minimize default or credit risks.

Interest Rate Risks

Prior to maturity, bond prices fluctuate on the open market. They rise and fall inversely to the interest rates. If interest rates move upward, your bonds' market value will decrease. If you need to dispose of your bonds prior to maturity, it could be at a time when interest rates have risen and the bond prices have declined.

Currency Risk

If you hold foreign pay bonds, you have a currency risk if this currency falls in relation to the domestic dollar, depending on your country of origin.

I know there are a lot of ins and outs to bonds. It may seem a bit more complicated than stocks, isn't it? Often this is where professional financial advisors come in handy. Later on, we'll talk about how to pick one if you desire. Next, we will talk about cash flow from mutual funds.

CASH FLOW

FROM MUTUAL FUNDS AND ETFS (EXCHANGE TRADED FUNDS)

Who should buy mutual funds? Mutual funds are great for busy investors who want to spend their time on activities other than managing their money. You save time since you have your money managed by a professional. A fund manager chooses the stocks or bonds in your portfolio. You avoid the day-to-day decisions. Mutual funds require little involvement for the purchasers.

The power of mutual funds is in their flexibility. You can do so much with mutual funds. You can generate income, obtain growth, and provide liquidity and safety. They are one of the best and easiest low-maintenance ways to invest your money in the stock market compared to buying individual stocks.

In our apple tree analogy, mutual funds are kind of like the water your seed needs to grow. Water is essential for your seed to sprout into a large productive tree. Many different sources can provide it. Water may come from the spout of a bucket, an automated sprinkler system, or even from natural rain in the sky.

The right amount of water is critical to a successful harvest. Water needs to be applied consistently and in the right balance for a seedling to grow large. This is why some of the best watering systems are placed on flow meters and timers.

What are mutual funds?

What are ETFs (Exchange Traded Funds)?

*Mutual funds are kind of like the exact amount of water
your seedling needs to grow.*

Mutual funds allow easy and inexpensive diversification. Diversification reduces risk. It also allows average income earners to own multiple stock portfolios. Mutual funds can be equity, stock, fixed income, or market-based money.

Investment fund managers pool their clients' money to invest in these funds. A bond fund is a mutual fund that consists primarily of bonds. For example, Canadian equity funds consist of Canadian stocks. Global Equity funds contain international funds. Asian or Far East Funds include Asian stocks.

Mutual funds are an excellent way to invest overseas without the work of deciding which countries to invest in. The main benefits of mutual funds are:

- Professional management.
- Inexpensive investments.
- Convenient and low maintenance investing.
- Expertly controlled and managed foreign stock market purchases.
- Diversification through the purchase of a wide-cross section of stocks and bonds.
- Convenient reinvestment of gains to build up your wealth.
- Flexibility to move from other funds within the fund family.
- Returns are reported daily.
- Easy liquidation if you require cash and have systematic withdrawal plans.
- Excellent collateral for bank loans
- Holding in safekeeping by the securities for no additional cost.
- Purchasable monthly, therefore an easy savings and investment program.
- Good tax treatment when purchasing equity mutual funds and dividend funds.

Global mutual funds are a key to power investing because you can earn excellent capital gains. Income funds that payout interest and capital gain are an excellent way to earn monthly, quarterly, or annual income. This is all done without making investment decisions and retaining your principal.

Many investment portfolios use mutual funds as a foundation. Then government bonds, some preferred shares, treasury bills, and common shares are added to provide additional benefits that mutual funds alone don't offer.

Mutual funds assist the buyer with automatic savings programs. Buyers are assisted by allowing forced savings programs. An automated savings program of 10% of your monthly income can be programmed to buy mutual funds. The significant advantage is that you do not have to time the market. If the markets are down, you benefit by getting more units for the same dollar.

In other periods you will buy when the units are higher priced. The net benefit of buying mutual funds monthly is that you do better in bad markets than in good markets. You are rewarded during those down markets. This principle is called dollar-cost averaging.

Mutual funds are an excellent investment for those people who want to save regular amounts every month. You can invest small amounts (a minimum of $50) monthly into different funds, such as international, stock market, or bond funds. The effect of dollar-cost averaging makes monthly mutual fund investing an excellent way to make low-risk gains in value even in a declining market.

Now that we've explained mutual funds, I want to give you an example. In this example, I'll be talking about Martha:

Each month Martha buys $100 in mutual funds. In January, she buys 10 shares at $10 a share. There was a massive market downturn in February, and Marta could buy 20 shares at $5 a share. In March, the mutual fund units recovered to $7.50 a share, and she received 13.33 shares. After three months, she has seen a terrible downturn in the price of her shares. She had a 50% drop in share prices in the second month.

Even after the recovery, the shares are still down 33% from January prices in the third month. Martha's investment was $300 over three months. She now has 43.33 shares worth $7.50 a share for a total of $324.98. In just three months, her initial investment increased in value by $24.98 ($324.98 minus $300) or 8.33%. This increase in value was despite the market decline.

To better understand how mutual funds work, imagine you are a member of an investment club. You enlist a financial manager to choose investments for your club. Each member puts in a lump-sum amount and then invests a few hundred dollars each month. The manager then buys stocks and bonds for the club members. This manager is paid a small fee for managing the club's money. This is a simple explanation of how a mutual fund works. The mutual fund is like a financial manager.

When you buy a mutual fund, you are purchasing the skills of a professional money manager. Individual professional money managers are expensive and require large sums of money to access. When you buy a mutual fund, you get the services of money managers, which most people could not afford to hire individually. You must be careful when choosing a fund because when you are choosing a fund, you are selecting the skills of that manager. With good managers, you tend to get better performance.

Income mutual funds are an excellent way to receive effortless income for your retirement. Global mutual funds are ideal if you want to invest in international markets. They provide expert advice and management for international markets. They allow currency diversification and political diversification. They allow you to invest in some of the hottest and highest growth investment opportunities anywhere in the world.

For example, take one of my clients, Jim:

Jim is 24 years old. He had just started working as an engineer for a large company. I started him on a $100 a month retirement plan on a well-run Canadian dividend mutual fund. The total investment was $50 a month into two international funds. I chose two funds because dividend funds benefit from getting many years of dividend reinvestment and global coverage in world markets. This is an excellent way to invest and save in a low-maintenance manner.

Except for money market funds, most mutual funds are long-term in nature. To obtain the maximum benefit, investments in mutual funds should be for a minimum of three to five years, with ten plus years being the preferred investment time. Mutual funds are inappropriate for short-term speculation. Occasionally, a precious metal or resource fund can be held as a shorter-term strategy.

Mutual funds are not exciting investments because they only change in value by small amounts (around a dollar) on good or bad days. On the other hand, stocks can double in value in a very short period. This is why playing stocks can be very engaging.

Mutual funds can be complex to understand because there is a wide assortment of mutual fund types with different management fees, expense ratios, management styles, and rear and front loads. Many investors, including inexperienced investors, buy mutual funds. A typical investor mistake is to choose the wrong fund for their needs. Professional investment advisors understand the different funds and help investors choose the appropriate fund for their needs or goals. This book will allow investors to select the most appropriate funds.

Mutual funds provide quick and easy tracking of pricing. You can check your unit prices online every day. Performance of your funds is provided monthly on internet services. The pricing of mutual funds is called the Net Asset Value or NAVPS = Total market value less liabilities divided by the total number of units.

Mutual funds offer the most flexibility, choice, diversifications, ease, and are excellent for saving small amounts of money using an automated program. Mutual funds should be a big piece of your wealth portfolio. Using a combination of stocks and mutual funds for your portfolios will make for the best portfolio returns over the long term. Another big reason to use mutual funds is the ability to internationalize your portfolio. It allows easy access to growth in world markets like Europe, Asia, and the U.S.

TIPS FOR DOING WELL WITH MUTUAL FUNDS

Invest in domestic and international mutual funds monthly, even if you can only invest small amounts of money. Regular monthly investments allow investors to take advantage of the highs and lows of the cycles. When market prices are low, you can purchase more funds for your money. However, when the values are high, you can buy fewer funds. In the end, it balances out to your advantage.

Try to be patient and focus on the long term. Regularly evaluate your portfolio, but don't sell your investments when the stock market drops a few points. If you have bought good companies, learn to stay with them.

Diversify among mutual funds for optimal results, so your money is invested in various funds with different fund managers. Fund managers run mutual funds from different companies, each with different investment approaches. Some approaches work better than others during different market conditions. Managers are only human and can make mistakes, so diversification will keep you safe. Also, a top manager may leave a fund and be replaced by a less skilled manager.

Choose mutual fund managers that have good track records. These managers have been successful over the long term (past five or more years), not just the last year. There are well over a thousand funds to choose from. Take time to learn about the mutual fund manager's investment record and style. Like professional athletes, not all fund managers are considered equal. Some managers rise above the pack. Seek out these managers.

Another tip is to choose a mutual fund company with a complete selection of funds. You want to have the ability to switch between various fund options. Not all fund families offer the buyer a comprehensive selection of investment options. Some fund families do not offer many international funds. Others might have a limited selection of Canadian or U.S. funds. Why limit your options?

THE ENDLESS HARVEST RULE:

Equity mutual funds are generally less risky than individual stocks because they do not have unsystematic risk. This is the risk of losing your money in a stock that goes bankrupt. Mutual funds do not have any insurance or guarantees by the government. The value of mutual funds will fluctuate with the investment held by the fund. Although they fluctuate and are not guaranteed, mutual funds cannot go to zero value. To go to zero, all of the assets held by the funds would all have to have zero value. (Extremely unlikely)

The security of mutual funds is due to many stocks, bonds, and other investments held by the mutual fund. Often hundreds of stocks or bonds are held within a single mutual fund. An equity fund can never have zero value, and you can never lose 100% of your money without all the stocks or bonds going bankrupt simultaneously. Even a significant correction such as the crash of 2020 can only temporarily reduce the value of your fund.

There are both systematic and unsystematic risks associated with stock market investments. Systematic risks are general factors that affect the stock market, such as political problems, tax changes, and economic downturns. Risks from market declines, crashes, or corrections can drop the value of your stock. Mutual funds can protect you from these risks.

Unsystematic risks are less predictable, and stocks seldom recover. These risks affect all mutual funds and equities. There are three main unsystematic risks:

1. Risk that the company in which you have stocks will go bankrupt. You can avoid this risk by purchasing mutual funds rather than individual stocks.
2. Industry risks result when one industry falls out of favor. For example, oil and gas company stock might drop in value if oil and gas prices fall. Gold stock could drop for similar reasons. Retail stores may post poor returns during recessions.
3. Individual stock prices could also drop if the company you invested in has management decisions that result in major mistakes.

You should now understand what mutual funds are, why they are purchased, and the value they bring to your portfolio. Like the last chapter, where we spoke about different types of bonds, there are different types of mutual funds. Next, I will list the different types and explain the characteristics of each kind. Follow these general guidelines to perform well with your mutual funds.

TYPES OF MUTUAL FUNDS / ETFs

Mortgage funds are investments in mortgages. These are low-risk income investments when interest rates are high.

Bond funds are domestic bonds or global bonds for global bond funds. The best time to buy bonds is when interest rates are high because you receive a high return rate with a low-risk level.

Money market funds are investments in treasury bills that mature in one year or less. These short-term investments keep your funds liquid while looking for the right long-term investment opportunity. They are not recommended for long-term investments because while the rate of return is better than savings accounts, it barely exceeds the inflation rate. Any interest earned from money market funds is taxable.

Resource funds invest in natural resource companies. These funds are risky because when there is little demand for natural resources, the resource funds do very poorly. Resource companies then have large ups and downs with the business cycle. If you own resource funds when resources like gold, silver, oil and gas, and nickel are rising, then your fund can do unbelievably well in a short period. Only buy resource funds when there is a rising market for resources. Do not hold resource mutual funds over the long term because they tend to peak and fall many times over a ten-year period. Market timing is very critical for purchasing resource funds.

Foreign equity funds broaden the investor's portfolio and create much richer investment opportunities. They provide the investor with the opportunity to participate in the growth of the international markets. They also allow the investor to invest small amounts of money into multiple global funds covering the entire world.

There are global, international, emerging market, regional, Asian, and European funds.

- Global funds cover the stock markets of the entire world.
- International funds cover the entire world except for the United States.

- Emerging market funds cover the entire developing world, including some countries like India, Mexico, Latin America, Southeast Asia, and any other nation in the developing stage.
- Regional funds cover specific regions of the world and focus on areas like European funds, Asian funds, and American funds.

These allow the investor to focus on the specific market potential of particular regions. You might invest more into European funds if you expect Europe to experience good growth. If you like the Pacific Rim of Asia's long-term potential, you might invest more money into Asian funds.

U.S. equity funds cover the stocks of American companies and do well when America is doing well. The U.S. has some of the world's most successful companies and has 32% of the world's market capitalization. By adding American funds to your portfolio, you increase your gains while reducing your risk level.

Sector funds focus on a small category of companies. For example:

- Medical companies constitute a health care fund.
- A telecommunication fund buys stocks of telephone companies.
- A financial service fund buys shares of banks and insurance companies.
- A technology fund buys computer, software, and computer-related stocks.

These funds are an excellent way to invest in a specific industry group that you believe will do well in the future. You should buy a technology mutual fund if you think the future is in technology companies. Holding a diversified group of technology stocks through a mutual fund is less risky than buying one or two technology stocks. There are many technology and health care stocks, and choosing one long-term winner is very difficult. This is why it is best to buy a fund specializing in these areas.

Precious metal funds invest in gold mining companies, silver companies, precious metal bullion, gold, and silver certificates. The two main times to buy precious metal funds are when inflation rises or when there is a rising demand and price for precious metals.

There are different opinions on holding precious metal funds over the long term. I believe in buying and holding precious metal funds only if there is rising inflation and fear of inflation; or if there is a shortage or excessive demand for gold, silver, and precious metals. Uncertainties like wars and currency crises are also a good time to buy precious metal funds.

Precious metal funds should be held only during certain times in the business cycle and not throughout the entire cycle because the funds do not pay dividends. Interest can also go sideways for years without the shareholder making any money.

U.S. dollar funds are held in U.S. currency and grow in U.S. dollars. The key advantage of a U.S. dollar mutual fund is that you can travel to the U.S. and not worry about the U.S. and domestic dollar exchange rate. Another advantage is having your money in more than one currency.

Open-end funds are the most commonly bought mutual fund. They are the traditional funds bought by brokers or at banks. Close-end funds are less commonly purchased. They are traded like stocks on the stock exchanges. The New York Stock Exchange is the best exchange for buying closed-end mutual funds because it offers many shares from many countries. The advantage of a closed-end fund is that you can buy a fully diversified portfolio as easily as a share on a stock exchange.

Country funds purchase stocks of one country and allow investors to obtain good coverage of the stock market of the specific country. Investors can buy country funds that are American, Japanese, or German, to name a few. Investors buy country funds when they believe the country offers excellent value and want 100% of their portfolio in one country, rather than diluting the fund with the shares of other countries.

Since country funds provide coverage of the stock market of a specific country, you may want to buy a country fund to properly invest in countries with large stock markets. The two largest stock markets in the world are Japan and the U.S. markets, with 21% and 32% of the total world market capitalization.

I want to break up the definitions of the different funds by giving you a case study. Yes, there are more types of funds to explain. Before we do, let's take a look at Michael. We can see what he decides to do with his country fund:

Michael believes that the Japanese stock market is undervalued. He decides to buy a country fund that emphasizes Japanese stocks. He puts $1,000 into a Japan fund. He looks forward to the long-term growth of the Japanese economy.

Now back to the different types of funds.

Income funds provide the purchaser with monthly or quarterly income using interest from bonds. This is different from dividend funds, where income is from dividends. The best time to purchase income funds is during times of high-interest rates because when rates are low, you receive a poor rate of return. Income funds are good choices for retired people who want investment income. The disadvantage of income funds is that they tend to be taxed as interest income. Interest income has the worst tax treatment of all investment categories.

Here is an example of how income funds can be used:

Cary and Sarah are retired. They want monthly income. Their broker decides to invest their money in 2 income funds. They put their $400,000 into income funds and decide to draw out 5% a year to supplement their pension plans. The $20,000 helps pay for their holidays, gifts to their grandchildren, and other expenses.

Balanced funds offer both bonds and stocks within the same mutual fund. The specific fund breakdown may vary, but generally, it is split equally between stocks and bonds. The advantage of balanced funds is that they provide low volatility. The disadvantage of balanced funds is that the rate of return is diluted because when equity funds do well, the bond portion lags and vice versa. Rather than buying balance funds, buying equities when interest rates are low and buying bonds when interest rates are high is more efficient.

Asset allocation funds are high-tech versions of balanced funds since they attempt to switch between money market, bond, and equity funds. Some use computerized models to decide what percentage of the fund to invest in each of the three categories. In contrast, others rely on fund managers to determine what percentages to invest in each of the three categories. Both methods have had mixed results.

This is difficult because of market timing in equity, bond, and money markets. One of the best times to buy asset allocation funds is when you are uncertain which direction the markets are heading or wish to invest without spending time evaluating where to allocate your money.

There are two main styles of asset allocation. Tactical asset allocation actively moves your assets between stocks, bonds, and cash. Strategic asset allocation has more of a static approach and can maintain a fixed percentage between set percentages in each of stocks, bonds, and cash.

Real estate funds invest in real estate companies and holdings. Due to real estate's cyclical nature, only buy these funds when real estate holdings or companies are poised to go up or are going up. Timing is critical for real estate fund investments because you can make significant gains or losses if you buy at the right or wrong time.

When real estate booms, your real estate funds boom. Investments in real estate company stocks are an excellent alternative to investing in commercial or real estate projects. You can quickly liquidate your funds by selling them, whereas it may take months or years to sell real physical estate property.

Canadian equity funds are complex because there are different types—some conservative, others quite aggressive. There are two main types of Canadian equity funds, growth, and blue-chip funds.

Canadian growth equity funds are bought for capital growth and do not pay dividends. Newer companies that are not yet established are often selected for growth funds. They offer the best growth potential with a high risk. They are made up of aggressive, smaller stocks. Growth funds do not tend to pay dividends. Growth funds are at their best when interest rates are low and stock markets are either low or are stable. During stock market downswings, they do poorly.

Blue-chip funds are less vulnerable to market downswings than growth equity funds because they tend to consist of bank shares, pipelines, utilities, and shares of well-established and financially solid companies.

Blue-chip equity funds buy an extensive range of well-established Canadian blue-chip companies. This fund purchases a broad group of investments: oil companies, gold mines, financial institutions, retail stores, computer companies.

There are also dividend funds in the Canadian equity fund category. They purchase stocks, like banks, utilities, or pipelines, which pay monthly dividends or compound into more shares. Dividend funds are solid conservative performers, often even in market downswings.

Dividend funds are one of my favorites and provide a source of income outside retirement savings plans that are considered favorable tax treatment. It is also one of the lowest tax rates for investment income. Buy dividend funds when interest rates are low because they provide a source of conservative income while also providing advantages of equities.

For example, if you reinvest the monthly 4% fund dividend while the fund increases in value from $10 to $12 a unit, you will receive a capital gain of $2 a unit over and above the dividend. The result, in this case, is a 24% rate of return.

By understanding the many varieties of mutual funds, we can fit the exact type of mutual fund to fit each investor's specific needs. We can use sector funds for someone who wants higher growth and higher returns. We can use dividend funds for someone who wants more conservative growth with income. Mutual funds are an excellent way for most investors to build their portfolios.

MUTUAL FUND MECHANICS

We've defined what mutual funds are and why people purchase them. We've also explained many types of mutual funds to choose from. The last part of this chapter will be dedicated to telling you a bit about how mutual funds work.

Some mechanics of mutual fund purchasing are commissions and management fees.

Commissions

A no-load mutual fund does not charge a commission fee. Banks and a few mutual fund companies offer these. There are no commissions charged. Most brand-name funds are not offered as no-load funds. A limited number of funds are offered at no load. Most common banks offer no-load funds.

Management Fees

There is a management expense ratio. All mutual fund firms charge clients a management fee for the investment manager's services. This is the management fee or cost to the company of the investment manager plus the cost of regular reports and brochures to the client. It is the total and complete summary of all costs and expenses to the client by the mutual fund company.

Management fee + additional fees for brochures and statements sent to the client = Management expense ratio. A common mistake is for the client to add the management fee to the management expense ratio. This duplicates the cost and is incorrect. The management fee is already included in the management expense ratio. Although, it does not include any commissions charged by the salesperson.

The broker or bank purchasing the fund can explain most of the mechanics. The details of mutual fund mechanics are found in the mutual fund prospectuses. A mutual fund prospectus describes management fees, expense ratios, investment risks, redemption policies, commission structure, distribution policies of dividends and interest, and tax ideas.

Mutual funds are pretty interesting, right? And we aren't even done with all the methods of cash flow you can fuel your Endless Harvest with. I know it's a lot to soak up, but that's a great thing, isn't it! Next up, we'll talk briefly about cash flow from real estate.

CASH FLOW

FROM REAL ESTATE

Real estate is one robust way to profit that has been around for centuries. The fantastic thing about real estate is that it will always be a source of income because it is a commodity that will always be necessary. Unlike other things, real estate is finite and cannot be mass-produced, ensuring there is always demand as long as humans continue to thrive.

Real estate profits you in two ways. They are paid rental income, and if the property goes up in value.

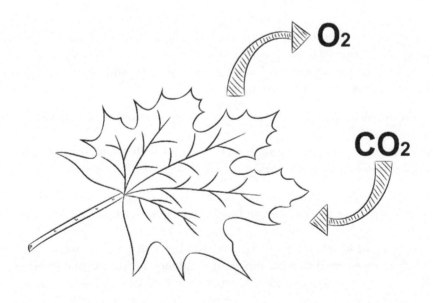

Real Estate is kind of like the carbon dioxide plants use to perform photosynthesis and grow large.

Real estate can pay in several ways. One of the best ways to profit from real estate is to use Real Estate Investment Trust or (REIT'S). The Canadian Securities Course defines REITs as an investment vehicle that invests in various real estate investments, including mortgages, purchase-leasebacks, construction loans, and real property.

They are sponsored by financial institutions such as banks, trust companies, and other groups.

Investors profit by receiving payments, often quarterly, of the income earned from the trust's real estate. If a REIT consists of shopping centers, some of the rental income might be paid to the trust's shareholders.

I consider owning rental properties not part of The Endless Harvest unless you use a property management company. Rental real estate should be considered in the same category as owning a small business. It is not a passive investment but must be managed actively with effort on your part. It can be an excellent way to build wealth but is not considered a passive income for the purpose of this book.

Having previously owned rental properties, it is not a simple case of showing up once a month to pick up a rent check. It is also cutting the grass, doing maintenance work, paying property taxes, and upkeeping the structure to find renters who will pay the rent on time and not damage the property. It is a form of active income.

I want to also talk about homeownership. Some people will consider this to be capital. Your home is not an asset but is an expense. This is because, at retirement, your home costs you money for items such as property taxes, utilities, and maintenance.

Capital is anything that produces income through capital gains, dividends, or interest. Since you live in your home, you cannot earn any returns unless you sell your home. Even then, you have to live somewhere. Having a roof over your head is always an expense whether you rent or own a home. The expenses are different, but your residence needs are that expense. Remember, you have to budget for these home expenses when you retire.

THE ENDLESS HARVEST RULE:

Never keep all your money in one asset, especially having your home
as your only asset.

It is a big mistake to think your home is your only important asset. Often people will ignore their retirement savings plans to pay off their mortgage. In their retirement, they may have a paid-off house but no money to spend. In this case, they must sell their house to have money. You can see the unbalance there, and having balance is the key. Never sacrifice everything for your house. Your house is necessary for living, and always save some money for your retirement and emergencies.

Unlike in the past, real estate will not be the most viable investment in the future. As the population ages, many cities will have an oversupply of real estate because people in retirement will leave colder climates to retire in milder climates.

Real estate is actually at the top of most investment pyramids. But most people fail to realize the risky nature of real estate and real estate prices. Just because it is a tangible asset means very little when prices fall suddenly.

For Alberta in the early 1980s, energy prices fell, and Toronto and New York real estate prices crashed dramatically. Learn a lot about real estate before putting any money down on it.

Whether you buy your home or rent, it has little to do with your financial independence. Homeownership is more of a lifestyle choice. It is great to live in a nice home. For investment purposes, if you rented rather than bought and invested the difference in mutual funds, you could be better off by retirement. For example, at 4%, a 25-year $400,000 mortgage could cost you interest on a home worth $120,000.

If you decided to invest that money into mutual funds, you could be much better off by retirement. Don't assume that your home is always the best place to put your money, such as a newly added pool, landscaping maintenance, and other endless home renovations. Balance is the key. Put some money in your retirement plans, some into your savings plan, and pay off your debts as soon as possible. Although real estate is necessary for living, it is not the best way to create financial stability.

Keep in mind that you cannot spend your living room. If you live by real estate, consider buying shares in major real estate companies or buying some global real estate mutual funds. You can benefit from only growth in the real estate market and be a part-owner of real estate companies. Yet, you can simply sell your shares or your real estate mutual fund if you want out.

You can also invest in real estate shopping centers by buying real estate investment trusts (REITs). I should also caution purchasers that owning real estate stocks is a high-risk venture since they are very vulnerable to swings in the business cycle. Recessions hit real estate and real estate companies very hard. On the other hand, a significant upswing is possible as well.

For most busy people today, REITs are one of the only ways to invest in commercial real estate without owning the actual real estate. The advantage is the liquidity. Unlike real estate, you can quickly buy and sell real estate stocks. You know what I'm talking about if you have ever had to buy or sell your own home. Sometimes it can be easy, but other times it can be very hard. Also, the time frame is not immediate in either circumstance.

Again, when considering real estate, balance is vital to a successful investment approach. You need to put some money into your retirement savings plans while trying hard to pay off your mortgage as quickly as possible. The number one priority for most people should be to put money into retirement savings plans first and then work on the mortgage.

MONEY MARKET AND CASH STRATEGIES

Money market investments are short-term interest-bearing investments (one year or less) and, therefore, very liquid. They include treasury bills, savings accounts, money market mutual funds, and interest-based funds.

Money market and cash are interest-bearing investments that mature in one year or less. The most common is the savings account.

Suppose you must buy a car, pay for a vacation, or make a short-term purchase. The biggest mistake of money market is poor returns after inflation. A tip: Longer-term retirement funds should not be kept in money market as the returns are low after inflation. Your return minus inflation is called your real return. This is the actual net return you make.

Cash and money market products are kind of like the soil your tree extracts nutrients from to grow.

Money market products are the best investments when you need quick access to your funds at an undetermined future date. For example, if you are planning to buy a house but haven't yet found the perfect one, or if you wish to buy a car or expand a business sometime in the future. Money market should be seen as a parking place for money. It is for money that is not committed yet. You can use treasury bills or mutual fund money market funds to earn a better savings rate return.

The three main types of money market products are federal government treasury bills, savings accounts, and money market mutual funds. They are perfect short-term purchases when you want a better rate than savings accounts; or if interest rates are climbing and you don't want to lock in an investment until rates stabilize.

Savings accounts are good places to build up your money to buy GICs or treasury bills. Their best usage is for day-to-day purchases of groceries, gas, and other living expenses.

Treasury bills are government-issued. They are issued in 30, 60, 90, 180, and 365 days in length and are liquid (same day). Minimum balances range from $5,000 to $100,000, depending on the investment term. They are backed by the issuing government and tend to have no limits on the default protection level. You could purchase $1,000,000 in federal treasury bills and be fully protected.

Let's look at some different scenarios for money market investments:

Scenario 1

Joe is planning to buy a car next year. He has saved $10,000 but needs another six months to save the additional $7,000. Joe purchased a six-month treasury bill to have a decent rate of return and still have quick access to his money if he stumbled on the perfect deal.

Scenario 2

Jill wants to buy her first house. She has the necessary down payment but does not want to lock her money in a term deposit if she finds the perfect house. She is frustrated by the low returns from her savings accounts; yet is scared to buy a stock or anything risky in the short term. Jill invests in a 30-day Treasury bill.

Scenario 3

Mike is worried about potential downsizing at his place of employment. He has saved about three months' worth of living expenses in case of a layoff. Mike bought Savings Bonds to keep his rainy day money accessible and earn him a better return than a savings account.

Scenario 4

Robyn likes to buy and sell stocks. She looks for undervalued stocks and buys them. Robin recently sold a stock for a profit and is waiting for the next opportunity to arise. She purchased a 30-day treasury bill to obtain a reasonable rate of return while keeping her money liquid as she looks for the next stock opportunity.

Scenario 5

Rick is a retired and conservative investor. He typically buys government bonds as an income investment. For the last six months, rates have been climbing steadily higher. Rick is rolling his treasury bills at higher and higher rates until rates level off or start to decline. He then plans to lock into a 10-year bond with an excellent rate of return.

There are some common mistakes people commit when using money market products. Never use money market products for your Endless Harvest accounts since the rate of return tends to be relatively low. You should move your short-term money from savings accounts to treasury bills since these can earn double or triple the interest rate without any additional investment risk.

Another mistake is to keep large amounts of money in checking and savings accounts if you have no immediate need for the money. Government strip bonds, mutual funds, and stocks provide better long-term growth, especially when you can lock in your investment and take advantage of high-interest rates.

Over the long term, stocks will generally outperform bonds and the money market. For endless wealth, this is a better place to invest. However, stocks and equity mutual funds rise and fall a great deal in the short term. For short-term cash needs, you want to invest in money market products. Since they do not earn much return, there is no decline in principal value. Therefore it is a better short-term storage vehicle for down payments on houses and other expensive items.

A significant weakness of the money market is the higher tax rate on interest-bearing investments. This can drastically reduce the amount of after-tax returns from low-interest rate short-term investments.

The biggest weakness of money market is the poor gains after inflation.

This brings us to the last part of the section, Becoming a Cash Flow Millionaire. You have just seen how inflation can hit our short-term cash, but I want to tell you about the law of compound interest for our long-term investments. I know you will find this very exciting. Inflation as of April 2020 is 6.7%.

USING INTEREST INCOME EFFECTIVELY

As defined by the Canadian Securities Course, interest is any money paid to a lender by the borrower to use their money.

Interest is a percentage of return usually paid annually, semi-annually, or quarterly simply—the person who owns the bond, term deposit, or interest-bearing investment benefits from a predictable return.

Interest income is best for people who want more growth. Since interest rates rise and fall regularly, it is best to buy long-term bonds when rates are high. Alternatively, purchase short-term bonds when rates are low.

Typical debt instruments are savings accounts, term deposits, guaranteed investment certificates, and federal and corporate bonds. To explain this further, I will give you a few cases of interest income:

WHAT TO INVEST IN AND WHEN

To wrap up this section, I want to touch on some main points I have not mentioned. One of the most important is effective asset allocation.

This is one of the keys to achieving poor, average, or superior portfolio performance. It comes from the asset allocation of stocks, bonds, and cash. The portfolio weighting should vary with the stage of the business cycle.

THE ENDLESS HARVEST RULE:

Investors waste time researching the wrong decisions.

Take, for instance, this short story:

Four friends are together at their company's annual Christmas party. They are discussing their investments over dinner.

Mary is happy because her bank gave her an extra half a percent. Her money grew by 5.5%. By shopping around, she could pressure her bank into a better return.

Tim put his money into a balanced fund. His fund consisted of half bonds and half stocks. His equity half matched the market average of 10%, while his bond half only produced 4%. The overall return on his balanced fund was 7%.

Jeff put all of his money in the stocks that he chose. Half were blue-chip conservative stocks such as bank shares and pipelines. The other half of his stock portfolio consisted of penny stocks selected from many hot tips from his golf buddies. His return was 10% from his blue-chip stocks, while his penny stocks gained only 4%. His overall return was 8%. Jeff intends to do more research next year.

Michelle did not pay much attention to her investments since she is a long-term investor. She put half of her money into well-run international mutual funds and the other half into blue-chip equity funds. Her performance was about 12%.

What is missing is a more scientific matching of the percentages in stocks, bonds, and money market to the economic environment and business cycle.

The performances of each of their portfolios directly follow the economic environment. The economic environment determines the rate of returns each person receives from their portfolios.

The first lady, Mary, might come out with the best return from her portfolio with her bond strategy during recessions.

Jeff would do very well during stock market booms with his heavy equity position. His portfolio would suffer during market downturns. Michelle would do well when international and domestic stock markets are booming.

One solution would be to follow Tim and have a balanced fund. You could permanently be half in stocks and half in bonds. The problem with that method is that it does not consider peaks in interest rates. It is better to overweight bonds during high-interest rate periods to lock in these great rates (put a higher % in bonds). When interest rates are low, move more cash into stocks (put a higher % into stocks and a lower % in bonds).

THE ENDLESS HARVEST RULE:

Tend your money but make decisions based on a reason,
not emotions of fear and greed.

In 1995, one broker I know decided to move all of his clients into savings accounts. He did this because he felt he could predict the movement of interest rates. He mistimed the market, and interest rates stayed low and did not change. During that time, the stock market soared, and his clients missed out on the best stock market gains in a decade.

Tactical asset allocation works because you choose the weightings of bonds based on actual achievable interest rates. This is easily found by looking at the term deposits, Treasury Bills, and offered bond rates. The prime rate or bank rate is another possible measure to use when deciding on your bond to stock weighting. The higher the achievable rate you can get for a bond, the more you should shift stock assets to bond assets.

It is best to use asset allocation based on:

1. Changes in economic growth using Gross Domestic Product (GDP). GDP is the total value of all goods and services produced by a country as a whole. Economic growth is the GDP increase or decrease over a specific time expressed as a percentage.
   a. A declining GDP shows that the economy is slowing down or is recessionary.
   b. An increasing GDP number indicates that the economy is booming or is in a recovery stage of the business cycle.

2. Gross National Product (GNP) is used as a measurement of economic growth. It represents the sum of all goods and services produced in a country within a single year.
   a. Negative GNP indicates a contraction in the economy.
   b. Positive GNP indicates an expansion in the economy.

Generally, a positive GNP is good for the stock market. A negative GNP usually indicates a bearish or poor indicator for the stock market.

3. Durable goods orders like refrigerators, machinery, cars, etc., reflect consumer confidence in the future. They can also indicate future trends in consumer and business spending.

Here are some examples of asset allocation for over and under-weighting asset groups*

Interest rate for 10-year bonds	% in bonds	% in stocks	% in cash
1%	0%	100%	0%
2%	0%	100%	0%
3%	5%	100%	0%
4%	10%	95%	0%
5%	10%	90%	0%
6%	20%	80%	0%

Interest rate for 10-year bonds	% in bonds	% in stocks	% in cash
7%	50%	50%	0%
8%	75%	25%	0%
9%	100%	0%	0%
10%	100%	0%	0%
11%+	100%	0%	0%

*% is for illustration only. The portfolio design should include personal risk tolerance and other factors.

Other factors are the level of political stability. A change of leadership in Japan might lead to a market downswing. Political crises in Russia can lead to a drop in the Ruble. This can create panic, such as in the fall of 1998. The start of the Persian Gulf War in the early 1990s caused some disruption in the stock markets.

There are four base ways you can allocate your investments:

1. Allocate based on the term.
   Long-term (10+ years), medium-term (3-9 years), and short-term (under 3 years)

2. Allocate by the level of risk.
   High risk, medium risk, and low risk

3. Allocate by mutual fund manager style.
   Allocate by buying different mutual fund companies.

As we summarize this section on becoming a cash flow millionaire, I want to summarize the two most popular types of investments we spoke about in this chapter. Simply put, I want to tell you when to buy them.

WHEN TO BUY BONDS

Bonds are low-risk investments. The best time to buy bonds is when interest rates are high, especially at 5%+, because you are obtaining a high rate of return at a low risk. Invest in stocks rather than bonds when interest rates are low.

When interest rates are high, stock markets tend to do poorly because people cash in their stocks and buy bonds or term deposits. Recessions are a prime time to buy long-term bonds because of the high-interest rates.

WHEN TO BUY STOCKS

There are two types of stocks—cyclical and non-cyclical. The non-cyclical stocks are called buy and hold stocks because any downswing in value tends to be temporary and provides a good buying opportunity to purchase more shares. You can buy non-cyclical stocks at any time because the stocks tend to increase in value over the long term. Some good examples are Coca-Cola, Disney, and Procter & Gamble.

Timing is critical to making money in cyclical stocks because they are highly vulnerable to recessions. The key to doing well in cyclical stocks is to purchase them in the early stages of an upswing for that particular sector. With cyclical stocks, you should carefully watch for supply and demand in the business cycle to help predict the direction of stock prices. Gold shares, mining shares, and automobile company stocks are examples of cyclical stocks.

For example:

Mark is a stock trader. Although gold-stock prices were low last year, he believed gold would increase in the near future. He invests $20,000 in some of the largest and highest quality gold companies. This year gold prices soared, and his investment is worth $40,000.

Susan is very interested in the oil and gas markets. Last winter, stock prices were low because of the mild weather. She purchased some excellent oil and gas stocks at low, depressed prices. This winter is colder, and prices start to rise to normal levels—Susan's investment doubles in value.

Asset allocation uses intelligent rules to seek superior results from markets with superior growth while avoiding risks. Do not arbitrarily leave your money into a set % of stocks, bonds, sector weightings, and geographic regions. Make changes when necessary.

Here is what I believe. When bond rates are 5% or over, buy them. Consider dividend-paying stocks and mutual funds when the rates are lower than 3%. This way, you get some return on your money and a little more security. A rough figure of 25% might be a good starting point for most investors.

This section was a bit technical, but it needed to be written. If you don't understand the basics of what you are investing in, how can you make a good decision? Or how can you ensure your financial advisor makes the right choices for you? I'm not saying you need to understand the ins and outs of the market and all the financial terminology. If so, you wouldn't be reading this book. I've spared you a ton of other information I've learned over my decades of experience.

Also, I want to add a list of seven things to be cautious of owning in any intelligent stock portfolio:

1. Penny stocks.
2. Avoid buying stocks on rumors or hot tips.
3. Futures and options trading.
4. Any stock or investments that you do not understand.
5. Jewelry, gems, coins, and stamps. (expertise required)
6. Cryptocurrencies

This section has the basics you need to know. A wise man once told me, "You don't have to be an expert at everything. That is impossible. You need to be educated on the elements of life so you can make the best decisions on what to spend your time on and what to hire out."

I'm going to end this section with a short story I recently experienced, based on that simple lesson:

I was having trouble with the electrical breakers at my home. Sometimes certain items would work as expected, like the garage door opener and outside lights. Other times, they would be very fickle and seem to have a mind of their own. This seemed to be a minor issue and would be a simple fix.

So I went outside and proceeded to investigate the control box. After countless hours searching through user manuals, browsing the internet, and watching do-it-yourself (DIY) videos, I gave up and called the electrician. (I tried to solve this problem for about one month before doing so.)

The electrician came to my house, spent 18 minutes at the control box, fixed the issue, and charged me $420. Now, you might say, $420 for 18 minutes of work sounds ridiculous. But let me remind you, I spend countless frustrating *hours trying to figure it out myself. What I did know was the right electrician to call, so I was sure he would fix the issue. I was educated enough to call the right man for the job. I was paying for his expertise plus 20 years of experience.*

This is why you have just read this section on becoming a cash flow millionaire. You need to know the correct tools and how to use them to build wealth. We are growing your money tree for an Endless Harvest. Whether you decide to do this on your own or hire an advisor is up to you. Both options work exceptionally well when done right. Throughout this book, it is my job to keep you informed to make the best decision for your unique situation.

We'll discuss how to hire an advisor, if you wish, later in the book. But we have two essential sections coming up on protecting your wealth and managing it. Next up is Staying Rich. In this section, we will discuss avoiding self-sabotage and understanding some elements that endanger our wealth and are beyond our control. See you in section two.

STAYING RICH

T he second part of The Endless Harvest is staying rich. It's one thing to get your apple tree growing and another to ensure it keeps growing. We are only human, and often our emotions get in the way. This section is focused on how to hold onto our wealth.

Do this so you can:

Protect the financial progress you have worked so hard for. Risks to your wealth come from yourself and also from outside forces.

In the analogy we use of planting an apple tree, this is the part where we protect its growth against any forces trying to knock it down. Constant forces will attack our harvest like pests, natural disasters, and even an unbalanced weight from our growth.

The same is true with our finances. It's tough to grow them, but I can assure you that it is effortless to destroy them. Things always take longer to build than they do to break. This is true when growing a tree and also building your wealth.

In this section, we will discuss some of the things you want to watch out for and how to protect against them. That's why it's immediately essential right after becoming a cash flow millionaire.

"Hire the right people with the right knowledge. The most expensive advice is to learn the hard way. The most expensive advice is free advice from unqualified people. Don't confuse someone's confidence with competence."

– John Yamamoto

This is kind of like watering a tree to keep it alive and healthy.

You'll want to pay close attention to this section because any little mistake can cost you many months and even years to rebuild.

Before starting this section, I want to present two case studies from my past experiences. I call the first case:

Helmond and Killing the Golden Goose

Helmond was a student of mine. He had sold his business and had received a million dollars after taxes. His wife had also inherited a million from her parents, who had passed away. They now had two million in total investment capital.

Helmond was interested in the stock market, particularly day-trading strategies. He considered himself very intelligent and was at the top of his graduating class. As an experienced business owner, Helmond felt he did not need investment advice and was very condescending, looking down at other people he felt were not as intelligent.

He subscribed to every investment newsletter and used the internet extensively to search for hot opportunity stocks and real estate trusts. He felt every cent should be invested and moved from stock to stock putting large bets on his hottest stock picks. Within six months the $2,000,000 had become $1,400,000, a loss of $600,000. That's over 25%!

Helmand wanted to make up for these losses, so he would spend all night looking on the internet for possible day-trading big profit stocks. Ignoring any warnings and refusing any advice from others, he continued to day-trade. His wife also felt very comfortable managing their inheritance as he was confident in his ability.

By the end of his first year, he was down to $400,000, a total loss of $1,600,000. He further ignored suggestions for taking his remaining $400,000 to help fund their retirement as he planned to make up his additional losses with his next stock picks. By the end of his second year, he had lost the remaining $400,000 and had nothing left to trade. He went back to work to earn enough to fund their daily expenses. Both of their inheritance were gone. I saw them at a trade show, and they were working just "to put food on the table." It was nice to see that her loyalty and belief in him were intact and they stayed married.

They are a lovely couple, but does this sound a little like gambling in Las Vegas? Here is the lesson from this story. Be wary of overestimating your ability. Do not learn through losing money. This is the hard way to learn your limitations. Instead, try interviewing and hiring a portfolio manager.

When using a portfolio manager, you should remain involved with your money and informed of your results. Use those people with expertise in managing money. Also, manage risk actively. Each loss is a little piece of feedback. The investment world is much more complicated than reading a newsletter or using the internet. It's taken me over 32 years of hard work daily, and I continue to learn and will never stop. Do not learn your limitations the hard way, and do not overestimate your ability to pick and manage investments.

Sometimes, the truth is learned the hard way, but don't let that be you. I want to share another simple case study with you about someone who had experienced the opposite. They experienced an exponential gain. I call this case study:

The Retired Engineer

Sometimes the stream of income is ignored by clients. The income streams paid out are often forgotten when calculating returns. For example, Steven and Greta, age 60, retired, and we invested their $900,000 into a maximum income portfolio. For the next 25 years, they received $3,000 per month to fund his and his wife's retirement. This $3,000 plus their pensions allowed them to travel and maintain their home and lifestyle.

One day he wanted a report to see how he had done. The following was the case, $36,000 a year x 25 years = $900,000 in income received. His current portfolio is now worth $1,300,000. This sum less his original $900,000 equals a gain of $400,000!

His portfolio even went through multiple crashes and Black Swan crises; yet the bottom line of his original $900,000 still generated $900,000 in income received + $400,000 in growth = $1,300,000 from his original $900,000. Steven and Greta still have their original capital plus inflation while living their desired lifestyle.

The lesson here is an awesome one. Always consider the income you have received when evaluating your overall return. We often forget to consider this amount, which surprises us greatly.

Between these two cases, you can see how important it is to protect your investment and live or spend wisely. This is why section two is dedicated to staying rich. Ensure you keep your apple tree growing, healthy, and free from harmful forces.

This is step two of The Endless Harvest. By the time you finish this section, you will know how to keep your wealth and avoid the large traps.

What we will do in this section is talk to you about the many steps you can take to protect your wealth. You must protect your main portion of money that keeps you alive and the multiple sources of cash flow you have. Risks come in all shapes and sizes. They come in personal or internal risks and can come as non-personal or external risks.

This section is dedicated to protecting what you have labored so hard for. Keep watering your money tree and protect it against everything harmful. The world is tough, and you need to keep your guard up.

PROTECTING YOUR WEALTH

THE 3 TYPES OF RISK

Protecting your wealth is essential to the health of your Endless Harvest. Many friends, colleagues, and even advisors will focus all their efforts on how to get rich. But not many focus on how to stay wealthy. For example, take any team sport. It could be basketball, baseball, hockey, or football. Every sport needs both offense and defense to win the game. You would lose every game if you only focused on scoring points but paid no attention to stopping the other team. The same is true for your finances. Protect your wealth because losing your money is ten times easier than making it.

First, let's talk about risk management.

The first type of risk is called controllable risk.

Controllable risks are typically risks we cause to ourselves. One of the most significant risks I find is letting fear and greed decide what you will invest in. Fear and greed are two of the worst emotions to use for your investment choices because you typically will not buy the right investments when you are scared. Because of fear, many people sell low and, because of greed, buy high.

One of the solutions to fear and greed is to have a mix of safer investments with more growth-oriented ones. Replace fear and greed with structure and diversification. This is called asset allocation.

The third emotion I find that is difficult but controllable is the emotion of impatience. We all face impatience. Impatience is wanting results immediately. For example, losing 10 pounds in 10 days or making a fortune in investing using some get rich quick system. We live in an immediate gratification society, and because of impatience, we tend to get into debt using credit cards. Why? We want that item, so we charge it and worry about paying later. That is a big mistake we make based on impatience.

Impatience in investing can also increase risk. We invest and get some results, so we get impatient for more. This causes us to make unwise decisions. For example, the problem with saving is that a savings plan at ten percent does not look like much at the beginning. We get impatient and pull out our money because we think, "I have been saving ten percent, and it hasn't been doing anything. The solution is to think long-term. You remember the chapter on compounding and what Albert Einstein taught us, right? My view is that if you believe from today to age ninety, that is your correct time horizon. Therefore, we need to build wealth over a longer period. This money has to last you for the rest of your life.

Another risk that we talked briefly about was over-confidence. Overconfidence is a form of greed. Overconfidence is when we take big risks because we are confident in the outcome. Therefore, because we take big risks, we take big losses when wrong. One of the keys is to balance overconfidence with being careful. We tend to be overconfident during times when markets are good.

Another controllable risk is our savings rate. Our savings is a controllable factor somewhat. Savings are tough because every dollar we save is money we do not have in our pocket today. Again, it takes a bit of maturity and discipline.

The last controllable risk is our spending using debt and credit cards. Again, we tend to be impatient and worry in the moment. We are one of the highest indebted generations in human history. One of the reasons is credit cards. We need to look at whether we should be using credit cards. I believe most people should not be using credit cards if they cannot pay them off at the end of the month.

The second type of risk is called uncontrollable risk.

To some extent, in your portfolio design and financial planning, we must ensure that you are appropriately diversified. One of the keys to diversification is to prevent against market crash risk.

Market crash risk is common now because markets are more volatile than ever. Something like 9/11 or the financial crisis in 2008 can trigger up to a forty percent drop in the market. Again, market risk is number one to avoid.

The second uncontrollable risk is inflation, as the cost of living increases consistently.

The third uncontrollable risk is currency going up. For example, we have seen the US dollar at an all-time high, followed early in 2008 by an all-time low. Again, we must diversify globally to have different currencies in the portfolio. We need a controllable strategy of currency risk.

The fourth uncontrollable risk is taxation. We all pay taxes. One of the things we need to do is maximize our registered plans that shelter our portfolio gains from income tax. Here we are trying to reduce the taxed income the best we can. Income tax is another risk we would want to mitigate, if possible.

The third type of risk is called financial planning risk.

Financial planning risk is having no plan and running out of money at retirement. Those are the three major risks we try to mitigate. In your financial plan, these should be built into your strategy.

MONEY DOES NOT MAKE YOU WEALTHY CASH FLOW DOES

I want to bust a myth most of us have been told ever since our youth. Do not mistake having money with being financially independent. They are two different things. We all have read about someone who has won the lottery and in a few years is broke because they spent all of their money. We have all seen movie or rock stars earning millions and later filing for bankruptcy. These people confuse having money with being financially independent.

Being financially independent is when you have set up your investments so that the growth of the investments equals your needs. If all you take is growth, then your principal will last forever. I want to say that again. If all you take is growth, then your principal will last forever. Ideally, your money's growth should be greater than your withdrawals since this additional growth will help your investments keep pace with inflation. This is what The Endless Harvest is all about.

I want to give you two opposing case studies so this sinks in:

Case 1: Mr. Rock Star

At age 35, he earned 20,000,000 from the sale of his hit records. His expenditures are $5,000,000 a year. He has an agent, maid, yacht, and rents apartments in Paris, London, and New York. He expects his next tour will *be even more successful than the last one. Unfortunately, his type of music becomes unpopular. His tours fail to sell any tickets or records. Within five years, he is back playing in small bars and never achieves success again. He now has no savings, so he is forced to work for the rest of his life.*

A solution to this problem would be to have Mr. Rock Star invest in an income-generating portfolio paying him a 5% income on his 20,000,000. He will have an income of $1,000,000 a year. He must also drop his expenditures to $1,000,000 a year from $5,000,000. If he does this, he will be financially independent even if his next few years are unsuccessful. The rock star will never have to work again unless he wants to. He will also have the option of pursuing higher education or training to create a dream album since he does not have to constantly work to pay his bills. Financial independence ultimately will make him a better musician.

Case 2: Miss Normal

At age 35, Miss Normal saves 10% of her income in quality dividend-paying stocks, international and dividend-paying mutual funds, and interest-bearing investments. At age 55, she wishes to earn $60,000 a year. At her current rate of growth and savings, Miss Normal will be financially independent at age 55.

To become financially independent, you must set up your investment portfolio to generate income to cover expenses without depleting the principal. Once your principal runs out, you are "dead in the water." Beware of the danger of outliving your money.

FINANCIAL NET WORTH WORKSHEETS

Now that we have discussed some of the risks to your money, let's talk about a simple way to protect your wealth. Many famous movie stars and professional athletes retire in poverty or go bankrupt because they do not have positive cash flow, spend more than they earn, have bad luck financially, and acquire more debts than assets. Doing a net worth worksheet is vital no matter who you are. This will give you a baseline to keep track of your real-time financial status.

You can tell if your debts are out of control when you:

- Loose sleep because of debts.
- Feel stressed about receiving bills.
- Argue with your spouse about money.
- Feel helpless and hopeless because of your debt level.
- Give up any restraint or control over your spending due to hopelessness.

Here is an interesting fact. Your bank first looks for your debt rating and net worth statement to evaluate your status. To become wealthy, you must find ways to increase your net worth. If this is what banks are looking for, don't you think it should be important too?

You must know where you are financially and where you are going. To begin with, you need to look at your current net worth. Your net worth is defined as your assets, less your debts. Anything that makes your assets higher will increase your financial security. Each time you make a payment that lowers your debts, your financial security increases.

Increase your net worth and hasten financial independence by:

- Building a cash reserve in your retirement plan, Tax-Free Savings Account (TFSA), bank account, or pension will eventually allow you to stop working because your assets cover your expenses.

- Paying down debts because your net worth increases each time you pay off a debt.
  (The ultimate goal is to be debt-free at retirement.)

- Owning your home.
  (Your home can also be an asset enabling you to obtain a loan for credit purposes quickly.)

- Accumulating money outside retirement plans with an investment portfolio using international mutual funds, bonds, and stocks.
  (This pillar of financial security is the first line of defense against unexpected financial threats. It acts as a rainy day fund and later on will act as retirement travel money and an additional buffer of financial security.)

Anyone who has gone to the bank for their first car loan knows the first question they are asked—*What is your net worth?* This question is important because your ability to qualify for a loan depends on your net worth.

You can calculate your net worth by completing the following exercise:

Defining your net worth: Net worth = Estimated Current Value - Estimated Debts

A helpful hint would be to fill out this net worth statement once a year to track how well you are doing. Even though there are fluctuations in the stocks and mutual funds, your assets should grow while your debts decline over the years. You need to have a positively growing net worth over the long term.

ENDLESS HARVEST NET WORTH WORKSHEET
(update annually)

What You Own	Est. Value	
A. Liquid Assets	Today	1 year later
Date		
Cash (checking, savings)		
Treasury Bills		
Money Market Funds		
Cash Surrender Value of Life Insurance		
Canada Savings Bonds		
Total Liquid Assets		
B. Investment Assets (outside retirement savings plans)		
Term Deposits		
Stocks		
Bonds		
Global Mutual Funds		
Canadian Mutual Funds		
Real Estate (other than Residence)		
Tax Shelters		
Total Investment Assets		

C. Other Assets (outside of retirement savings plans)
Business
Partnership Value
Tax-Free Savings Account (TFSA)

D. Retirement Funds
Retirement Savings Plans
Stocks
Term Deposits
Equity Mutual
Bond Mutual Funds
Bonds & Savings Accounts
Employer Pension Plan
RRIF
Annuities
Total Retirement Funds

E. Personal Assets & Chattels
Residence
Vacation Property
Boat, Car & other vehicles
Coins, stamps, art, antiques
General Furniture, TVs etc.
Jewelry
Total Personal Assets

TOTAL OF ALL ASSETS

Debts
F. Short-term Debts (under 2 years)
Credit cards
MasterCard
Visa
Others
Total Credit Cards
Personal Loans
Back Taxes owing
Other Obligations
Total Short-term Obligations

G. Long-term Obligations (3 years and over)

Mortgage on Personal Residence   _____   _____
Other Loans   _____   _____
Total Long-term Obligations   _____   _____
Total Obligations   _____   _____
Totals Asset $ _____ Less Total Obligations $ _____ = Net Worth _____

THE ENDLESS HARVEST RULE:

Avoid surprises by determining how much money you will need
for your retirement lifestyle.

The rule of $20. Earning $1 per $20 can be a target assuming a 5% dividend and long-term gain from your investments. A simple rule of thumb is to set a goal of a 5% return from each $20 invested.

Take the income you desire at retirement. For example:

If Mary wants $50,000 a year at retirement, what amount will Mary need in investments to generate $50,000 a year in income for life?

Mary would divide the $50,000 by approximately 5% = $833,000 in principal assuming no inflation adjustment. Mary will need $1 million in principal to get an approximate amount. Mary may need less than $1 million in capital if she has a pension plan and government benefits.

The net worth statement is an excellent guide to evaluating your debt to equity ratio. Are your debts growing faster than your assets? Plan to reduce your debts and increase your assets over the next five years. Over time, you will grow wealthier by paying down debts and investing even small amounts of money into your permanent wealth accounts. Time will become your friend rather than your enemy. This is how you can protect your wealth.

We've spoken about the risks to your wealth in this chapter. It's important to know what they are and the current status of our wealth year after year. Next, we will talk about the ways to manage these risks.

THE FOUR METHODS FOR
MANAGING RISKS

N ow that we know the different risks to our wealth, let's talk about managing them. Risks, as you know, will always exist whether we like it or not. However, we are in control of the way we manage those risks.

It's kind of like guarding your growing apple tree against harmful pests and rodents. Things will come at your tree to try and harm it. This is inevitable, and we can't stop them from happening. What we are in control of is how to manage those risks.

For instance, we can wrap our tree trunk with a rodent guard to prevent animals, such as mice or squirrels, from harming the tree or climbing up to eat the leaves and fruit. Keeping all rodents off your property is nearly impossible, but you can successfully manage them from harming your Endless Harvest.

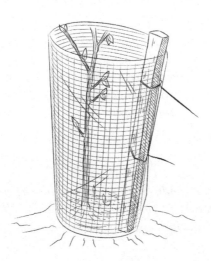

Managing your financial risk is kind of like using guarding to protect your tree against harmful rodents.

There are four strategies for managing risks. These are valuable to know since you can choose the most appropriate risk strategy that suits you best. Although they seem like common sense approaches to managing risks, do not underestimate their importance in helping you control or prevent severe financial losses.

THE FIRST METHOD TO MANAGE RISKS: AVOID THE RISK

The best way to explain this is to show you some real-life case examples:

Case 1

Johnny Cass enjoys gambling. He sometimes cannot afford groceries for his children because he loses his money at the casino hours after payday. The solution worked for Johnny to have his checks directly deposited into his family's joint bank account. Since his wife had some say about where the money got spent, Johnny no longer had the cash in his hands after payday. This helped him avoid the temptation of the Casino. Johnny eventually lost his desire to gamble and could adequately feed and clothe his children. He avoided the Casino and therefore avoided the risk of losing his money to gambling.

Case 2

Martha Stew, age 43, enjoys playing the penny stock market. She often acts on hot tips from the ladies club she attends. Although she has had some big winners in the past, her losers have resulted in her having a minimal retirement savings plan. She wanted to leave teaching earlier but worried she would never retire in style on her teaching pension.

Since starting teaching late in her career, she has had a small pension plan and a small retirement savings plan. Martha had recently opened an account with a conservative investment advisor and is now saving in a well-balanced portfolio of stocks and bonds. She now avoids buying penny stocks and is rebuilding a solid investment portfolio. By age 55, Martha hopes to retire or be semi-retired from teaching.

Case 3

Rick, age 34, smokes half a package of cigarettes a day. His cost is about $6.00 a day. Up to now, Rick has not saved any money for retirement. With no pension plan, Rick worries about his future. He knows a registered retirement plan would reduce his taxes and help provide him some security if he loses his job.

He can avoid three risks by quitting smoking. The first risk is obvious. Since he knows cancer runs in his family, he can help avoid or reduce his chances of dying early. He also will have an additional (365 days x $6.00 = $2,190) in cash per year to buy a registered retirement savings plan.

Rick can now build up his retirement plan, reduce his vulnerability to a job loss, and reduce his chances of a fatal health problem. He avoids a poverty-stricken old age by quitting smoking and investing the money. He lowers the financial risk from a sudden job loss while simultaneously preventing the potential of a self-inflicted health problem. Even on top of that, he can also avoid paying more tax than necessary since a registered retirement plan contribution also reduces his income taxes payable directly by the amount of $2,190.

Case 4

Nick loves to drive her car fast. She has had a significant increase in her car insurance recently. She has had three speeding tickets in the last year, which cost her $250. She also had a minor fender bender which was her fault. This cost a deductible of $500 on her insurance to have her car and the other cars' fenders repaired. The additional cost is over $300 per year.

Suppose she avoids driving fast in the future. In that case, she avoids severe consequences, such as a disability to her back or neck from a car accident, being killed, or killing/injuring someone else. This would also include the financial costs such as losing her driver's license, the cost of speeding tickets, and higher insurance premiums.

You can manage risks by avoiding the causes of negative consequences. Avoidance is an excellent way to prevent severe financial and personal consequences.

THE SECOND METHOD TO MANAGE SEVERE RISKS: TRANSFER THE RISK

One of the best ways to transfer the risk is through insurance. It is the best solution when the consequences of the loss could be damaging, but the chance or probability of the loss is slight. One example is fire insurance on your house. This cost is small but necessary since the consequences of losing your home and its contents in a fire are financially severe. Transferring the risk using a fire insurance policy makes sense in this case.

Alternatively, the risk transfer strategy does not make sense if the consequence of the loss is minimal. Since the cost of premiums may be too high to justify the policy.

Some clever ways to transfer the risk are shown in these cases:

Case 1

Two years earlier, Kurt, age 31, took out a life insurance policy for $800,000. He had two daughters, aged 3 and 5, and a stay-at-home wife. He loved to fly his plane on weekends. On one tragic day, his plane crashed, and Kurt left his wife and two children without any financial support. Since his registered retirement savings plan was only worth about $24,000, they would have been financially devastated except that their mortgage of $250,000 was life insured at the bank. They also had an additional $800,000 life insurance policy.

Consequently, the surviving spouse and two infant daughters were covered by the million dollars in life insurance. She got to keep her house and used the $800,000 received from the life insurance policy to raise, feed, educate, and clothe her children. She also had time to return to school and regain her career to support her in her old age. Without the insurance proceeds, they might have ended up homeless and living off of handouts from relatives until they could get their finances together.

Case 2

James and Karen, age 60, owned a successful trucking business. They also had three children. Only one child, Michael, had an interest in the business and, from the age of 14, had worked in the trucking business, doing everything from cleaning the trucks to helping with the bookkeeping. The other two children, John and Peggy, went to university and worked in other occupations.

138

The problem occurred when the parents passed away suddenly within a year of each other.

Since Michael was the only family member who wanted to keep the trucking business and the other two children, John and Peggy, wanted their money from the estate, a court battle ensued. Two years and thousands of dollars in legal fees have not resolved the family battle to sell the business.

A better way would have been to transfer the problem using life insurance. A joint last-to-die policy would pay the children tax-free for their portion of the business while allowing the business to continue in the hands of the interested parties. Michael would receive the business while Peggy and John receive their cash value of the estate, tax-free, from the life insurance policy. Since life insurance proceeds are paid out tax-free, it is an easy and acceptable way to pay out members for the value of a farm, business, rental property, or cabin.

Case 3

Roger, age 58, is a self-employed industrial designer who plans to retire in two years. He currently has no legal problems or customer complaints about his designs, although he has had some complaints and lawsuits during his long 25-year career.

When Roger retires, he is concerned that an unexpected lawsuit might damage him financially during his retirement years. He has taken the usual precautions and protected himself against creditors and lawsuits by taking out errors and omissions insurance and putting his investments into permanent insurance and segregated funds. These types of investments have some creditor proof and lawsuit protection.

Since Roger has consulted on hundreds of designs over the years, he is worried a lawsuit could arise when he leaves his association which had a group liability plan. As a retired member, he has lost some entitlement benefits and was also concerned about the high costs of maintaining his membership status. Since he and his wife planned to spend most of their money golfing and traveling, he wishes to protect his life savings. Insurance allows him to transfer some of the uncertain legal liability risks.

You can reduce risks with nominal costs by transferring your risks using insurance products. As long as the costs are small compared to the consequences of loss, you should consider transferring risks as a great strategy.

THE THIRD METHOD TO MANAGE RISKS: REDUCE THE CONSEQUENCES

"There is no such thing as a risk-free investment."
– George Hartman, *Risk Is a Four Letter Word*

For example, investors can reduce investment risks in their portfolios by diversifying well. By having foreign stocks, US stocks, Canadian stocks, bonds, and cash, you cannot eliminate risks, but you can reduce the risks.

Since eliminating all risks is impossible, I seek to provide you with top ideas for minimizing risks.

Case Example:

Wilma and Fred Flintrock, age 36, have registered retirement savings plans. Wilma is conservative and wants her entire plan in term deposits, while Fred is a risk-taker who wants his whole plan in stocks. Wilma sees the large monthly fluctuations in Fred's plan while her plan grows steadily. To Fred, her plan is growing too slowly. Her current five-year average is only 3.74%. They constantly argue about the right portfolio strategy. She was uncomfortable when Fred ran her portfolio. He also does not want her to run his portfolio.

The best approach is to look at their portfolios as one extensive portfolio with a 50% bond and GIC and 50% equity or stock portfolio. The funny thing is that they have a balanced and shared portfolio by accident. Since Wilma's portfolio is not keeping pace with inflation, she is losing real purchasing power since when they retire and she wants to buy a new car or travel. A 100% term deposit strategy will not buy very much. Her risk is inflation eating away the value of her money. Her plan does provide greater stability, and there are times when a term deposit plan will outperform the stock market. (Such as during bear markets or declining years in the stock markets.)

The advantage of Fred's plan is that his plan beats inflation over the long term. Since a 100% equity plan has always beaten inflation over the long term, it does not suffer from inflation risk. It does suffer from other risks, however. The one risk might be market decline risk. Fred is okay with market declines if he is diversified in an equity mutual fund or a diversified portfolio. Stocks would hurt Fred if he decides to put all his assets into one stock that goes down or if he panics and sells during market declines and crashes. As long as Fred contributes to a well-diversified equity plan that he continues to hold during bad times in the stock market, he will do quite fine over the longer term.

The strategy of reducing the risks is best when there is no way to eliminate the risks. (Risks will always be present in one form or another.) This is the best strategy for managing financial investments. In reality, investments perform similarly to metal in that the best approach is an alloy. Stocks, bonds, and cash all have specific strengths and weaknesses. They each face a different type of risk. For example, iron feels strong yet has the weakness of rusting away. Aluminum seems weak yet is resistant to rust and the effects of water.

To say one material is stronger than the other is incorrect. They are stronger against certain risk factors and weaker against other risk factors. It would be risky to restrict yourself to building a large and complex structure using only one metal. That is why you would choose an alloy or a combination of different types. Similarly, it can be risky only to consider one asset class, such as bonds, stocks, or cash.

THE FOURTH WAY TO MANAGE RISKS: ACCEPT THE RISK

For some people, the cost of disability insurance is too high for their budget. They have to accept the risk of disability impacting their ability to earn income. Avoiding unnecessary risks might be used in combination with accepting the risk. For instance, avoiding extreme sports reduces their chances of an injury or disability.

In investing with having a 100% stock portfolio, most people have to accept the risk that their portfolio can fall during down markets. History has shown that when people invest during down markets, they can benefit from the low prices when the stock market recovers. History has also shown that the stock market always recovers from a crash. By understanding this possibility, a successful stock market investor simply accepts the risk of a down market.

I have two cases I would like to highlight:

Case 1

Doug and Amanda, age 42, are long-term investors. Doug knows the stock market will achieve higher growth than bonds, term deposits, or cash over the long term. When Doug and Amanda buy a stock, they accept that the short-term prices of the stocks can fall. By simply accepting the risks, they can comfortably invest in stocks.

Case 2

Wilber, age 55, is single without kids. He has decided against buying life insurance since he has left his sizable registered retirement plan and stock portfolio in his will to his favorite charities. He has simply accepted the risk of dying without life insurance. This seems perfectly appropriate since Wilber has no dependents and sizable assets in his estate.

The best strategy in some cases is to accept the risk. Avoidance is the best strategy when the cost of covering the risk does not justify the potential loss. It also works when the probability or chance of the loss is small.

As you can see, there are four different ways of managing risk. Again, risks will be present throughout life and in your investment portfolio. There are ways we can address those risks, however. Use these simple strategies to protect yourself while putting your mind at ease.

In the next chapter, we will go into more detail about non-personal risks. These are risks that are often way out of our control. Let's talk about what they are precisely and how to manage them.

NON-PERSONAL RISKS

I n this chapter, we'll go over a few non-personal risks to be aware of. Non-personal risks happen no matter who you are or what type of investing or spending habits you may have. These are also classified as environmental or external risks.

You can think of dealing with these risks, like using a supporting stick or tree stake to grow your apple tree. Not all trees grow straight up. They will grow and lean more to one side more often than not. This can happen because of an unlevel terrain, winds predominantly coming from a single direction, the flow of natural water underground, or an uneven distribution of weight from the branches. Tree's don't always grow straight up, so we use supporting sticks to ensure they grow straight and tall.

This is also important if you plan on growing multiple apple trees. You can't have your trees crisscrossing each other. They need to be organized and in line for optimal production.

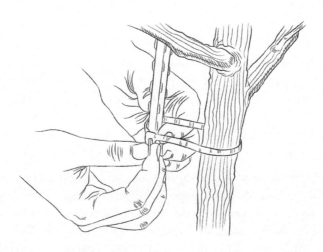

Non-personal risks are kind of like the many forces that will make your tree grow crooked, so you are required to use a tree stake.

Here is an index of environmental/external risks:

1. Job Loss
2. Injury or Disability
3. Taxes
4. Inflation
5. Lawsuits
6. Business Cycle Risk
7. Stock Market Risk
8. Currency Risk
9. Geopolitical Risks, such as Natural Disaster risks, War Risks, Terrorism risks, Random Risk
10. Bank or Institutional Failure

The best way to describe these risks is by real-life case studies. Some of these may hit close to home, so please don't be hurt by them. I use these case studies to show the reality of non-personal risks. Some of us have experienced these risks or have close relatives that have. Reading these case studies will allow us to understand each situation best. These risks are not just things that may happen, but they are really happening. Don't let them take you by surprise.

JOB LOSS

This case is about Michael and Sarah:

They were married at age 25. Today they are 34 years old. They have two children, Courtney, age 4, and Bobby, age 1. Both of them held good jobs at the time they were married. She was an Administrator at a hospital. He was a Sales Manager at a local car dealer. Sarah decided to stay home when her second child was born since the cost of daycare was equal to her take-home salary. (The amount of money left over after paying taxes and work-related expenses.)

When their second child was born, they needed a second vehicle and bought a new minivan on a 48-month payment plan. They also spent a large sum of money to renovate by expanding the house and developing the basement as a play area. They have a total loan on their line of credit of $40,000. They have a mortgage left of about $150,000 since they only bought the house three years ago. They also use their monthly credit card bills to build up their Airmiles points. They routinely use their credit cards rather than paying cash.

Michael and Sarah have not invested any money into their retirement savings plans for the last three years because money was tight after Sarah left her job to stay at home with their children. The total amount of their retirement savings plans totals $24,000. Sarah also has a small pension plan at work which will pay her about $200 per month at age 55.

They have no life insurance and no will, and Michael was recently let go at work due to slow sales at the local car dealership. They have recently started to take out the money from their retirement savings plan but worry about when that money runs out. Sarah and Michael are frantically searching for work, but employers have declined them because they are overqualified for many positions. Michael was even denied from working at the local burger restaurant.

UNEXPECTED INJURY OR DISABILITY

Here is a story about Craig, a successful engineer:

Craig's specialty is petroleum engineering in the oil and gas industry. Craig was doing so well that he decided ten years ago to go out on his own as an oilfield consultant. He made very good money and bought a large house, three sports cars, and a cabin in the mountains. He also has six children and a stay-at-home wife. He has expanded his business recently and has a large office with a five-year lease. Craig has recently taken on five junior partners but still makes all of the big decisions. In addition, his company also has a staff of 30 who work with him. He works seven days a week and has demands on his time from his six children.

Craig recently was injured in a skiing accident that left him unable to move due to a back injury. He has been off work for two months, and many projects at work have been postponed or delayed. He worries about the possibility of lawsuits or critical staff and key clients leaving. Since he never expected to be injured, he has no disability or overhead insurance. Furthermore, he has not delegated enough responsibility to his staff so they can carry on business without him. His wife recently expressed worries that she and the six kids are concerned about the future.

TAXES

I once attended a presentation by David Chilton, the now-famous author of *The Wealthy Barber*. Many people were asked, "What is the biggest financial expense you will have in your lifetime?" The answer was typically, "My mortgage." The real answer is taxes. In your lifetime, between federal taxes, sales taxes, provincial taxes, gasoline taxes, corporate taxes, and property taxes, you will pay about 50% of your income to income taxes. It pays to do your best to reduce the amount of unnecessary taxation on your hard-earned money.

We must pay taxes for good roads, schools, safe streets, etc. I support intelligent tax planning to avoid unnecessary payment of taxes. This tax planning is called "tax avoidance." Do not confuse "tax avoidance" with "tax evasion." Tax evasion is the illegal avoidance of taxes. Tax avoidance is the smart use of income tax laws to reduce your taxes legally. Tax avoidance, tax advisors, and a wise investment strategy are advised when reducing your taxes.

Consider the following cases:

Case 1

Herman and Gertrude own several rental properties. Although considered to be a resident of Canada for tax purposes, Herman earns his income overseas on projects all around the world. He is frequently doing consulting work in Saudi Arabia and Mexico. His primary source of income is a Texas-based oil company.

Herman has a bank account in Houston he frequently travels to on business. He and Gertrude are considering buying a small condo in Houston to save on hotel costs. When asked about their tax strategy, they answer, "We only take time once a year to fill out our tax forms with our accountant. Otherwise, we never consider other strategies for reducing our taxes."

Recently, Herman was surprised by a threatening letter from the IRS (US Internal Revenue Service). As a Canadian citizen and resident of Canada, he is surprised that the US tax department is questioning him. He is distraught since he received a similar letter from Revenue Canada about his Canadian tax report. They meet with their accountant as soon as Herman gets home from Singapore.

Case 2

Fred and Wilma are both retired. They recently received a significant increase in property taxes in their home and their cabin at the lake. This is a major concern for Fred and Wilma since they are on a tight budget on a fixed income from Fred's pension plan. This large increase in their property taxes means they might have to cancel their annual January trip to Hawaii to escape the harsh winter. Fred and Wilma look forward to going to Hawaii to golf and swim. They did not budget property taxes into their retirement plans.

Case 3

Lynda and Stanley, ages 55 and 58, have spent their lifetimes building their business empire for their three children to continue after retirement. Their three children are Dora, age 22; Ryley, age 26; and Wilber, age 28. They know the business will either pass to their children in their will, or they will sell it to their children. They have not consulted anyone on the best way to pass the assets down to their children with the least taxes payable.

Lynda and Stanley are concerned that the tax bill could be huge if they pass away unexpectedly. When they retire, they won't need money from their sizeable registered retirement savings plans because they have a large sum of money in their corporate account. Their accountant recommends drawing this money out since their retirement plans do not need to be withdrawn until they are age 69.

Case 4

In 1998 Larry, who worked for a major software maker, had stock options worth $1,000,000. He could exercise the options and walk away a millionaire. Larry and his wife Mary discussed it with their accountant and decided not to exercise the options because they did not want to pay the hefty tax bill by taking the million dollars home with him. He also saw no reason to exercise the stock option since his software company and shares continued to grow.

In 2000 Larry read the morning paper and saw his company was close to bankruptcy. He rushed to work and called the payroll department to exercise his options and sell his shares. He found that his stock options were worthless. He is now unemployed and has only his pension plan worth $40,000.

Although he would have had to pay taxes on his stock options, he would still be far better off than he is today.

INFLATION

Ken and Linda were conservative people:

They believed that the best security was no debt, term deposits, and a solid pension plan. When they retired, they started to draw Ken's pension and found they were comfortable. Over the next five years, his pension plan seemed to buy less and less. They wanted to buy a new car this year but found they would have to borrow to buy it unless they sell a quarter of their term deposits. If they did this, they would reduce their "rainy day fund."

With a recent increase in auto insurance and property taxes, they may have to forget about buying a new car this year. Their trips to Palm Springs are growing shorter and shorter. With the rising cost of their golf club memberships, Ken and Linda were forced to reduce their contribution to their daughter's wedding. Ken mentioned that his one mistake was never considering the prices of food, fuel, and more would keep rising over time.

Inflation is the invisible killer of wealth. It takes a $10 bill to buy the same amount of goods (2020) as a $1 bill from 1967. Small increases in your grocery bill, gasoline bill, insurance bill, and property taxes mean you need more and more money to maintain your current standard of living.

Since I also am a consumer, I find that living costs for basic necessities are rising continuously. Each year I see an increase in my property taxes, gasoline, utility, and food costs. From talking to renters, rent prices have risen over time as well.

A big mistake of most investors is to confuse the safety of capital with the certainty of capital. This means that inflation can eat away the spending power of your investments. While you still may have the same $40,000, it buys less ten years from now than today. Therefore, you are losing money if you earn below the price increases or inflation rate. Since you may look in your bank book and see the same amount of money plus a modest increase over time, you may make the mistake of feeling that your money is "safe." Do not confuse "safety of capital" with "certainty of capital."

LAWSUIT RISK

Case 1:

When Mike was downsized from the local telephone company, he decided to form his own home renovation business with his wife, Edith. He put small flyers and classified ads in his local newspaper. He received many home renovation jobs and went to work almost immediately. One of his first jobs was a basement renovation job. He felt he did an excellent job renovating the basement because he was careful to ensure the homeowners were happy with every phase of the project. It took Mike about a month to complete the job, and he was paid $5,000. The homeowners seemed very satisfied with Mike's job on the basement renovation.

He was midway into another renovation project when the first homeowner served him a lawsuit notice. They were suing him because there was a flood in the basement and extensive damage from the water. They claimed in the lawsuit that Mike had damaged the water pipes when he did the carpentry work to renovate the basement. Consequently, the toilet flooded, causing damage. Mike claimed another person installed the toilet, whom the homeowner hired to install a bathroom in the same basement.

Mike claimed that he did not do any of the work on the bathroom project except installing the bathroom cabinets. The toilet was not even installed when Mike did the job. Mike had completed his phase of the basement renovation after the toilet was installed. The claim was for over $26,000. This seemed unreasonable since Mike only earned $5,000 for his carpentry work on the basement project. Mike and Edith did not have any liability insurance, so they would either have to go to court or settle out of court as recommended by their lawyer.

Case 2:

Martin, age 28, graduated at the top of his computing science class. He has quickly risen to a top position in a major computing company as the head of programming. Recently he bought a brand new, jet black, imported sports car. Single with no kids, Martin's future looked unstoppable until one evening, Martin was speeding down a street and hit another vehicle.

Martin's car was a top design for safety, and he was unhurt except for a minor neck sprain. The people in the other car were not wearing their seat belts and *suffered extensive injuries. Although Martin had some liability insurance at $500,000, he was unprepared for the over $2,000,000 lawsuit against him.*

Martin is meeting with his lawyer and is very worried about his future. He is unsure whether to go to court and risk an extensive, multi-million dollar loss or settle out of court for a large debt he may have to work years to pay off. His plans for traveling or buying a new house are looking dim at this point. At only 28, Martin is apprehensive about his long-term future.

BUSINESS CYCLE RISK

"Ignore business cycle risks at your peril. In my experience, this is one of the most important risks to business owners."

– John Yamamoto

Business cycle risk is the risk to our job security, sales, portfolio value, or income arising from our economy's recessions and boom cycles. Just as we have physical seasons of the year, such as winter, spring, summer, and autumn, we also have economic seasons such as recessions, recovery, boom, and decline or crash cycles in our economy.

The risks caused by the business cycle are huge if you are planning a business expansion. Technology jobs can be very high in demand during booms such as during 1997-2000, only to fall in large numbers between 2000 and 2003. It can also be significant if you work in a cyclical business such as oil and gas.

Let's consider a case about Bill's business:

Bill had inherited a large hardware chain from his father. He, as managing director, planned to expand his hardware chain during an economic boom to better serve the local oil and manufacturing industry. The expansion would take about 18 months to complete the new store. During that time, the economy seemed to be weakening. By borrowing a large sum of money at reasonable interest rates to expand the operation, Bill seemed to be making a smart business move.

Bill did not follow the decline that was happening in the general economy. Interest rates rapidly rose. The original loan at 7.25% was 10.25% a year later. Being on a variable rate, which changed daily, the increase in the loan might have been prevented using a fixed rate which would not change for the set time. The loan rate was at 13.75% when the store was completed. They then met with the bank and tried to set the loan rate on a fixed five-year term. It eventually got set at 15.25% for five years.

On top of the increased interest charges, the new store opened during a recession in the oil, gas, and manufacturing world. The sales were half of what was projected. Sales fell in all of the stores. The heavy debt of the loan payments and the lower sales resulted in the eventual bankruptcy of the entire hardware chain. They became victims of the recession.

STOCK MARKET RISK

There are two types of stock market risk. The most common stock risk arises from a specific stock falling due to factors like accounting fraud, declining sales, and management failures. These can cause a stock to go down in value, become bankrupt, and become worthless in extreme circumstances. This is the main reason to diversify your portfolio properly. Having your money divided amongst a larger number of different stocks in your portfolio avoids the danger of significantly declining your wealth due to one stock going bankrupt. This type of individual stock risk is called "unsystematic" risk.

Case 1:

James is a sophisticated investor. Having a degree in business and banking experience, James knew how to analyze stocks. By age 45, James had built a sizable net worth with a paid-off house and a stock portfolio worth over half a million dollars. He was doing fine until 1999, when he decided to invest a large amount of his net worth in a new technology stock IPO or initial public offering. Since this was a no-lose deal with thousands of investors buying into this stock, James felt he had a chance to make a massive amount of money from this stock.

Going against his usual policy of being diversified, James decided to liquidate his portfolio and place a large piece of his net worth into this technology stock. Since all of the analysts had glowing reports on the massive potential of this technology stock, James felt quite fearless in his purchase of this stock. At first, the stock rose quickly. Then it started to fall. James bought more and more of the stock as its price fell.

While trading, the exchange froze the stock, and James felt a jolt of fear. He heard rumors that the internal company management had overstated their cash reserves and understated their debt. The official confirmation came out in a press announcement that the stock was in serious trouble. By the time James had sold out, he had lost most of his fortune. He realized that diversification is still the best way to reduce significant losses.

The second type of stock risk is general stock risk. This general stock risk is called "systematic" risk. This is the risk of the general stock market falling. Anything that affects investor confidence, such as a terrorist attack like 9/11 or the assassination of President Kennedy, would affect all stocks.

A minor form of stock risk would be sector risk. Sector risk is when a particular stock market sector falls, such as oil and gas in 1998 or technology stocks in 2000. All stocks in either sector fell significantly while other stock market sectors rose during those periods. The best solution to stock market risk is to diversify your stocks broadly and own bonds and stocks from other countries.

A common risk people mention is general stock market risk. This is due to a particular stock falling to zero or a sustained stock market decline such as 2000-2003, when most stocks fell in value.

Case 2:

In 1999 Edith and Archie, age 51, had bought growth equity mutual funds. They took some money Archie received as a small inheritance and invested it into mutual funds. Archie had read about the high returns from growth equity funds. Not sure what growth equity funds were, Archie and Edith, put all their money into them in 2000. They fell 30% after the September 11, 2001 attack a year later. With the uncertainty of this event, accounting scandals, and wars, they were panic-stricken that they would never recover their money.

History has shown that their funds will eventually recover. They may need to reconsider their risk tolerance level and consider a more balanced approach to investing in the future. The best strategy for them at this time would have been to buy more of the same mutual fund as the prices continued to fall. They could also add a bond or fixed-income fund to complement their aggressive stock portfolio.

GEOPOLITICAL RISK

Geopolitical risk comes from decisions and actions by governments. A change in tax laws could dramatically affect the amount of taxes you may pay in the future. The British and US governments' decision to go to war against Iraq impacted the stock markets. A decision by a government to nationalize or take over oil fields previously owned by private companies is a risk of dealing with foreign governments. The need to follow global political decisions is vital to formulating investment strategies.

If you do not want to follow the events of foreign governments, an excellent way to deal with geopolitical risks is to buy global investments. These investments are professionally managed by experts in that particular country or region. For example, let a Far East manager decide which stocks to buy in Hong Kong, Japan, S. Korea, or China.

Geopolitical risks are also the main reason you should look at a balanced portfolio of stocks and bonds. Bonds and stocks are affected differently by the same geopolitical decisions. Stocks may rise while bonds fall due to a government decision to raise interest rates to fight inflation within an economy. Bonds will often be unaffected or even rise, while stocks may fall dramatically during a political crisis.

The emotional stress caused by geopolitical risks is difficult to deal with because they cannot be forecasted or planned. A terrorist attack happens instantly and affects the markets without warning. High levels of emotions such as fear or grief often accompany a geopolitical risk. Therefore, the best practice to reduce the effects of geopolitical risk is to remain diversified. Another approach is to ignore the temporary impact of the geopolitical risk.

Natural Disaster Risk, War Risk, Terrorism Risk, and Random Risk are all forms of geopolitical risk. Things such as Mad Cow Disease, SARs, and global droughts are random risks that affect the stock market.

CURRENCY RISK

I experience this risk whenever my wife and I travel together. We end up at the foreign exchange windows seeing large numbers of domestic dollars turned into small numbers of Yen, Euro, or other currency. Since most of my income is in one currency, I must diversify my investment portfolio into foreign currencies.

153

A danger to consider if you are diversifying into foreign investments is the specter of foreign estate taxes. Be careful to plan, read up, or assess foreign estate tax risk.

Case 1:

Al and Margaret loved to travel to San Diego, California, each year to golf and escape the Canadian winter for a few months a year. The problem was that their entire portfolio and pension were paid in Canadian dollars. They have, in recent years, only been able to go to San Diego for a few weeks a year due to an unfavorable exchange rate. They are waiting for a favorable time to buy US dollars for their portfolio. Maybe then they can travel more during the winter. They regret not buying more US dollar investments when the Canadian dollar was higher.

Case 2:

Fred and Ginger are in the trucking business. They buy an average of two trucks a year. Since the trucks are imported from the US, they take on foreign exchange risk every time they buy a truck. From 1994-2003 they paid a large amount for each truck since the US dollar was firm. My recommendation is to build up a US dollar account when the US dollar is weak.

BANK OR INSTITUTIONAL FAILURE

Let's talk about Marion, who lives in Alberta:

Marion is a conservative investor. She did not buy stocks because she was afraid of any losses or fluctuations in the value of her portfolio. She had her life savings in term deposits at a smaller trust company. One day she read the newspaper and finds her trust company going bankrupt. Her portfolio is still recovering from a loss ten years earlier.

Since this trust company was covered by CDIC, or Canada Deposit Insurance Corporation, for a maximum of $100,000, Marion's $350,000 went down to $100,000. After ten years of savings, her net worth is back to $350,000. She now keeps her money only in large banks and purchases government bonds from her broker. She now stores most of her money in government bonds with unlimited guarantees and competitive rates on term deposits. She felt safe by missing a major risk to her wealth but took on institutional failure risk. She has learned from her mistake the hard way.

These are some of the non-personal risks you have to consider during your lifetime. Don't worry, as all of them won't occur at once. But you can see that non-personal risks can take an enormous toll when they come along. The world has been full of its ups and downs for many centuries. It will also continue to have more ups and downs in the future.

This chapter's key is understanding non-personal risks and planning for them in advance. We can't predict precisely when exchange rates will be favorable, when a global crisis may occur, or when we will have a dramatic fluctuation in the stock market. What we can predict are things like inflation and taxes. Take all of the non-personal risks into consideration by assessing what we know now and being prepared for things that may come in the future.

In the next chapter, we will discuss financial problems from our behavior. These problems or issues are personal. If we had a winning algorithm and traded like robots, everyone might be a successful investor. The truth is, we are human beings. Many act based on emotions, take gambles, and make risky decisions. The next chapter will explain what kinds of problems can come from these emotions and what to do about them.

FINANCIAL PROBLEMS FROM OUR BEHAVIOR

Here we are going to talk about financial problems from our behavior. This is also known as personal or internal risks. You are reading this chapter to find out how to identify and manage psychological risks to our wealth caused by the emotions of fear, greed, and other illusions.

You can think of these internal risks, kind of like over-trimming your growing apple tree. Maintenance to your growing apple tree does need to be done over time. Trimming branches weighing down uneven sections of the tree, cutting off limbs that have died, or scraping away mold that may be growing in some areas is important. What we do not want to do is over-trim our tree.

This is also called tree pruning. It's one thing to provide the right amount of tree maintenance with cutters, but it's different to cut almost everything off. Doing so will ruin your harvest and result in an unhealthy apple harvest or perhaps no harvest at all. Don't let your internal fear or greed get in the way of properly maintaining your apple tree or investment portfolio.

"We are our worst enemy."

– John Yamamoto

Financial problems from our behavior are kind of like over-trimming your growing apple tree and hurting the harvest.

The new approach to investing is based not on economic and financial analysis but behavioral science. This may not have been what you were thinking. Behavioral science helps us understand why people make investment mistakes. We can make logical investment decisions that can be very profitable by controlling our emotions. By avoiding the "lemming syndrome," in which we do the same things as our friends and neighbors, we can take control of our money. A lemming is known as a mindless creature that follows the pack. Would you jump off an unknown cliff just because someone else did?

Investing is a very emotional experience. Despite many textbooks full of mathematical ratios, many investors still rely on their emotions to make major investment decisions. Volatile periods allow you to buy very cheaply or sell very high during periods when the stock market is driven by high fear or high greed. The key to faster wealth building is understanding and controlling your own emotions. The best way to handle those times that may drive you to make rash emotional decisions is to hire and use a top investment advisor and rely on professional money managers to make your buy and sell decisions.

You can pick up huge bargains by controlling your emotions, leading to enormous profits from the stock market, mutual funds, or even real estate. You accumulate more for the same money by buying when things are low. By avoiding buying what is in high demand, you prevent the inevitable crashing from previous highs to more normal prices.

One of my financial heroes, Warren Buffett, built his wealth on "contrarian buying." Contrarian value buying is based on buying investments at a sale or discount prices and avoiding buying anything considered overpriced according to mathematical and logical analysis.

Here is an index of behavior/internal risks to your wealth:

1. Fear
2. Greed / Impatience
3. Procrastination
4. Group Thinking
5. Hindsight Risk
6. Making Investment Decisions Based On Feelings
7. Extrapolation Risk
8. Impatience
9. Overconfidence
10. Short-Term Thinking

We will do the same thing, just like in the last chapter. We'll use real-life examples just like before to best explain these risks. Doing so will allow you to look inside your life, emotions, wants, and needs.

FEAR

Here is a situation that happened to a young adult, Ken:

Ken, age 28, started to save money for a down payment on a house. Since he lived at home, he could save ten thousand a year. He had accumulated

$20,000 by the second year. He wanted to buy a house but did not want to carry any debt with a mortgage. He continued to save money. The problem was that after four years, the original house he wanted to buy had increased in the same time from $135,000 to $165,000. Although he had saved an additional $20,000 for his down payment, he was no closer to buying the house without a mortgage.

Another year later, his down payment had increased to $50,000, and the house had gone up in price by another $8,000. Ken was even further from buying his house than before. At that point, I pointed out two factors. The first was that mortgage rates were at the lowest point in thirty years. The second factor was that he would be an old man before buying the house with cash. He eventually bought the house and placed a $55,000 down payment. He did a good thing since the economy boomed in his area, and his house has climbed an additional $38,000 since he bought it.

GREED AND IMPATIENCE

Here is a case about a couple and their business:

Mr. and Mrs. Andros were 58 years old when they sold their construction business. Excited to have some money, Mr. Andros decided to play the stock market with the $1.2 million proceeds he received from the sale of his company. He chose to go with his friend's broker. He wanted to double his money through aggressive investments. They both decided against blue-chip stocks. Instead, they invested the entire amount into junior oil, gold, and other penny stocks. Since this broker worked for a penny stock company, this became their investment strategy.

The stocks started to slide downward immediately. Mr. Andros decided to sell some at a considerable loss to buy another penny stock, which he sold when it also fell. He did this until the amount was down $800,000. At this time, we met and discussed his account. He refused to listen to any advice about preserving his capital and diversifying away from penny mining stocks. He decided to open a discount account and day trade the remaining amount. He returned to work a year later and is now broke. Mr. Andros was his worst enemy.

I consider impatience the most expensive financial cost to you because impatience leads us to sell too early before our investments have paid off.

PROCRASTINATION

The emotion of procrastination is one of the most expensive emotions because it can put off saving money. This leads to having to work longer.

Procrastination affects us just as much in investing as it does daily. If you've ever procrastinated on a house chore, only to find yourself spending more time than initially necessary to complete the task, you know exactly what I'm talking about.

GROUP THINKING

Following your friends and neighbors can be financially devastating. Group thinking is "lemming syndrome." Don't blindly follow the pack and hope its leader does the right thing. You can get yourself into trouble quickly this way, and you only have yourself to blame.

HINDSIGHT RISK

Hindsight risk is thinking that a win or a mistake in the past was more predictable than before. Don't trick yourself into thinking that "if you would have..." or "if you kept doing..." will always be right in the future. Make educated decisions based on an analysis of your past choices, but don't convince yourself if it is not proven based on hard numbered facts. Our emotions often trick us into believing what we want to think is correct when it may not be the truth. It takes away from our happiness to second guess and analyze regrets about our past.

MAKING DECISIONS BASED ON FEELINGS

"The biggest mistake investors make is buying what is comfortable, not what is appropriate."
– George Hartman, *Risk is a Four Letter Word*

Do not choose only comfortable investments. Instead, select suitable investments to achieve your financial goals and dreams.

I started an exercise program two years ago. It was challenging to keep up the gym routine twice weekly for the last two years. I found it difficult because it was often uncomfortable or even painful. I have kept up the program for two reasons.

The first reason is that I know I will be better off health-wise and keep my weight under control in the long term. I am actively preventing the weight-related diseases that affected my father. The other reason I go is that I have a personal trainer who will charge me whether I go or not. He is also there to keep me on track and prevent me from taking a few months off whenever I get busy.

You may be asking what this story has got to do with investing. It is similar to many financial planning interviews I have had with clients over the years. It is a huge benefit to convince many of my clients to stay in the market during uncomfortable periods. This occurred mainly during bad times in the stock market. Although it can be uncomfortable, buying low and selling high is the right thing to do. To succeed in business and life, you must be uncomfortable at times.

EXTRAPOLATION RISK OR HAVING A HUNCH

This type of risk is unfamiliar to most people, but you may have heard the terms "educated guess" or "hypothesis." Extrapolation is the risk of using an educated guess to make investing decisions.

Using data is great to decide, but not if that data does not specifically correlate with your decision. Having hypothetical guesses does make us feel better, but in reality, it is just a guess. Go with hard facts or data when making your financial decisions.

OVERCONFIDENCE

Overconfidence is a risk to investors who have been successful or just have a strong type A personality. Just being confident in your investment choices won't make them successful.

Stocks, bonds, and the market, in general, don't care about how confident you are in what you put your money into. The market will go its way regardless of how you feel about it. The trick here is not to believe you always have the right choice just because you think so. Again, make your decisions based on hard numbers and facts.

IMPATIENCE

Immediate gratification is a problem today. Everything seems to be instant today. Learning when to harvest an investment is vital. Avoid selling because you do not get short-term returns. Immediate gratification hurts success.

We are getting into debt with credit cards due to impatience. We want it now and pay the price in high-interest rate credit cards.

Have you ever done something you usually wouldn't have, just because you didn't want to miss it? For example, did you go on the London cruise because you didn't want to be left out of the picture? Did you go on the fishing trip because your friends planned to catch "the big one"? How many times did you end up going, but the reward wasn't there like you wanted? Or possibly you had to sacrifice something personal or financial to take that risk?

Impatience can be a big player here. Sometimes we are too eager to jump in and take the risk without proficiently analyzing the facts. We are too anxious to get the reward, and our incompetence leaves us at a loss. This is how impatience can be a considerable risk to take.

Learn to put your investments in a separate long-term account, which I call your permanent wealth account. This is your "serious" money for your senior years.

SHORT-TERM THINKING

Short-term thinking is a killer risk, especially with The Endless Harvest. I've said it before, and I'll repeat it. If you want short-term wins and are willing to risk it all, this isn't the right book for you. With The Endless Harvest method, we are talking about winning long-term. That means winning for life. I don't want you to risk everything you have for a 1 in 1,000 shot at being successful.

This is short-term thinking. Short-term thinking is exciting and can even be fun. Some people even make some short-term trades because it is a fun game for them. This is what they enjoy doing as entertainment. It's kind of like having a $500 limit when you gamble in Las Vegas and being prepared to lose it to enjoy the experience. It is not ok to bet your life savings in Vegas.

Short-term thinking will lead to short-term results. The Endless Harvest is about long-term thinking for long-term results. You decide what is more important to you.

NOT UNDERSTANDING APPRECIATING VERSUS DEPRECIATING ASSETS

I wanted to discuss appreciating versus depreciating assets in this chapter because our emotions have much to do with this. We spoke about internal problems based on investing strategies, but I also want to discuss internal problems based on our personal asset spending. There is a big difference between having money and being financially independent. Being financially independent means the returns earned from your investment income equals your living expenses. Having money means you have a lump sum of money available to spend or invest. What you do with that money determines whether you will be rich or poor. It is your emotions that run this decision. To have an Endless Harvest, you must invest so that you can live off the principal for the rest of your life.

THE ENDLESS HARVEST RULE:

To become financially independent, you must focus on putting your money into assets that appreciate over time. Learn not to confuse depreciating with appreciating assets.

With so many advertisements telling you to buy, buy, buy, it is important to discuss one of the main reasons people retire broke. A depreciating asset is worth less and less every year until it is eventually worthless. Cars, clothes, and stereos are examples of depreciating assets.

When I was a young boy, some parents' friends constantly bought new cars, fur coats, and other luxuries. In their later years, they had financial hardships because they could not work for health reasons. They did not plan and save for retirement, so they had a tough old age. To become wealthy, we must acquire appreciating and not depreciating assets.

Depreciating assets do not increase in value over time. To offset your investments in depreciating assets, you need to also save a certain amount of your income in appreciating assets. Investing only in depreciating assets is closely related to having no savings plans.

Investing most of your money into appreciating assets will make you wealthier with time—it becomes your ally. With depreciating assets, time is your enemy. You can see why spending money on clothes, cars, fine food, and drink can lead to poverty when the money or salary runs out. There is no momentum from depreciating assets. Some lottery winners and celebrities make millions of dollars but invest in depreciating assets. In doing so, they often go broke after a few years.

Here is an example:

	Appreciating Asset	Depreciating Asset
Before Tax Income	$20,000	$20,000
Purchase	Registered Retirement Savings	Boat
Amount Spent	$10,000	$10,000
Tax Benefit	$4,000	Nil
Growth or appreciation in value	$800 @ 8%	Nil
Value in 9 years	$20,000	$1,000*
Increase in Financial Independence	$24,000	$1,000

Using assumed depreciation rate, for example, only.

Appreciating assets are what are serious money assets. Also called capital, serious money is your investment wealth. You live off the returns of your serious money.

If you borrowed to buy the boat, your cost would be even higher. You can see why appreciation-orientated people can retire earlier and are wealthier.

Focus on investing your hard-earned money into appreciating assets that grow in value over time. Avoid putting most of your money into depreciating assets that go down in value until they are worthless. Since they decline in value over time, time is your enemy. Since depreciating assets always go down in value, they are temporary or short-term forms of wealth. Appreciating assets are endless forms of wealth.

Next, we will discuss the danger of not fully understanding tax risks. So far, many of our numbered examples haven't included tax considerations. So let's take a look at this quickly.

TRUE COSTS OF BEFORE AND AFTER-TAX DOLLARS

You ou pay for everything in after-tax dollars. Therefore, understand the actual cost to your pocketbook. This is perhaps the most giant monetary illusion we have. Just consider:

- The price of a house
- A winning lottery ticket
- Your vacation flight tickets
- College tuition
- Your house's net worth
- The value of your company
- Even how much money you need to retire

We almost instinctively think about the cost before taxes when we think of these factors. The truth is, we need to consider the cost after taxes. This goes for both what you buy and what you wish to sell. When purchasing an item, you often consider tax more quickly. The after-tax dollars will hit you much later when selling something, such as a house or a business product.

Let's even take this a step further. When you make a purchase, you are using after-tax income. When you buy a depreciating asset like a stereo for $1,200, it costs you $2,400. Why is that? It is because you have to earn $2,400 to have an after-tax amount of $1,200. When making a purchase, mentally double the cost of the items you buy.

Now, you have the reverse situation with purchasing appreciating investment assets like retirement savings plans. Tax credit against income means that for every $1,000 contribution, you receive $250 or more (depending on your tax bracket) in tax savings, plus tax-free investment growth. This is the power of appreciating investments!

Focus on accumulating quality stocks, bonds, and mutual funds that grow over time. This is a compelling way to build your wealth and financial strength. You can build a wealthy future by using your after-tax income to purchase appreciating investments with tax-saving benefits such as registered savings plans, dividends, and capital gain investments.

It is a good rule of thumb to divide your gross income in half to get your after-tax or true cash flow. You get your net income by subtracting your taxes and other expenses from your gross income. The net income figure is the figure you need to know.

Most people spend after-tax income to invest. But, because all of our purchases are after-tax dollars, we must spend our money wisely.

For example:

Kate, age 33, buys a new car. She has found an excellent car for $26,500. She feels that because she earns $55,000 a year, she can easily afford to pay for this car. After a year, Kate still owes $23,800. She is frustrated by how long she must make car payments. She also wants to pay the car loan off as quickly as possible. Her other priorities, such as her mortgage, credit card bills, retirement savings plans, and daily living expenses, take all her remaining money. She is barely able to make the minimum car payments.

Kate is frustrated because her car will be worth very little at the end of the four-year car loan if she decides to sell it. With interest, she will have paid $32,000 for a car worth about $12,000 by the time it is paid off. She also did not consider the before-tax cost of the car. Because she is in a 40% tax bracket, the car did not cost her $26,500. Its actual price was $32,000 because the car loan interest was an additional $5,500.

Furthermore, because of her tax bracket she had to earn $32,000 + (.40%) $32,000 = $44,800 in before-tax earnings to pay for this car. The car's true cost was that Kate had to work 75% of an entire year just to pay for this car. If she knew the true cost of almost a year of her life for this car, she might have bought a second-hand car or a less expensive model.

Always double the costs of any purchases to get the true cost in before-tax dollars. If possible, try to buy items using before-tax dollars. Be aware that buying things on credit also makes items much more expensive. Continually evaluate the true cost regarding how much time and money it takes to pay for any purchased item.

Now that we have spoken about taxes and their effects on our wealth, let's take a moment to talk more about debt. We've discussed this briefly before, but I want to go into more detail. I have a list of commandments you need to understand about debt. Many websites even have national debt counters. It can be an easy hole to dig yourself into.

THE DANGERS OF DEBT

T he single biggest threat to maintaining your wealth is spending money using debt. This chapter is going to be quick and straightforward. I have some hard-set rules and commandments you must follow. No if's, and's, or but's here. It's not a story-driven read, but you must follow the below if you want to stay rich.

ENDLESS HARVEST RULE:

You will never be Permanently wealthy until you:
1. Control your spending
2. Eliminate consumer debts
3. Invest in assets, not possessions

After paying yourself first, put in extra money to reduce your bills using the Endless Harvest method. You need to avoid the temptation of spending by avoiding shopping centers and avoid incurring new debts. The next step is to start paying down the smallest debts first.

ENDLESS HARVEST RULE:

Learn the habit of shopping for capital investments in stocks, ETFs, and mutual funds rather than possessions or stuff.

ENDLESS HARVEST RULE:

Since you are less secure after buying that extra item on credit, you are borrowing against the future. By paying off those loans, you are buying back your future earnings.

ENDLESS HARVEST RULE:

Pay cash for everything. Think about paying cash as paying for something now. Think about a credit card as borrowing from and hurting your future.

The Ten Commandments of Credit

1. Pay off your credit card balance each month to avoid finance charges.

2. Pay your bills on time to avoid late fees.

3. Use cash to buy consumer items.

4. Borrow only to buy investments and avoid borrowing to buy consumer items.

5. Shop for investments, not for consumer items.

6. Think about credit card spending as borrowing against your future.

7. Use coupons and join frequent user clubs.
   E.g., Airmiles and other free benefits for buying your groceries, gas, and other necessities.

8. Be patient and look for sales for items you want to own.

9. Do not pay for vacations using your credit cards.
   Do not take it on credit if you cannot pay for the vacation. Find a cheaper vacation destination. Instead of a four-star hotel, rent a condo. Better a less expensive vacation than a six-month credit headache long after the break ended. This is hardly relaxing. Paying for a vacation on credit is not worth the worries for months afterward.

10. Cut back on eating out.
    Cook more of your meals. Eat out less often, so when you go out, you should eat guilt-free. When you go out, treat yourself in style. Simply do it less often. It becomes a treat when you eat out less often and is much better for your financial security. Pay for the meal with cash.

I even have a few more tips that will help you manage your credit correctly:

1. Find a credit card with a benefits program such as air travel points, or replace your expensive card with a card with no annual fees.

2. Consider consolidating your debts with one large consolidation loan at a lower interest rate.

3. Cut up all but one credit card.
    This will simplify your payment schedule by having fewer bills to pay.

4. Go to matinees or cheap Tuesdays when you are going to a movie. Consider renting or streaming it for your home viewing.

5. Examine the expensive golf or health club membership.
    Are you using it enough? If you rarely attend the club, you should consider canceling or switching to a cheaper club.

6. Have a rummage or garage sale to sell off any unnecessary clutter in your home.
    Take this cash and pay down your loans.

7. Drive your cars for a long time.
    One of the biggest money wasters is to replace your car every few years. Make sure to remember that your car is a depreciating asset. It falls in value every year.

8. Review your home.
    Is your home too big for your needs? Consider the amount of money you are paying for your mortgage. Is your mortgage too large a debt for your salary? Can you pay it off earlier? If you can, it will save you thousands in interest charges. Could you downsize your home to a smaller one without hurting your level of happiness?

Stop borrowing against your future. Stop unnecessary spending and start to pay off your consumer debts. Do not add more consumer debts. Sell off unneeded items and use the cash to pay down your consumer loans.

It may seem like I was a bit harsh in this chapter, but that was on purpose. Debt is a considerable danger to your wealth. It is a huge danger to your Endless Harvest.

Next, I will list out what are called Black Swan risks. I'm not talking about the Hollywood movie or Natalie Portman. I'm talking about large economic events that are unpredictable.

BIG BLACK SWAN RISKS AND FINANCIAL HEADWINDS

B lack Swan risk is a term for unexpected or unpredictable risks that have massive consequences or effects on our lives. Negative consequences can cause large drops in the value of investment portfolios. The Black Swan risks also have a substantial downside risk which can cause panic selling on stocks.

Black Swan risks are kind of like big disasters that endanger your apple tree. Some things can be predicted, like rainy weather, wind, rodents, or a dry summer. Then, there are other things that no one can predict. An example of this would be a wildfire.

Wildfires can come and wipe out entire apple orchards in an instance. Black Swan risks in the economy are also unpredictable. We don't know when they will come and what effect the Black Swan event will have on your investments.

Examples of Black Swan events are the 2020 Global Covid-19 Pandemic. It is an unpredictable event with massive negative consequences for our wealth and lives.

Black Swan risks are kind of like unpredictable wildfires that can endanger your apple tree.

Some examples of Black Swan risks we have seen in our lifetime may be:

- World War 1
- The 1918-1919 Pandemic
- The 1929 stock market crash
- World War 2
- The assassination of President JF Kennedy in November 1963
- The rapid rise of interest rates in 1982-1984 from hyper-inflation led to 16% mortgage rates.
- The Black Monday stock market crash of 1987
- The Dotcom crash in the late 1990s
- The 9/11 Terrorist Attack
- The 2007-2009 Banking and Mortgage Crisis
- The 2019-2022 Covid-19 pandemic

During Black Swan events, you have an opportunity to turn lemons into lemonade. Lemons are often thought of as sour and not a delicious fruit. But when done right, lemons produce a refreshing lemonade drink. You have the greatest opportunity and the greatest risk during Black Swan events.

For example, Warren Buffet frequently purchased high-quality stocks and great prices during these events. The events often produce a panic in the market, where stock values will decline. If you can get high-quality stocks at "discount prices" from the panic, you must hold onto them until they rise again. World War 2, the 9/11 terrorist attack, the Dotcom crash, and other events will not last forever. Once the world recovers from these periods, high-quality stocks rise in value and often keep rising. This is where you can make great money by buying low and selling high.

Having a diversified portfolio is best because Back Swan events are unknown. These are the things that keep me awake at night. I have a strategy of what to do when these events happen, but I still cannot predict when they will come. These are unforecastable and usually have devastating effects on the economy, but you can take advantage of these situations.

With the recent pandemic of Covid-19, I have seen up to 27% return in some cases. How about that return for a short period? Isn't that superb! In the good times, you plan for bad times, and in the bad times, you plan for good times.

The specific event that made me come up with a strategy was 9/11. After this event, my focus on Black Swan events went from avoidance to future gain. This event specifically stood out to me because I was in the United States then and could not return to Canada via airplane. This was not bad, but it made me realize exactly how life-altering these events can be.

I remember sitting in the hotel room for a few days before I could fly again. Even when I returned to the airport, the airline agent said my tickets were expired! Well, of course, they were. All flight was suspended because of the terrorist attack. This specific Black Swan event has affected air travel worldwide. Because of 9/11, air travel has never been the same.

The Covid-19 pandemic was a big Black Swan event because it affected the entire world. In 2021, even the Tokyo Olympics had no one in the stands. Everyone was watching on television. That has never happened before in history.

My main lessons from past Black Swan risks are to have an investment strategy for dealing with sudden and unpredictable events that have a short-term but massive impact on the value of your portfolio. My advice is to have a Plan B for your investment plan. Consider that sudden and rapid drops in the value of your investments can happen, and use risk management, portfolio structure, and tactical buying and selling to counteract.

There are many things to consider when trying to maintain your wealth. I could talk on and on about them, but in the next chapter, I want to highlight the most important things to think about as we move forward, from reducing the negative to enhancing the positive.

I'm not trying to be a downer in this section, but you need to know what can harm your Endless Harvest. All it takes is one wrong blow to take you out. Avoid these at all costs.

CONVERSION OF MONEY TO CAPITAL

The entire purpose of the investment world is to facilitate the transfer of money between its physical forms. The principal is the seed money we have received from savings, business sales, and other things. Gains are the result. I call this the physics of money management.

Money exists in three forms. These forms are **solid, liquid, and gaseous money**.

Solid money is in the form of cash and coins. This is the money you carry in your wallet or purse. Because this money is bulky and inconvenient, we must use other forms of money to store our wealth. The solid form of money also provides zero growth or active income.

Liquid wealth is created when we hold wealth in the form of short-term capital. This form of wealth is harder to spend, and we must use checks, instant tellers, debit cards, and other intermediaries to spend this money. This form provides us with a slightly better rate of return than solid money. Liquid cash is temporary in nature and does not lead to financial independence.

Gaseous wealth is the most un-spendable and least liquid form of money. Gaseous money offers the best growth potential with higher risk potential. Examples of gaseous wealth are stocks, businesses, real estate, and mutual funds.

Gaseous wealth is also defined as capital. Most capital is not liquid. It is much harder to cash in gaseous wealth. Capital is the permanent form of money. We can only become financially independent for life by converting money to capital. We must be much more careful in selecting capital since the value of capital can fluctuate. Capital is the most fickle of all forms of money since it can expand and contract very quickly. It is also the quickest way to grow your money since it offers the greatest growth potential. The conversion of money to capital must be done wisely.

Most investment mistakes occur at the conversion of money to capital. For example:

Michael sold his business for $1.2 million. At age 58, he wanted to get the best growth out of his portfolio. He foolishly decided to play the stock market by investing his money into shares of highly risky gold mines. Gold had a bad year and plummeted in value. His shares also fell massively in value. Some of his shared companies had drilled for gold and did not find any. These shares became worthless.

Over two years, Michael had lost all but $400,000. His wife decided to take control, and we met and reinvested the remaining $400,000 into blue-chip stocks in banks and conservative mutual funds. The changes have stopped the losses, and her account is starting to earn back some of the principal lost in the gold shares. Michael had incorrectly converted his money into capital.

All investment decisions come from the conversion of money to capital. To create an Endless Harvest portfolio, we must learn to convert money from solid and liquid form to gaseous capital in the safest way.

Most investment mistakes come from the incorrect conversion of money to capital. All investment decisions are solely the decisions on how to invest money into permanent wealth best. Permanent wealth occurs when we convert money into capital. We then earn investment returns in interest, dividends, or capital gains from capital. We hope never to spend any of the principal by living off the profits. We must focus on the safest and best way to convert money to capital. The basis for this book is to locate the best ways to create a permanent base of capital.

THE DIFFERENCE BETWEEN MONEY AND FINANCE

Money is the paper and coins in your wallet, purse, and pockets. (Solid Money) Money becomes finance when you invest it into income-producing assets at the bank or brokerage house. Finance becomes capital when it produces income, dividends, or capital gains while you sleep. (Gaseous Money)

Money in the paper or coin form is temporary wealth. The money in your bank account to write a check or access through an instant teller or Internet banking is also temporary wealth. Anytime you can spend money or principal is temporary money.

It is essential to realize that it will never make you rich until this temporary money is converted to permanent capital. You could have a million dollars in your checking account, and you still are not permanently rich.

The keyword is "Permanently" rich. What I am talking about is your Endless Harvest. History is ripe with examples of temporarily rich people who die broke. Tragic stories about the former actor, athlete, or business owner with dreams of making a comeback so that they can be rich again... The tale is as old as time.

The key is that they had the potential to be permanently wealthy. These tragic stories could have been avoided if they had the knowledge, discipline, and strategies to convert their temporary wealth into permanent wealth.

ENDLESS HARVEST RULE:

Permanent Wealth =
Conversion of Money to Capital

ENDLESS HARVEST RULE:

Permanent Wealth =
Conversion of Temporary Capital to Permanent Capital

To become permanently wealthy, you must convert money to permanent capital that generates some long-term income. This income can be interest, dividend, or capital gain income.

USING CAPITAL GAINS FOR BUILDING YOUR PERMANENT WEALTH

We will end this section on a high note by describing how to use capital gains to build your permanent wealth, which produces your Endless Harvest. According to Deloitte Touche Accountant Guide to Personal

Financial Management, capital gains are when the selling price of capital property is greater than the sum of its adjusted cost base plus any costs of dispositions. You have a capital loss if the selling price is lower than this sum.

That is a bit of a mouthful. But to strip it down, capital property is defined as shares, bonds, and real estate you hold as an investment. Once again, the best way to teach this is in real-life cases.

Capital Gain Case 1:

Sam, age 71, has been a client for the last ten years. Ten years ago, he invested $280,000 with me and wanted $2,100 a month in income from this money. Since $2,100 x 12 months = $25,200 a year income, he would need to have a 9% return on his investments. Since bond rates were 5% in the last seven years, he would need to earn his growth using a capital gain strategy. We invested in stocks and international mutual funds to get a higher than 9% return annually. We earned about 11.6% over the ten years, and he now has the liberty to take out more than $25,200 a few times over the last ten years.

He currently has a portfolio worth $312,000. If we relied on interest or dividend income, he would have spent much of his principal over the last ten years. We could protect his principal from being consumed using some capital gain strategies.

A point of caution when using capital gains is that there is a much greater amount and fluctuation of the value of a portfolio using a capital gain strategy. We did not have his portfolio go straight up in value over the last ten years. We saw the portfolio value drop for two years since we took out 9% when there was no growth. We did find that good years could make up for the bad ones.

Capital Gain Case 2:

Susan and her husband plan to retire in 10 years. Since they recently paid off their mortgage, they wanted me to create a low-maintenance and high-return portfolio. They also wanted a portfolio that generated low taxes. I invested their former mortgage payment of $700 a month into five mutual funds. I put $200 a month into a well-run international fund that covered the entire world's stocks, $100 a month into a European mutual fund, $100 into a Far East mutual fund, $100 a month into a U.S. mutual fund, $100 a month *into a technology fund, and $100 a month into a global health care fund. They paid almost no taxes since a fund must be sold or switched to create a taxable situation.*

Since they received no interest or dividends, they paid very little tax. They also had experienced good growth over the period. They intend to create a systematic withdrawal plan to sell a small percentage of their mutual funds when they retire. All the sales of their funds will be taxed at low capital gain rates when they retire. They pay little to no taxes while building and accumulating their funds and pay little to no taxes when they eventually cash out the growth from their funds at retirement. Since the tax department treats capital gains with a lower tax rate than regular employment income, it has tax advantages and more considerable potential gains than interest income.

Although capital gains offer greater growth potential, they are more volatile than interest or dividend income. There are tax advantages to accumulating growth without paying much taxes until you decide to cash out the investment. While earning your investment life cycle, little to no capital gain tax is necessary. The capital gain strategy is excellent for people who want higher growth and lower taxes. The downside of capital gains is that the investment's value fluctuates, and the rate of return is not set or guaranteed. It is best for people who want growth more than safety.

Now that we have spoken about ways to stay rich, we move on to managing your wealth. You need to:

- Grow your wealth
- Protect your wealth
- Manage your wealth

Just as you would:

- Grow your apple tree
- Protect your apple tree
- Manage your apple tree

Let's move on to the last part of The Endless Harvest. How to manage your millions.

MANAGING MILLIONS

The third part of The Endless Harvest is managing millions. You've gone through the hard process of growing your apple tree from a little seedling and have protected it from the elements during its growth. This is the time to reap the benefits of your hard work. But what do you do now that everything is working properly?

Do this so you can:

Get reports and measure how you are doing. By understanding what you have and how you have progressed, you can then learn how to build it further in a predictable fashion.

Let's think back again to our golden apple tree analogy. So, we've planted the seed. We've protected it. Now your apple tree is flourishing and is producing fruit. This is what we have been waiting for all along. But this is not the time to stop working and think we've arrived at the finish line.

There is no finish line in The Endless Harvest. This is a good thing. If I was writing this book to get you to a certain monetary number, and that's it, it would have been called *The Harvest*. No, this book is *The Endless Harvest*. You will continue to reap the rewards of your hard work year after year, even into the years of your children or the next following generation.

We must pick the fruit we have grown and not let it go to waste. Don't let it hit the ground and spoil or go rotten. Can you get family or friends to help you pick the fruit? What will you decide to do with it afterward? Maybe you can dry some apples for the future or eat some the very next day at a picnic.

This is kind of like picking the delicious fruit off your tree.

I've got two case studies I'd love to share with you about people I have associated with.

The first case study looks at everything we own and ensures we are organized, or rather, diversified. I call this case:

Keep Your Investment Liquid

Biff and Buffy sold their business for $10 million. (No, I'm not talking about Biff in the movie Back to The Future or Buffy The Vampire Slayer.) Initially, they decided to spread it around. After a few years of retirement, they grew restless and decided to invest all their money in a single piece of real estate.

They had plans for a vacation resort and invested all $10 million in the land and development of the property.

A decline in the town occurred as the minerals in the nearby town fell dramatically in value, and the worldwide demand fell. Technology advances made the mineral less valuable. People left the area for jobs elsewhere. The result was that no one wanted to buy the properties in the resort.

Unfortunately, the property became worthless, and Biff and Buffy are now looking at a future with minimal funds. They lowered the prices three times and still got zero offers to buy. Biff and Buffy still have to pay thousands in property taxes and maintenance of the resort year after year. Their future remains challenging as the mineral prices have remained very low ten years later, with no hope for higher prices. No money can be taken out of the project as no buyers exist, so they are stuck with the situation.

The lesson here is simple. Ask whether you can get your money out of an investment. This is called liquidity. Liquidity is how easily you can cash out of something. One solution is the concept of diversification. You've heard the saying, "Never put all your eggs in one basket." Never have an overconcentration in one or two things.

Diversification is investing in many things in case something goes badly. These things happen, so you have to manage your wealth properly. Avoid the temptation of over-concentration in a few investments just because it is easier. No matter how lucrative something may seem, things can go wrong. Expect and plan for the unexpected.

The following case study focuses on financial planning. No, it's not sexy. Yes, it is numbers, math, and things that may not seem important during the present moment. But see what happened to Fritz in the following case I call:

Will You Outlive Your Money?

Fritz, age 55, attended one of my retirement workshops. After the session, Fritz asked me to do a financial plan as he wanted to retire. The plan results were not what Fritz wanted. The plan showed that Fritz would run out of money if he retired at age 55 at the income level he wanted. The income level Fritz wanted was $5,000 per month after-tax income. This was the amount necessary for him to maintain his current standard of living.

Taking his current investment value and pension income at that income level, he would run out of his investment funds in only seven years. I suggested working for another seven years, saving 15% of his after-tax income. He refused and did not want to follow any of the plan's suggestions.

Circumstantially, I ran into Fritz ten years later, and he was working for minimum wage at a local hotel. He mentioned that he ran out of money seven years into his retirement and had to sell all his possessions to keep his home from creditors.

It was a harsh lesson for Fritz, and here is the takeaway. Always do a regular financial plan and use conservative projections to see if your goals are realistic. With current lifespans growing longer, the danger of outliving your money is more real than ever.

One of the most significant risks rarely discussed is the danger of outliving your money. This is also called longevity risk. Market crashes get the news headlines, but outliving your money may be the bigger threat. Do a Financial Plan.

During my first meetings with clients, I suggest a financial plan to look for any danger of outliving their money. Longevity risk is caused by taking out more money than the portfolio earns. Over time every portfolio falls and falls, eventually turning to zero if you spend more than you make. Try to avoid running out of money in your 60's, 70's, 80's, or even 90's.

In these two cases, we see precisely how important it is to properly manage the money we make from our investments, just like growing our apple or money tree. Once the growth is complete, we are not done yet. You have to take care and harvest your hard-earned money or delicious fruit.

This is the final step, step three, of The Endless Harvest. (But I have a secret step four to share with you after. This step will teach you how to speed up your successful process.) When you finish this section, you will know how to properly manage the millions you labored so hard for.

In this section, we'll talk about a few things, from how to read and manage your financial report cards to continue to build your wealth. There are many options like creating your financial network, organizing your finances, and even knowing how to change your portfolio.

When harvesting an apple tree, you will need to know how to do it best and what you can do with your harvest. Taking this step ensures you properly use your money to the best of its ability.

Here is the truth of this section. There are infinite ways to manage your millions, but there are only a finite number of things you can manage. I will give you the roadmap or blueprint of what to do. You don't have to make it up yourself. Follow this section and if need be, just ask for help.

READING AND GETTING FINANCIAL REPORT CARDS

Questions:

How am I doing now?
How have I done in the past?
How much income am I receiving?
What money did I put in, and what did I earn?

L et's start this section by discussing reading and getting financial report cards. Here is an interesting fact. Many of my new clients have never read or even received a financial report card from their financial advisors. This is entirely unacceptable, as this is how you measure your progress.

Financial progress can only be measured in dollars and cents. Do not settle for these kinds of statements from your advisor or even from your analysis:

- *You're doing good...*
- *Your financial future is healthy...*
- *We'll discuss the report later, but let's grab a drink...*
- *Meet me out on the golf course to review how you are doing...*
- *You are way up from where you started...*

These statements are positive, yes, but what does it mean? There is no validity, and your financial report card needs to be reviewed seriously and in detail.

Reading and getting financial report cards is kind of like analyzing your new apple harvest. Until you examine the apples you have grown, you will have no idea how you are doing. Here are some questions you may want to ask yourself:

- *How many apples did my tree produce?*
- *How crisp and fresh are my apples?*
- *Do they have the best sugar content?*
- *Are my apples free from mold and insects?*

By analyzing your harvest, you can tell how your newly grown apple tree is producing. This is just like analyzing your financial report card to understand how you are doing financially. Even though money is one of the essential aspects of life, clients often settle for just understanding if they are doing "good" or "bad." This is unacceptable, and you need to get out the paper, grab your calculator, and do that math.

Reading and getting financial report cards is kind of like measuring your new apple harvest for quantity and quality.

An excellent time frame to analyze your finances is tracking how you have done in the past ten years, five years, and the last year. Ask yourself:

- *What is your yield or income stream from it?*
- *What does the diversity of your investment portfolio look like? (On a pie chart)*

This report is not figurative. This is actual data. In finance, figurative counts for precisely nothing. Actual data is what matters. Why do you think we have weight scales at home? It's not good enough to just say, *I think I'm losing weight,* or *I think I'm gaining more muscle mass.* You need to prove it on the weight scale.

So let's jump into the different sections of a financial report card. I want to tell you what they mean and why they are important. I'm going to list out some key indicators you need to know to understand your past and your present results accurately:

1. Portfolio Composition – What do you own?
    How much are Foreign stocks, US stocks, Canadian Stocks, Real Estate, Bonds, etc.?

2. Time-Weighted Returns – What are your total returns in % return and dollars?
    How much have you made in your time investing? (in the last year and the previous five years)

3. Monthly and Yearly Income Generated by your portfolio – How much is your annual cash flow from your investment portfolio in dollars by the month?

4. Market Value History – What has been your annual return in dollars for each year you have invested?

5. Net Contributions and Return History – What is the total amount of money you have invested, and what is the total amount of money made by the portfolio?

6. Portfolio Performance – Gives you the return by % for each invested year.

7. Summary of Terms gives you definitions to understand key investment terminology.

These are the identifiers I give my clients on their financial report cards. If you are doing one yourself, please look at this list. If you have a current financial advisor, ask them for these metrics.

Financial report cards are usually reviewed one to four times per year. This frequency depends on how aggressive your goals are and how volatile the market is. When reviewing the report card, the key metrics are important to note. An example would be time-weighted returns on how much you have made in dollars and by percent returns. Typically it's best to check no more than quarterly. Doing so will get you too focused on the short term when you want to be thinking long term.

When checking your time-weighted return page, keep an eye out for sudden drops in your portfolio value. A view of the portfolio composition may cause some adjustments to be made. A sudden drop in the value of your portfolio may provide opportunities for you to change your financial plan for the better.

Your Financial Report Card is just part of a bigger picture of your finances. Because they should be consistently updated, there is no need to hold on to old report cards. Also, as a Financial Report Card is for viewing past and present results, it should have a regularly updated Financial Plan which looks at your future financial picture. (We'll go into more detail about this in the next chapter, but I want to give you the big picture list related to your report card.)

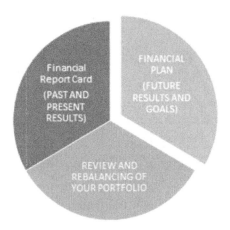

Parts of a future financial plan are:

1.   Projected Future Net Worth of the value of your investments in the future and how long your money will last in retirement.
     (It answers the big question, *Will you outlive your money?*)

2.   A Cash Flow Report provides a future net income or cash flow expected from your investments during retirement.

3. A Savings Rate Report provides different outcomes based on your savings rate.
    (How much do you have to save each year to achieve your retirement income and goal of not outliving your money?)

4. An Expenses and Outcome Report provides you with a ceiling of maximum withdrawals before you deplete your capital.

5. An Assumptions Report provides you with rates of return, inflation rates, and retirement dates.
    (Different rates of return can be used. Suggestions are to keep it very conservative between 4-7% as rates of return should not be set unrealistically high. Incorrect assumptions can make a financial plan less accurate.)

6. Total Income is your entire cash flow to be received at retirement, including government pension plans, private pension plans, retirement savings, corporate income, tax-free savings, and any other sources of income such as rental properties.

7. Plans should be made every time a major event happens, such as retirement, inheritances, job loss, and divorces, or I suggest doing it at least once every one to five years.

We'll come back to the future plan in the next chapter. For now, a financial report card is a tool you need to get a crystal clear picture of your situation. This goal is to find out if you have a bigger or smaller future than you think.

One thing to consider is the time frame of reading your report card. For example, we just had the Covid pandemic, so this is only short-term data if it went up or down. Make sure to look at the whole picture depending on how much data you have and over what length of time.

This report card will allow you to assess your current situation accurately and make intelligent decisions about what to do about the future. I can't tell you how much data you have, whether fifty years or one year. But ideally, it is best to have report cards with data from the past ten years. This will give you the most accurate assessment of your current situation.

I know I've given you a lot of technical data in this chapter, so I'll try to end this as easy as possible. When reading your financial report card, ask yourself two simple questions:

1. What are your goals?

Be aware of your goals and the risk you are willing to achieve them. Don't compare yourself to your friend's or family's goals. Everyone is different, and you must understand the risks for different goals. These are your goals and what you want to achieve.

2. Are you confident with your current plan or advisor to reach your current goals?

Only ask this question if you have a current advisor or are considering working with a new one. These financial report cards are critical for advisors to give to you. That is unacceptable if your advisor shies away from giving it to you or even hands it to you without explaining. They are your financial advisor, and finances are measured by reports in dollars and cents.

Next, we'll move on to your financial future. Let's take some time to discuss how effective planning can mold a better tomorrow.

POWERFUL FINANCIAL PLANS FOR YOUR FUTURE

What is the big value of a financial plan? Michael J. Fox in the movie *Back to the Future* is a great metaphor or example of the power of a financial plan. Like a time machine, a financial plan allows us to see into the future years ahead of where we are. We can see "gaps "or shortfalls in our financial plans. The gap is the difference between what we want to happen and what will happen to us financially.

Even with these problems, a financial plan is invaluable in detecting problems in our finances years in advance. No plan is perfect, and plans should be super conservative in the growth rate, say 4-5%. They should also be updated every two years in case the world changes dramatically. This allows us to alter our financial actions and prevent or reduce financial gaps.

Let's take Frank for example:

Frank, age 45, made a financial plan to retire at age 55. He planned to spend $50,000 a year in retirement. He saved $300,000 and put another $2,400 or $200 per month into his retirement plan. But, assuming a conservative growth rate of 5% a year, Frank could not retire at his planned age of 55.

Frank would run out of money in the first eight years of retirement. We found this out early, so Frank had time to alter his plans to reduce or mitigate this from happening. Without a financial plan, it would have come as a surprise to Frank when he ran out of money. This could be a common event if people retire without having the benefits of a retirement plan. Don't let this be you!

To have a highly successful financial plan and avoid gaps, I've created:

8 Steps To Building an Effective Financial Plan

1. Physical organization of statements into a financial planning binder
2. Consolidation of current investments into self-directed income-generating portfolios

3. Reorganization into well-diversified financial plans
4. Future-based investment plan to locate gaps
5. Gap analysis to see if you are on track to achieve your financial goals
6. Re-balancing and course corrections
7. New updated plan
8. Repeat the previous 7 steps as needed

WHY SOME FINANCIAL PLANS FAIL

You might be saying to yourself, *John, I have a plan. I'm ready to rock and roll.* Not all financial plans are created equal. Let me talk a bit about why some financial plans fail. In my 30+ years of experience, I see that procrastination is the number one reason financial plans fail. People put off saving enough and do not take the time to seriously examine their retirement until it is almost too late. Why does this happen? The number one reason is that they have no savings plan in place.

The book, *The Richest Man in Babylon*, talks about this. It says to save 10–20% of your after-tax income in a long-term permanent savings plan. People usually know they should be doing this, but the reality is that a lot of them simply don't. I think it's because they feel like they have more urgent needs that take precedence. Saving for their future is very important.

The second recommendation is to take another 10% of after-tax income, pay down debts, and then live off 80%. This includes both long-term and short-term debts.

The other reason financial plans fail is that they have no debt plan. In other words, people have debts that accumulate, and instead of going down over time as they should, they are rising over time and are compounding debt. One of the main reasons behind this is buying too large a house. They cannot afford the house, and all of their money goes to service the debt on the house. This then feeds into the first problem: they do not have any money to save for the future.

Another reason financial plans are not successful is disorganization. I often see clients who have money in five or even ten places. Therefore, they do not know how they are actually doing. They are not actively managing those investments, which means they don't have a plan for how much they are worth. Organization is one of the areas in which financial planning helps by putting all of your statements into a binder and having tabs within the binder. The tabs include wills, estate plans, debt, mortgages, credit card bills, retirement plans, and pension plans. All of this is organized in a physical binder. Physical organization comes first, then financial organization. This is how you build your portfolio the proper way.

For example, typical tabs in your binder should hold:

1. Retirement Statements
2. Government Pension Statements
3. Your Will, Enduring Power of Attorney, and Personal Directives
4. Your Investment Statements (nonretirement plans)
5. Tax-Free Savings Plans (TFSA)
6. Auto, House, and Fire insurance
7. Life Insurance
8. Your key contacts (lawyer, accountant, etc.)
9. Location of your safety deposit box, if any
10. Others such as Employee Stock Plans, Timeshare information, deeds on rental properties or vacation properties

THE DREAM PLANNER
SETTING YOUR LIFETIME FINANCIAL DREAMS

The exciting part of money management is that we can design our future since the future has not happened yet. If we do not design our future, then the future will just happen. It may occur in a way we did not want. We might be living in poverty because we did not save enough money. We must put our goals and dreams on paper to design our financial future. We also need to prioritize and date our dreams and goals.

When setting your dreams on paper, it is helpful to think about them this way. If you were to die tomorrow, what things would you have regretted not doing? Most of us often would not answer, "My biggest regret was not spending more time at my job." It would be things such as: *I always wanted to go to Rome, walk the Great Pyramids, play golf at Pebble Beach, or see a baseball game at my favorite stadium.*

The reason for setting clear financial goals is that having money is useless if we do not get to enjoy having it. We need to use the returns from our money to have fun and have the freedom to accomplish our goals and desires.

The key to successful financial planning is to balance the need to enjoy life today without worrying about running out of money when we retire.

One of the biggest mistakes people make is not understanding the true nature of retirement. Retirement is not about killing time. Retirement is when you get up in the morning and are free to do what you want with your day. It will be a time of great enjoyment and personal accomplishment when your day is spent doing what you enjoy most. Much information supports that people die prematurely when they retire without planning or objectives. Part of a successful retirement process is having sufficient money to achieve your goals.

Setting your financial goals on paper will help to motivate you to work towards these goals. If you won $100,000 could you spend it in a year; could you spend it in 3, 4, 5, or 10 years? How much money could you spend in twenty years? To provide for your financial dreams, you need to plan how much money you will need to save ahead of time.

Going through life without financial goals is like paddling down a river without a map—you might be heading for a waterfall. It is vital to plan where you want to go with your finances.

Setting goals and financial planning can ensure you have enough money for a comfortable retirement. You must determine when to retire, pay off your house, and how much you want to save each year. With a financial road map, you can develop a systematic plan for saving and investing and not drift around aimlessly. Take this worksheet on goals, for example:

Importance Level Goal	Low	Medium	High		
	1	2	3	4	5
Have life insurance	__	__	__	__	__
Take regular vacations	__	__	__	__	__
Pay off mortgage	__	__	__	__	__
Build trust account for kids	__	__	__	__	__
Buy investments outside retirement plan	__	__	__	__	__
Retire early (before 60)	__	__	__	__	__

Invest globally   ___ ___ ___ ___ ___

Have an emergency fund   ___ ___ ___ ___ ___

Have U.S. dollar investments   ___ ___ ___ ___ ___

Have an investment system   ___ ___ ___ ___ ___

Have clearly written investment goals   ___ ___ ___ ___ ___

Do not wait until retirement to assess your financial goals. That is way too late. If your goals are realistic and achievable, it is best to find out as soon as possible. The more time you have to achieve your goals, the closer you are to achieving those goals at retirement.

Now, let's relate this to investing. The clearer you are about your investment goals, the faster you can build wealth. You must decide how much money you will need to live the retirement you desire.

There is the famous Harvard Study that portrayed the power of goals.

The researchers took 100 students in the study and followed these students for twenty years. The students were divided into several groups. 3% of students stated they had written financial goals, such as having $20,000 worth of investments in five years. Another 8% of the students had financial goals set in their minds, and the remaining 89% had no financial goals. At the end of twenty years, the results were shocking. Although the individuals earned similar incomes in the twenty years since graduation, the 3% with written financial goals had a net worth larger than the other 89% combined. This shows the power of goals.

Take some time to complete the following goal-setting exercise. I'd do this now or at least mark this page and set a reminder to do it soon.

DREAM PLANNER GOAL SETTING WORKSHEET

I wish to retire in _____ years or the year _____ or I am retired _____

I wish to have income of $_____ (in current $) a year while retired.

I wish to travel for _____ days outside Canada when I retire.

I wish to pay off my house in _____ years.

My net worth that I need to accumulate by retirement will be $ _____

I wish to buy a larger house in the future _____ yes _____ no

I have to pay for my children's education _____ yes _____ no
If I answered yes, I will need approximately:
Children _____ X $40,000 per child = _____ Total

THE ENDLESS HARVEST RULE:

Be realistic about the amount of money you will need at retirement.
It is typically much larger than people expect.

If you want a point of reference, take this, for example. Assume you are 40 years old and want to retire at age 60. You want $40,000 a year at retirement, and assuming a 3% inflation rate, you wish to take out 6% of your money each year. You will need to have $XX,XXX in investments at age 60. (This number will fluctuate with inflation depending on the year you read this.)

Using a computer program, I can get some excellent estimates on how much money people will have and how much they need to achieve their goals. Do not just throw money into your retirement savings plans and hope it will be enough. You need to set some precise and solid financial goals.

I have two real cases for you to view:

Case 1:

Herb, age 42, provides an example of setting precise financial goals. His goals are to pay off all debts by age 50. Have $800,000 in retirement savings plans by age 60. Have a retirement income of $40,000. Travel one month a year to Hawaii. Have $100,000 of money set aside in U.S. dollars to help finance the travel plans.

Case 2:

Darryl and Pat, age 50, want to retire at age 55. They have saved a total of $200,000. They plan to save $7,500 a year for the next five years. Their goals are unrealistic after performing a financial assessment, given their lifestyle. They wish to travel and live with an income of $60,000 annually. Given *these variables, they will run out of money very quickly. Darryl and Pat could work longer, save more money, invest in more aggressive investments to get a higher rate of return from their investments, or plan to take out a lower income at retirement.*

There are several reasons you want to save money. One is simply to feed, clothe, and house you at retirement. Another might be to help out other people, such as your children or charities.

In my view, after necessities are met, the main reason you want money is to fulfill your dreams. If your dream is to bicycle across France, money will help you pay for the trip. If you want to hike the Great Wall in China or ride an elephant in Thailand, money can help pay for these trips.

Money is only useful because it allows you the freedom to do the things you desire. Money itself is useless. If you do not spend the money fulfilling your dreams, it is only a number on a statement. The starting point is to put down your dreams and goals on paper. This may seem like a life lesson, but it also applies to finance. Only you can decide your future lifestyle. By putting your dreams on paper, you can prioritize, price out, and fulfill each dream with a realistic budget.

Also, do not wait until retirement to start to fulfill some of your dreams. Use the big purchase account to save the money you need to fulfill your dreams. Your savings system allows you to achieve your dreams without sacrificing your long-term retirement accounts.

One more thing. Don't count on government help, or you will probably live at or below the poverty level. If the government kicks in and helps, consider that icing on the cake. Start setting goals and mapping out your financial future today.

MAKING CHANGES TO YOUR PORTFOLIO

FORGET BUY AND HOLD AND CONSIDER MAKING CHANGES WHEN NECESSARY

We just spoke about some powerful financial plans for your future. But what if you need to make changes to your portfolio to fit those plans and eliminate some risks you may have? This chapter will discuss some of the top strategies you need to consider to "course correct" or "get back on track."

When growing an apple tree, it's kind of like trimming dead and unnecessary branches. You have to maintain that nice productive tree you have grown. Unfortunately, your apple tree will not take care of itself and sometimes can grow out a little too wild.

When it does this, it may hurt the overall health of your apple tree. Growing too much to one side or another will unbalance your tree and force it to become unstable. Sometimes this can even damage the roots and the tree trunk. Although it can seem counterintuitive, trimming unnecessary tree branches is critical for the long-term survival of your healthy apple tree.

Suppose your tree is uneven, if the branches are dying, or if a specific section of your tree has a disease, you need to trim it away. This can also be an issue if you have multiple trees in your orchard growing on top of one another. Trim the weeds and harvest when necessary.

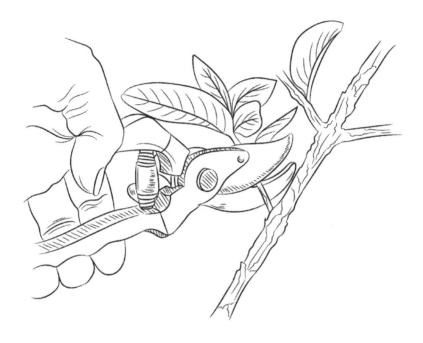

Making changes to your portfolio is kind of like trimming unnecessary branches off your apple tree to keep it healthy.

I follow four hard rules when making changes to a portfolio.

1. **The first thing you will want to learn is that the past is dead. Learn from your mistakes.**

Don't dwell on what has happened because you should focus on what is happening now and what will happen in the future.

Let me give you a case study about Chris:

Chris, age 30, came to see me. He was a professional hockey player who had not saved anything long-term. He had speculated into some businesses with family members, which had gone bad. He also played the stock markets, chose highly speculative penny stocks, and lost most of the trades. When we met, he had started to get arthritic joints in his knees and knew he had only a few more years of playing hockey. The clock was ticking for his professional career.

In my opinion, the biggest flaws in his investment approach were impatience and poor choice in evaluating investment risks. We eventually redesigned a long-term portfolio of government strip bonds, dividend stocks, and international mutual funds. I also projected how much money he needed to save to achieve his retirement goals at age 50. He is now building a long-term portfolio and will be comfortable by age 50.

The most important lesson to learn is that your investment past is over. You cannot change or reverse past investment mistakes. A more positive approach is learning from your mistakes and setting up detailed investment plans and portfolio designs to reduce your investment risk while achieving reasonable return targets set by yourself. The past is dead. Learn from your mistakes, and avoid being trapped there.

2. Plan for some problems with any investment.

The future is not set, or we can't predict the future—plan for some problems to occur because investing is partially out of your control. If you remember the chapter on mutual funds and diversification, this is precisely why these strategies are used.

For example, two of my clients, Robert and Michelle, experienced this firsthand:

Robert, age 48, was an employee of Enron. He had some of his money in the shares of the company. When an accounting fraud was found in his company, Robert lost the value of his shares. Circumstances outside his control meant these shares became worthless.

Michelle, age 32, was a flight attendant on a small regional airline. On September 10, 2001, her company was a solid investment. After the terrorist attack on the World Trade Center, the next day, on September 11, 2001, her company started having major problems as many clients canceled their travel plans. By Christmas 2001, the small regional airline went into receivership, and Michelle had to find another job. Her shares in the company were also worthless.

All investments have risks. Don't put all your eggs in one basket because it is easy. Or don't do it just because you think a single investment is safe. Even the job you may have with the government is susceptible to risk. The risk or potential for loss occurs for all investments.

3. Take a holistic view of risk and plan for many different types of risks.

It can be easy to think of just one reason to change your portfolio, but make sure you consider all aspects. We have discussed many different elements in this book, and each person's goals will be unique.

For reference, you would want to take into consideration:

- The risk of a Black Swan event.
- The possibility of a long ten-year trend.
- The volatility of the economy at the time.
- Your current health and expected life.
- The goals you have and how quickly you want to achieve them.
- Your family and their current situation.
- Your spouse and what they want and need.
- Etc.

As you can see, there is a list of aspects you need to consider before making changes to your portfolio. Make sure and have a holistic view, leading you to make the best overall decision.

4. Seek real returns, not nominal ones.

It is only money in your wallet that matters. You should always take off the cost of taxes and inflation when evaluating your investment decisions.

Don't convince yourself you are doing better than you are just to feel good. In the long run, this will increase your self-esteem but hurt your bottom line finances. In the end, you will damage your self-esteem.

A simple example of this is something I often see in news reports or on television. A news reporter will say, "Stock XYZ has made a 47% increase in value over the past four days. We could see the quickest forward trending stock of the year at this rate. Now is the time to buy; you won't want to let this opportunity slip away." What I do in this situation is stop and wait to let reality set in.

If this were a stock like Google, Amazon, Exxon Mobil, etc., it would be fantastic news and noteworthy to pay attention to. But if this is some penny stock no one has heard of, has no track record, and is selling for pennies per share, a 47% increase doesn't mean anything.

Just because something sounds good doesn't mean it is good. Always seek the real return and find your real dollar.

To end this chapter, I want to give you some sample long-term wealth portfolios and what they may look like:

Portfolio 1: The Income Portfolio
Purpose: Pay Income
25%   Dividend-paying stocks
50%   Dividend mutual funds
25%   Bond or income mutual funds

Portfolio 2: The Balanced Portfolio
Purpose: Some Income and Growth
25%   Global mutual funds
50%   Dividend mutual funds
25%   Growth stocks

Portfolio 3: The Growth Portfolio
Purpose: Growth of Principal
50%   Global mutual funds
25%   Dividend mutual funds
25%   Sector mutual funds and growth stocks

We've spoken a lot about risk, your portfolio, current report cards, and future plans. Let's change gears here and discuss other important aspects of managing your millions. Next, we'll talk about building a financial network.

You don't have to do this all on your own. I'm a financial advisor, and I even have a team that helps me with different aspects of finance. In the next section, we'll look into it, and I'll show you the types of personnel to use and why.

CHOOSING AND BUILDING A
FINANCIAL NETWORK

U sing finance professionals is not only wise, but it saves a ton of time and headache. Even as a financial advisor, I have a professional network that helps me with finances. Later in this chapter, I'll tell you exactly what types of professionals to use and why.

I learned a vital lesson through many networking groups I belong to. The lesson is this:

You can't be a professional at everything. A true master is skilled at one specific aspect and knows how to hire other masters to complete the job correctly.

Building a financial network is kind of like getting family and friends together to help pick your fruit. Yes, you could do it all yourself, but how long would that take? Would you get tired? Would you enjoy the experience as much? I think we can all agree that picking apples with your spouse and children would even make a fun day outside. Use the help of others, and you will make the experience ten times better.

Building a financial network is kind of like planting different types of trees.

I know what you might be thinking of these networking groups. There are so many out there. There are groups on Facebook, free meet-ups, and even some are just friends who get together and eat pizza. The networking groups I belong to have an annual fee of 5 to 6 figures for membership. These people are the real deal and know the importance of building a successful network. So let's dive into why it is so important.

Today's financial world is getting more and more complex. We need to work with financial specialists to keep control of our investments. One of the big keys of financial organization is to build a network of financial professionals.

210

For example, it is important to work with an accountant. The accountant files your taxes and makes sure everything is on track. A qualified accountant is valuable. In your plan, you should have a network of planners as well. You have an accountant and a lawyer who makes sure your will is set up correctly. You may have a banking relationship where you get loans and credit cards.

I am the investment planner and advisor for clients, what investments to buy, and so on. Then I have an agent specializing in fire, auto, and theft insurance. I have a network of financial professionals to tap into. I am just one of five or six key people I think all clients should have access to.

Some key financial specialists are:
(Definitions taken from Investopedia.com)

Financial Planner:
Financial planning includes help with budgeting, investing, saving for retirement, tax planning, insurance coverage, and more.

Financial Advisor:
Advisors use their knowledge and expertise to construct personalized financial plans to achieve clients' financial goals.

Accountant for Tax Filing:
Two important types of accounting for businesses are managerial accounting and cost accounting. Managerial accounting helps management teams make business decisions, while cost accounting helps business owners decide how much a product should cost.

Lawyer (who does wills and estate work):
Becoming a lawyer requires you to pass a state-sanctioned bar exam, which gives you the license to practice legally

Banker:
An investment banker works for a financial institution and is primarily concerned with raising capital for corporations, governments, or other entities.

Life Insurance Specialist

Fire, Auto, and House Insurance Specialists

You want to run your money with the least amount of work possible. Do things that you are competent in. Do not do something you are incompetent in. Although we want to, you can't be good at everything. Is Exxon Mobil, Apple, Google, Amazon, or NASA run by a single person? No. Behind every successful company is a team of specialists who produce a successful product or running service.

Do the same thing, just like these Fortune 100 companies. You are the head or leader of your finances, but you do not have to be the "one-stop-shop."

Next, we'll briefly discuss wills and estates for your loved ones. We don't always like to think about it, but it is vital for our family as we get closer and closer to retirement.

PRESERVING WEALTH FOR YOUR FAMILY

INTER-GENERATIONAL WEALTH TRANSFER

A t this point, I know you will have successfully grown and maintained your wealth. But enough about ourselves. What about your loved ones and the future generation? We want to ensure our family members, like children, have the financial stability they need. This is when you start to move assets to your children and grandchildren. The use of a will and trusts can be beneficial in reducing estate fees.

A tip is to use these experts:

- Tax
- Investment
- Legal advice

Life is fragile, but we can make sure our success passes along to our family in today's age. They may not have the same financial education as you; unless they are also reading this book.

In our apple harvest analogy, this would be kind of like preserving your apple harvest. There are multiple ways of doing this; two of the most popular methods are canning and drying the fruit. Canned apples can be easily made into a great apple pie filling, and dried apples are a tasty snack everyone in the family can enjoy for weeks on end. Your apple harvest is plentiful, and you now have many more apples than you can eat. Preserve them so that you can consume them at a later time.

Regardless of how you decide to preserve your apples, they will be safer and healthier to consume longer than if you simply leave them on the table or inside the refrigerator. Like the preserved apples, wealth can be preserved for your loved ones even if you are not around to assist.

Preserving wealth for your family is kind of like canning or drying your apple harvest to consume at a later date.

PRESERVING YOUR WEALTH THROUGH ESTATE PLANNING

Estate planning is defined as "arranging one's financial resources to provide the maximum overall benefit for oneself and one's heirs." It ensures your wishes are followed after you pass away and helps provide guardianship of children and smooth transfer and distribution of your assets.

Estate planning will help ensure you provide for the financial well-being of your loved ones should you pass away. Generally, an accountant, lawyer, banker, life insurance agent, and investment advisor are involved in the estate planning. By developing a sound financial plan, you can help reduce the cost and time needed to distribute your assets.

THE ENDLESS HARVEST RULE:

You don't have to be old and rich to do estate planning. Everyone needs
an estate plan to benefit their loved ones, not just themselves.
Wills, enduring powers of attorney, and personal directives
are vital for everyone 18 and over.

Write a will and always keep it up-to-date. You should update your will
when you have major changes in your life, such as a divorce, death in the
family, or when your children reach the age of maturity.

Many people falsely believe that if someone dies without a will, their
assets will simply pass on to the surviving spouse. This varies with the
province. A person who dies without a will is considered to die intestate.
It is difficult to have all of your wishes followed without a will since the
government has its own set of rules. These inflexible rules do not adapt to
your personal needs or goals.

What would happen is that the province will appoint an administrator to
manage and distribute the estate. This person might not distribute assets
according to the wishes of the deceased. The entire estate will be subject
to probate fees, which can be significantly high depending on the size and
complexity of the estate. There may be higher than average taxes payable
because there has not been any tax planning. When a person dies without
a will, a common-law spouse may have difficulty being recognized. If you
don't specify guardianship of children, they could end up with incompatible or undesirable relatives.

Thorough estate planning will reduce the amount of:

- Taxes the estate has to pay.
- Legal and accounting costs relating to the estate.
- Time spent managing and completing the estate because of good
  records of assets.
- Confusion required organizing and distributing the assets accord-
  ing to the owner's wishes of the estate.

Next, I want to write out some estate tips. A will is vital to ensure your
assets are distributed according to your wishes. While you can write your
own will, you should hire a lawyer experienced in estate planning and
preparing wills. An experienced professional will know many aspects of

estate planning you would never have considered, such as income tax and family law.

Make sure to take these three steps:

1. Maintain an update-to-date list of the location of all-financial assets, mortgages, liabilities, bank accounts, and important papers.
2. Ensure your family knows where your will and asset list are stored for safekeeping.
3. Plan to provide adequately for your family in the event of your untimely death or if you are disabled.

The main aspects of estate planning are to organize your assets, covering the below topics:

- Your will
- Guardianship of children
- Executor
- Marriage contracts
- Charity gifts
- Taxes and probate fees
- Life insurance
- Pension plans
- Business transfers

A will is a written document that provides instructions for the disposition of your assets in the event of your death. Your will is essentially a written record that:

I. States who will be the executor in charge of following your wishes as described in your will.
II. States who will take care of your children.
III. Ensure your wishes will be followed, and the government or a third party will not take control of your assets.
IV. Reduces conflict and confusion over the distribution of your children and assets.

THE ENDLESS HARVEST RULE:

Have a lawyer write up your will.

Most wills only cost a few hundred dollars. It is worth paying the money to ensure your will is thorough and valid if ever contested.

The main points of a will are:

- Distribution of cash.
- Distribution of proceeds from the sale of assets.
- Division of family heirlooms and other assets not for sale.
- Guardianship of children under the legal age, usually age 18.
- You choose a guardian to care for your children if you and your spouse die simultaneously.
- (Be sure to ask the people if they are willing to accept guardianship of your children.)
- When you specify guardianship for your children, make a first, second, and third choice.

You will also need to choose an executor. An executor is someone you trust and designate in your will to fulfill your wishes. The executor can be one or more people or a trust company. This person administers your estate according to your wishes, the law, and your beneficiaries best interests. An executor should also be competent and reliable to follow the will correctly.

When choosing an executor, do not automatically name your spouse, as you and your spouse could die in the same automobile accident. Make sure your choice is someone who has an excellent financial mind. You should choose an executor and a co-executor if your first choice cannot fulfill your wishes. Always ask the people you choose if they are willing to accept the responsibility.

The main duties of an executor are:

- Distribution of insurance proceeds.
- Probate your will.
- Sell off and distribute your cash and assets.
- Sell any real estate.
- Payoff creditors.
- Arrange guardianship for children.
- Close off bank accounts.
- Inform the government.
- Rearrange pension changes.
- Pay taxes.
- Make funeral arrangements.

If your children or grandchildren are to share in your estate, your executor may have to hold their share in a trust until they reach the age specified in your will or the age of maturity.

Most wills go through probate, a process of checking to ensure their validity and transferring assets to the estate. It is a common requirement for financial institutions such as banks, brokerage firms, and life insurance companies.

This briefly covers the topic of estate planning. Make sure to do some estate planning with a professional team. Use a lawyer to do your will, an accountant to help do the best tax planning, and a knowledgeable investment advisor and insurance specialist to do a thorough job of your estate.

There are ways and methods to save taxes, and a good investment advisor should act as a middleman or bridge to the other professionals. Since the estate planning area is so vast, no one professional can do the entire estate plan themselves. This is a wise area to spend some money or fees to be done correctly. Do not skimp on the estate planning area.

PRESERVING YOUR WEALTH THROUGH LIFE INSURANCE

The whole purpose of life insurance is to ensure that your dependents have something to compensate for the loss in income from the deceased person. A risk to many families is poor life insurance coverage.

Life insurance is very misunderstood. The whole purpose of life insurance is to act as a substitute for lost wages due to the early death of the wage earner. Would you drive your car without insurance? Not likely! Nor should you go through life without life insurance.

Typical life insurance mistakes are having no life insurance, being inadequately insured, and not understanding the details of a life insurance policy. Imagine a family with three young children. They rely on a principal wage earner that makes $50,000 a year while the other parent is a full-time caregiver. If the primary wage earner died, a $500,000 life insurance policy would allow the remaining parent to continue as a full-time caregiver to the children for at least ten years. Now that is peace of mind.

A case I encountered was James and Heather:

They owned a farm worth $1 million. They had two children. The son wanted the farm when they passed, while the daughter did not. The conflict was about what to do with the farm when the children disagreed.

James and Heather bought a $1 million life insurance policy payable to both their son and daughter in their will. The will included a clause for inflation in case the value of the farm grew above the $1 million policy. This way, the son can keep the farm, while the daughter will get a cash payment from the life insurance policy.

Remember to follow the K.I.S.S. principle when buying life insurance (keep it super simple) and avoid complex options and confusing contracts. It is important to buy a simple term policy and control the amount of insurance you receive. A disaster, like accidental death, is the wrong time to find out the clauses and small print in your policy.

Life insurance coverage should be like a bell curve and reflect the theory of decreasing responsibility. Purchase less coverage in the early years when you are just married, then more coverage during the middle years when the kids are young and the mortgage is high. Finally, lower your coverage again in the senior years when the kids are grown up and the mortgage is low or paid off.

It is important to shop around and look at reputable companies established for several years and will be around years later. Term life is the recommended choice due to its simplicity and lower costs. Term life insurance is for a specified period. The insurance cost varies by factors such as age, whether you smoke, or have any pre-existing conditions.

Universal Life is an insurance policy that is usually fairly complex, and its contracts tend to be long and wordy. It promises to pay a fixed amount or face value on death and combines a cash value that often only pays 3-5%.

An excellent strategy is buying term life insurance and investing the difference into a mutual retirement savings plan fund. In this way, you build up your net worth over time. This helps compensate for the higher life insurance levels you pay as you age. In other words, you drop your level of life insurance coverage as you get older because the retirement savings plans and other investments grow over time to balance out the difference. The growth of other assets and the net reduction in your mortgage and parental expenses will mean you can drop the term level quite significantly later in life when the term premiums start to get high in price.

I know some people with $1,000,000 in term insurance due to their high mortgage and dependents. Remember, you wouldn't drive without car insurance. Yet many people with small children and large debts walk around without life insurance protection. Term insurance provides you with some protection.

Look at insurance plans through your employer and any associations you belong to. These can be lower-cost alternatives to private plans.

Disability Insurance is often not considered by many life insurance customers. People working in professions where an accident can devastate a family's income should also consider disability insurance.

An example would be a dentist who has a hand damaged in a car accident. It is vital to consider some disability insurance if this is a concern. Check the small print and details of a disability policy. What does the insurance company define as disabled? Also, check what lengths of time the insurance will pay disability benefits.

Use life insurance to protect your loved ones in the case of an untimely death. The purpose of life insurance is to replace the income that the person would have earned over their lifetime. Life insurance can also protect your estate from capital gain and other taxes that would otherwise cause your beneficiaries to liquidate part of the estate.

Next, we are going to talk about organizing your finances. We've spoken a lot about the different investments you can make, risks you should avoid, and just recently, protecting your future. Let's look at organizing your finances into a simple savings system.

ORGANIZING YOUR FINANCES

I t is crucial that you set up a system for saving your money. We've made it and prevented it from disappearing, but let's discuss how to save it effectively. Most people fail in their investment program because they save without a system. A system is designed to work with little time and effort for the participant. You will continue to do the program almost on autopilot by making the system easy to use. That's even if you have a busy or complex lifestyle.

In general, here is what I suggest. Consider saving 10-20% in after-tax income yearly. For example, if Brad takes home $5,000 a month, he saves $500 a month for his investments.

With my saving system, you have five or six funds or accounts. These accounts are:

- **Account 1: Early Retirement Account**
  Purpose: Permanent Savings

  This account is your government-approved retirement account, where you get a tax deduction for investing. This may also include your private or company pension plan. This account aims to pay for living expenses such as food and shelter at retirement.

- **Account 2: Luxury Account**
  Purpose: Permanent Savings

  This is a non-registered account, which is subject to income tax on its gains. Be careful to keep the investments in this account in lower tax dividend and capital gain investments of stocks and mutual funds. The purpose of this account is an income stream for luxury spending at retirement. Traveling in the winter, golf holidays, fine dining, and shopping would be examples of items you could buy from income generated from your luxury account.

- **Account 3a: Big Purchase Account**
  Purpose: Temporary Wealth

Your big purchase account is used to save for purchases of big items. A new car, van, or boat would be a big-ticket item. If you plan to have a recreational vehicle at retirement or a vacation home in Hawaii, you must start a big purchase account immediately. Most people have to cash out their savings accounts at retirement to buy a new car etc. Doing this would reduce the amount of principal you have at retirement. Don't do this since a car is a form of temporary wealth. It is a mistake to cash out permanent wealth to buy a temporary item.

- **Account 3b: Education Savings Account (If You Have Children)**
  Purpose: This is also a temporary form of wealth since it will be spent before you retire.

  Although this account is a big purchase account, you might, for tax reasons, keep this account in a registered education savings type vehicle that receives good tax and government benefits.

- **Account 4: Debt Reduction Account**
  Purpose: Reducing Negative Wealth

  Since debts earn the opposite of an investment income, this account must be used carefully. Negative interest charged to you to buy boats, cars, and houses reduce your wealth, and they become negative assets. They cost you money each month. This account is used to reduce further your mortgage, car bill, credit cards, and other bills. By reducing your debts, you gain security by having lower cash flow demands. You want no outstanding mortgage, credit cards, or car loans by retirement.

- **Account 5: Daily Interest-Bearing Checking Account**
  Purpose: This is a temporary wealth account for daily living expenses.

  This account is where you need to keep your money to pay your bills and buy food and essentials for daily living.

After setting up these accounts, the next step is to set up pre-authorized checking accounts for direct debit from your savings or checking accounts.

The last step is to decide on the percentages to invest in each account.

Take, for example, an account I set up for a client, Sharon:

Sharon earned about $42,000 a year in income. After paying taxes, she took home about $30,000 a year. Out of this we budgeted the following:

1. *15% into retirement savings = $4,500 a year = $375 a month*
2. *5% into a luxury account = $1,500 a year = $125 a month*
3. *5% into a big purchase account since Sharon needed a new car in five years = $1,500 a year = $125 a month*
4. *5% into additional payment on her mortgage on each anniversary date = $1,500 a year = $125 a month*
5. *The remaining 70% or $21,000 a year went into her checking account and allowed Sharon to spend the rest guilt-free since she had done an excellent job in savings in accounts #1, 2, 3, and 4 each month. Her total disposable income per month = $1,750*

If the numbers are too difficult for you to survive, make the numbers match what you can afford. Instead of $125 per month for a car fund, maybe you only need to have $50 per month. You must set an amount into the five accounts and do it monthly.

If you are debt-free, you might take Savings Account #4 and put it into Savings Accounts #1 and #2. Although numbers or $ figures will be different for everyone, set up the accounts, so you have separate accounts for your permanent and temporary wealth.

To do well financially, you have to use a system. This system is excellent since it builds wealth over the long term by separating your long-term capital from your spending money. It also eliminates the need for budgeting since it automatically invests your money into neat wealth packages.

Organization takes away the guilt of spending money since you have paid yourself first. A great rule is to invest 30% into debt reduction and your long-term capital accounts. After that, you can spend 70% on anything you wish since you have covered your necessities.

We have spoken about what to do with your money and how you will organize it into your different savings accounts. You might be thinking, *Well, John, I know what I can do with my money. But what if I want to borrow money and start making a little extra on the side. Banks lend out loans, so what if I could take advantage of that and grow it even more.* Let's talk about this in the next chapter.

TO BORROW OR NOT TO BORROW?

We live in a world today where you can easily borrow money. Even in the ancient days, there was a "favor for a favor," which would leave you indebted to someone. Today, all of these favors come in the form of money and interest rates. This can be either a pro or a con depending on how it is used. Some people get rich by borrowing other people's money, and some are indebted for life because they borrow what they can't pay back.

You can think of this like growing multiple apple trees after your first one. If you can grow one apple tree, then why not grow another? Although this may seem like the logical thing to do, you have some factors to take into account:

- Do you have enough water, soil, and sunlight to provide for the new tree?
- Who will be responsible for the increased labor of your new trees?
- Is there space available so the roots of one tree don't overtake the other?
- What are you going to do with the fresh apples you will harvest?

Taking these factors into account is essential before planting a new tree. When borrowing money, you must consider factors like interest rates and the potential new investment earnings.

Be careful that you can pay back your debts or loans. Remember to take into consideration unexpected job loss and expenses that may occur. If there is an interruption in your income, could you still make all your payments?

Borrowing money to invest is kind of like understanding
what is necessary to plant new apple trees.

THE ENDLESS HARVEST RULE:

Buy cars and depreciating items with cash and borrow to buy your
investments if you are an aggressive investor.

Well, this is a book on investing, so let's talk about investing on this subject! Aggressive investors often borrow money when the potential for
investment gain outweighs the risks. Don't borrow when interest rates are
high unless the return far exceeds the interest rate. Never borrow if you
can't afford to pay back the money if something goes wrong. That's called
gambling.

When borrowing in a margin account, your assets are held as collateral for
the loan. Rates are often competitive and can, in some cases, be equal to
some personal line of credit through financial institutions.

Leverage can also allow the investor to pay down just part of the payment. Leverage uses borrowed funds to maximize the investment return by purchasing more investments or shares than you could otherwise. If there is an excellent investment opportunity, the additional borrowing power allows investors to multiply their returns many times. But if an investment goes bad, multiply the losses many times over.

Borrowing money to buy investments offers some advantages, such as tax-deductible interest. Be careful only to borrow to buy good long-term performing stocks and mutual funds. Your growth in the long term has to be large enough to cover the interest and put some positive growth in your assets over the long term.

Try only to borrow if you have a longer time horizon, such as five years. If you try to borrow and make a day trade, you may find the market moves against you too quickly. Then you may not be able to afford the interest payments. Be careful when borrowing money to invest. Use caution, but it can make sense if you buy good-quality investments with above-average growth.

You also need to be capable of having more debt. It is smart debt compared to buying cars, clothes, and vacations. Still, be careful and avoid using debt if you are risk-averse or very conservative.

CREATING YOUR FINANCIAL BATHTUB

This is the last chapter in this section on managing millions. Have you ever noticed that when filling up a bathtub with hot water, you must plug the drainpipe first? If you do not plug the drainpipe, the bathtub never fills up with water. The water quickly enters the bathtub, then just as quickly flows through the drain hole and disappears. Even if you increase water flow, the tub never fills up.

Isn't this like many people's finances? They work for many years and still have no financial security. Their finances are just like a bathtub with no plug. The money enters and then quickly drains down the hole. There are no assets or accumulation of wealth. If they work harder and earn more money, they may not get ahead financially because the extra money drains even quicker down the spending drain hole.

One of the fastest ways to improve your chances of financial independence is to keep your debts under control. Today, so many wants and needs can lead to little cash left over at the end of the month. Just charge it... "Charge it" becomes the solution. We all want it, and we want it now. The dream home, the cottage, the new cars, good education for the kids, traveling to exotic places, a comfortable retirement... "Charge it" becomes the lifestyle.

Investment planning and research are excellent, but it is useless if you spend more than you make. Money is the fuel of your investment plan. Without the fuel, your investment vehicles will go nowhere. Savings fuel your investment portfolio.

THE SOLUTION IS TO PLUG THE DRAIN! In addition to setting up the five savings accounts we discussed earlier, you need to look at where you are wasting your money. Are there places where you could reduce the money that is not spent productively? Do you have any recurring monthly subscriptions you are not utilizing?

Debt arises when you spend more than you make. Sometimes one of the hardest lessons to learn is not to spend more than you earn. You cannot accumulate wealth until you control your debts. You are in debt if you spend $1.25 while making $1.20.

If you cannot control your spending, you will never become wealthy. You will never have peace of mind because you constantly worry about paying bills. Just because you make more money doesn't mean you can increase your spending uncontrollability. You must maintain control of your debts—don't let your debts control you.

Drain Strategy 1: Consider using cash instead of credit cards. Spending using credit cards is even worse than spending money. Because when you use a credit card, you are spending money you do not even have. You borrow the money from the credit card company until you pay for the items later.

When you buy something with cash, you buy something without creating future debts. Wasting cash by buying items you do not need is a very poor practice. Wasting money by buying items you do not need on credit is even worse. Since if you do not pay for the items within a set period, you get charged vast amounts of interest.

Interest in spending is the opposite of wealth creation. It is negative wealth since you get poorer and poorer each month as interest accumulates. You owe more and more money each month. You must work harder to generate income to pay interest charges. It extends the number of years you have to work before retiring or can be a never-ending spiral downward.

Drain Strategy 2: Have a garage sale to sell off the clutter in your home. Turn this junk into cash to reduce debts and build your permanent wealth accounts.

THE ENDLESS HARVEST RULE:

Ask yourself, *Are you making efficient use of your resources? Is there cash in your clutter?*

Another aid to debt reduction is selling off unnecessary items taking up space in your home or apartment. Have a garage sale on the weekend to sell off those items. For cash, you can sell snowmobiles, cars, boats, stereos, and large ticket items. You can use that money to help pay off your debts.

Keep items that are valuable to you. Sell any items you do not care about. Turning the clutter into cash is a great way to clean up your physical space and financial world simultaneously. You do not have to be heavily in debt before you have a garage sale. I have had many of them to clear up space in my home and garage.

Take this case, for example:
Karen and Melvin have the following debts.

ABC Department Stores	*$800*
VISA Card	*$2,800*
XYZ Furniture Warehouse (Midnight Madness Sale)	*$3,000*
Line of Credit	*$1,200*
Dentist Bill for two children	*$900*
Master Card	*$3,500*
Mortgage (Monthly payment is $1000)	*$120,000*
Store credit card	*$22,000*

They feel discouraged because they have little money to pay off these debts. Their money is spent raising their two children and making all payments on their mortgage and other debts.

Karen and Melvin read this book and discussed the possibility of selling some items in the garage and their basement. They sold the following items:

1. *Melvin's old motorcycle: he wanted $3,000 but settled for $1,800.*
2. *Karen and Melvin sold their old furniture in the basement, which they did not use, for $120.*
3. *At the cabin, Melvin kept two snowmobiles. He sold one of them for $3,500. He also sold the old boat that he no longer used for $1,800.*
4. *Karen and her two kids organized a garage sale over a weekend. Garage sale items of old toasters, pictures, toys, bicycles, and clothes raised a total of $800. Each of their kids got to keep $100 each for their efforts. Total to the parents of $600.*
5. *Old books taking up space in their garage at the local second-hand bookstore sold for $50.*

Total cash from garage, rummage, and classified advertisements totaled $7,870. They went to their bank and paid off their ABC Department bill of $800, Dentist bill of $900, VISA card of $2,800, the furniture bill of $3,000, and had $330 for some clothes for their kids. They also had fewer payments *and more space in their house. Next month, they plan to have another garage sale and give some of these items to their local charity.*

There was cash in all of that clutter in their basement, yard, and garage. They turned useless items into a financial benefit for their family by selling them.

Drain Strategy 3: Start by putting your debts down on paper. Put your debts on one side, and then put dates you wish to eliminate the debts on the other side.

You will obtain financial independence when you have no debts and the interest income from your assets is large enough to live the way you desire.

I used this method to eliminate my debts. When I first graduated from University, I received my first credit card. At the same time, I bought a sports car. I went on a shopping spree, and "in the blink of an eye," I was heavily in debt. It is a terrible situation to have many debts. The solution is to cut up your credit cards and pay cash until your debt situation is under control. That's what worked for me.

Drain Strategy 4: Discuss the possibility of a consolidation loan to roll all your small debts into one big loan with your bank. This will reduce the number of payments you will have to make.

Drain Strategy 5: Start paying the smallest balances first. You might have to pay minimum payments on the remaining debts. Clearing and paying off your first debt is a big morale booster. No matter how small, the repayment in full of any debt is encouraging and means you are moving in a positive direction.

Take Michael, for instance:

Michael had just bought his first house and found that many debts had accumulated. He created a debt problem. His debts were:

Visa bill from hardware purchases	*$2,500*
Student loan	*$11,000*
Mortgage	*$135,000*
Automobile loan from bank	*$14,000*
Bill from Zellers for towels etc.	*$1200*

Michael should look at paying off the smallest bill first. Then he can pay off the next smallest bill. This would reduce his overall monthly payments and stress.

Drain Strategy 6: Give yourself a realistic time to clear the bills. If you try to pay off your bills in too short of time, you will create too much stress. You need to be realistic that this will take some time to accomplish. Be patient and clear one bill at a time. If you try to pay off the bills in too short a time, you could create a cash crisis and have to borrow more money to make your monthly payments.

Drain Strategy 7: Read books on debt reduction and how to stretch your money more efficiently. Taking your lunch to work once a week can save money and not burden your lifestyle. Parking in a less expensive spot a block further from your work might help you lose some weight and provide you with some exercise daily.

An excellent book on reducing debt and clutter is *Your Money or Your Life*. It should be available at your local bookstore. *Simplifying Your Life* is another excellent book that teaches ways to reduce waste.

Let me give you this worksheet to use:

DEBT ASSESSMENT WORKSHEET

Take a few minutes to look at your current debt level.

Do you feel comfortable with your level of debt? (CIRCLE) **Yes** or **No**

House Mortgage
Amount owing on 1st mortgage _____
Second Mortgage _____

Credit Cards	Amount Owing	Payoff Goal (DATE)
1. _____	_____	_____
2. _____	_____	_____
3. _____	_____	_____
4. _____	_____	_____
5. _____	_____	_____

Car Loans
Amount Owing _____ _____

Set a deadline (payoff goal) for paying off each debt and commit to these deadlines.

If you have credit card bill problems, consider cutting your credit cards. Credit cards are one of the biggest causes of personal bankruptcy. Pay cash for everything you buy. Paying money for items discourages impulse buying. It is easy to lose track of what you spend by credit card, but you physically hand your money away when you pay cash.

When your debt is decreasing, then your net worth increases. This means the bathtub is filling up! To increase your net worth, it is vital to lower your debts. By shrinking your debt level, you gain financial stability and reduce your vulnerability to job loss, an unexpected illness, or unanticipated expenses. Additionally, I suggest having an emergency fund of at least three months of expenses saved.

That wraps up this section on managing your millions. Next up is our secret bonus section on asking the right questions. This is where we put everything together and show you how to understand your plan and hire the right help you need. Up to this point, you have been able to do everything yourself. You can still keep going on the road alone, but in the next section, we will discuss further understanding everything we have spoken about and getting professional help.

Always understand your finances before hiring anything out. You don't need to be a master mechanic and understand how to rebuild an engine just to drive a car, do you? But you have to know enough about your automobile to know what to do when the "check engine" light goes on; or what type of fuel to put into your car at the gas station.

ASKING THE RIGHT QUESTIONS

The fourth secret part of The Endless Harvest is asking the right questions. In this book, we have walked through how to build your wealth, protect it, and then manage it. Some of you may be asking yourself, Isn't there an easier way of getting this all done? How can I just get someone to do it for me?

As promised, this book is filled with everything you need to grow your financial Endless Harvest on your own. I held nothing back, and you have all the tools you need to succeed. I decided to include this fourth step because not everyone wants to manage their finances. Even though this may be the case for you, you will still need to know how to ask the right questions.

Do this so you can:

Ask yourself the right questions and be prepared and knowledgeable about your situation. The more you know about your finances and what you desire to have, the better job you will do at hiring the right advisor for you.

Take, for instance, our analogy of growing an apple tree. This is the part where you would be interested in possibly hiring a team to take care of your tree for you, planting more trees, and turning your operation into overdrive. Before you can do this, you need to know your situation first.

What kind of apple trees do you want, and how many different types? Is the quality of apples what you expected, and how many years will your tree need to survive? The last and one of the most critical questions is, Who is the most qualified to take care of my tree, and how do I know they will do a great job?

This is kind of like putting the process into high gear and getting professional help.

In this section, I want to give you a case to consider. This case tells you about some of the truths of the investment advisement industry. You may remember the experience my father had with financial advisors. Yes, I am a financial advisor, and my goal from this book is to give you everything you need to succeed on your own.

But if you intend on going down the path of using a financial advisor, you will want to read this case:

Blind Trust and Poor Advice

Not all investment advisors are created equal. Clients tend to treat all investment advisors who hold the title as equal. Rudolf is a successful professional who has two advisors. One advisor trades penny stocks and small mining and speculative real estate trusts. I was the other advisor specializing in risk-managed portfolios of diversified income-generating investments.

For twenty years, we were given $1,000,000 in total cash. The advisor who traded highly speculative penny stocks and mining stocks had winners and losers. At the end of retirement, the client had $40,000 in total value, a loss of $960,000. The other advisor, myself, had $2,200,000 in retirement assets.

The total belief in both advisors was despite tangible evidence that one had a winning approach and the other had a losing approach. This was not a theoretical exercise. Investment strategies leave actual clues and evidence in dollars and cents. I'm not telling you this case study to brag or "toot my own horn." Instead, I only want to educate you on the reality of our world.

Here is my suggestion, no matter what advisor you have or choose to go with. Over the longer term of five years or more, decide if the advisor has a winning strategy or not. All advisors face tough times and recessions. The main criteria are consistently having bad results.

In the short term, three years or less, sometimes an unsuccessful approach may get lucky and provide good results. A winning or losing strategy will become very clear in the longer term. Not all advisors have equally good investment strategies. Do not have blind trust but evaluate the results periodically. Events such as recessions or pandemics should also be considered when evaluating results.

The lesson from this case is that not all investment advisors are the same. Do not have blind trust just because someone holds the title of an investment advisor. Periodically evaluate their long-term results. A losing strategy over the long term will become apparent. Do not stick with a losing strategy if it is consistently unsuccessful. The most expensive advice is bad advice.

This is my secret step, step four, of The Endless Harvest. By the time you are done with this section, you will know how to ask yourself and your potential advisor the right questions to get the desired results.

One key is that even though you want to put your finances and investment on autopilot, you cannot step out of the picture altogether. Have you ever hired someone to clean your house, redo your flooring, or even watch your children but never check up on them? When this happens, the other party will start not to care. Nine times out of ten, if you are not involved in the process, the other party will assume you do not care about your finances.

This is your money, your hard-earned money! It means a lot and has much value. Using financial advisors is one of the most innovative things you can do in life. But just like you would hire a team of workers to help harvest your crop, please keep an eye on your harvest. Know what is going on with your crop and keep everything running smoothly.

Remember when I said to run your investments like running a business? This is just the case. The best financial advisors love it when clients are as interested in their progress as they are themselves. In the end, you are a team. The right advisor can and will help you get to your goal quicker and faster than you could do yourself if you work together.

"Not all investment advisors are equal in knowledge, advice, and strategy."

– John Yamamoto

ASSESSING YOUR CURRENT PLAN

Financial plans help us choose the level of growth versus safety in a portfolio. This is the first decision you want to clarify. Once you can determine this, it is easier to move forward in a clear direction.

Let's talk about the building blocks of a portfolio. The primary issue with investing is that it is complicated. However, there are some basic building blocks of wealth management.

Let's talk about the first one. The most noticeable building block of wealth management is investing in stocks. Stocks should be the primary vehicle in every portfolio. Stocks are basically ownership of a business. If you own a stock, you are part owner of that business. If I have a hundred shares of Starbucks, therefore, I am part owner of Starbucks. When Starbucks makes a profit, it pays that profit to me in a dividend. As a part-owner of that business, I get a dividend that I could spend or put into more shares of Starbucks. The point is that I want to get stocks that pay dividends as the first component of my portfolio.

The second component is real estate or using real estate investment trusts. I am not trying to own physical real estate in this case. As an investment advisor, I am more interested in rental income. I will buy a well-diversified portfolio of apartment buildings or office buildings and get part of their rental income through a real estate investment trust. Again, I am getting a return from owning real estate, a "real estate investment trust." I am sticking to high-quality investments, not any that are speculative.

The third category that most people know is bonds, fixed income, GICs, or return deposits. These pay you interest sometimes yearly, sometimes quarterly, and sometimes monthly. It is a debt in which I lend my money to this company by buying a bond. Then I get interest payments. That interest payment is my return on capital.

The fourth category includes items like precious metals, such as gold and silver. Precious metals are an alternative, meaning there are times when you own gold. Why would you own gold? You would own gold during global uncertainty, political crisis, or paper currency concerns. After 9/11, for example, gold went up because of the fear of terrorism and global uncertainty.

The fifth type of your portfolio building block is commodities—things like oil companies, copper, sugar companies, and coffee companies. Again, commodities tend to go up during specific periods, usually periods of economic opportunities. Those are the main building blocks of a portfolio.

We will discuss a little bit about a sixth building block, which is emerging markets. Emerging markets are stocks of companies of newer or smaller growing economies, such as India and Mexico. China is a pretty sizeable emerging market stock. The advantage of emerging markets is that the growth can be high. The downside is that the risk can also be high.

Those are your primary types of investments, and you probably remember them from earlier chapters. We put them together in what is called an asset allocation mix. The percentage of stocks, bonds, real estate, metals, emerging markets, and commodities tend to vary with the economy. My view is that no set percentage should be throughout all time. I think you should make adjustments based on the economic conditions. There are times when gold is risky; there are times when real estate is risky. You want to adjust periodically.

When you adjust, it is called rebalancing. Rebalancing once a year would be sufficient. You don't necessarily want to buy and hold forever. I think you need to reallocate your portfolio. Part of your financial plan would be a pie chart with your estimated asset allocation model for this period. It is different for each individual based on goals, risk tolerance, and age. The asset allocation model for a couple may differ from another person down the street.

Those are the parts of a portfolio. I would have a plan, set aside a savings percentage, and create a debt management plan, an asset allocation plan, and a risk management plan. Those all fit together.

The five parts of a financial plan would be:

1. Goals
2. A plan that puts it all together
3. Your pie chart of what investments you own
4. A risk management strategy
5. A rebalancing strategy

That would constitute your entire financial plan.

When you rebalance your plan once a year, ask yourself, *What should I do now?* Your answer will vary depending on what kind of future you want to have. Three things will directly affect the answer to your question:

1. Longevity
2. Things you want
3. Unexpected circumstances

This is where you will assess your past, current, and future desired results. Doing so tells you where your future can be and what to do with your current situation. I know that not everyone will have past results or even current results. We should all have future desired results, in any case.

It is timely and logical for a financial advisor to move from left to right in the diagram above. But I often move from right to left with new clients. Talk about the future and then move backward.

Just to give you some reference, on average, if you are young, your plan may not change for a long time. If you are older, your plans may change more frequently. This is because your future is very far from you at a young age. You should be focused on the same things for a more extended period. When you are at an older age, living longevity changes quickly, and unexpected circumstances may arise.

Whether you are young or old, make sure to focus on the main goals you have in life. We can become indecisive or even change our minds frequently as human beings.

"The main thing is to keep the main thing the main thing."
– Stephen R. Covey

The investments you should be looking at in your portfolio and the five parts of your financial plan. You should assess your current plan once a year with these two elements. We already spoke about creating your financial plan. This is all about assessing it.

It applies to you if you have an investment advisor or if you do not. Make sure you know your numbers at all times. Only then can you quantitatively evaluate how you are doing year after year.

THE FINANCIAL HEADWINDS THAT CAN DERAIL YOUR RETIREMENT PLAN

I want to talk about financial headwinds last in this chapter. These are important because they can be a "curveball" to your financial plan. Things like longevity risks, running out of money while still alive, and outliving your money. There are also, what I call, encroachment risks to be leery of.

Encroachment risks are when you take out larger withdrawals than the portfolio's growth. In other words, people retire, take out a quarter of their money to buy a motorhome, and then find out they run out of money much quicker. One of the plan's encroachment risks is that if you plan to take out $50,000 or $100,000 a year to do something, include that in the plan.

Financial Headwind 1: Subtract taxes in your planning to show after-tax income available to spend in retirement.

Taxation risk is when people plan to retire but fail to prepare for the tax they will pay in retirement. They want $5,000 a month, but they forget that to take out $5,000 a month, you have to take out $6,000 because $1,000 goes to pay taxes. When they retired, they forgot to include taxes on their retirement income. In every plan, you should have some taxes held back on your government benefits, your pension plans at work, your retirement plan, and include the taxation risk in your budget.

Financial Headwind 2: The cost of living will increase by 2% annually.

Another significant headwind, and probably one that we never talk about much, is inflation risk. The cost of living typically goes up 2% a year. If you retire 15 years from now, you will have to take out 2% more a year for the next 10 or 15 years. If you think you need $4,000 today, you will need $5,000 in 10 years. In your plan, you always include 2% for inflation in your calculations for your income.

Financial Headwind 3: Falsely assuming your cost of living will decline as you age.

Let me give you an example:

Jim, age 60, assumes that after he turns 70, his cost of living will decline as he will travel less. Jim needs to consider that although he may spend less on his trips abroad, he may have to pay more on assisted living, health care, and drug costs.

Another significant headwind that can derail a retirement plan that many people overlook is health care risks. Will you have larger bills for health care when you retire? Will you need more pharmacy drugs? Will your health care plan at work stop when you retire and leave the company? Health care risk is a considerable risk you need to plan for.

Financial Headwind 4: Include any loan interest charges in your projections.

I've got another example to explain this headwind:

Mary and Scott have a mortgage of $350,000. They have not considered the interest charges on their loan in their financial planning. Interest charges on debts are another financial headwind to be aware of. Most people think they take out a $300,000 mortgage; they will pay the bank back $300,000. The reality is you will pay them $450,000 over a 20-year term at 4%.

These are a few financial headwinds I recommend you look at and make sure your retirement plan accounts for them. We've discussed assessing your current plan, rebalancing, and watching for financial headwinds. By now, you might think this is much information to consider. I won't lie. It is a lot, and yes, it is all necessary.

One of the best ways to get professional advice in this arena is from a financial advisor. But you've probably heard of that before. Now, I'm not telling you that you need to hire me. I just want you to know that hiring a financial advisor is very beneficial in many circumstances. Maybe you even had one, but they didn't work out. Or possibly you have an advisor but don't know how they are performing.

Every financial advisor will give you a pitch, telling you how they are the best. You must determine precisely how good they are and whether they have your best interests. In the next chapter, I will tell you exactly how to hire the right advisors.

HIRING THE RIGHT ADVISORS

Hiring the right advisor can seem tricky if you are unfamiliar with finance. You have been reading, and I can tell you that you are more prepared than 99% of others who want to hire an advisor. You know the foundation for becoming a cash flow millionaire, the risks you must avoid to stay rich, and how to manage your millions successfully. These are the basics that everyone should know before hiring an investment advisor.

When hiring an investment advisor, you may still have questions about picking the best one for your situation. Having been in the industry for decades, I can tell you that not all investment advisors are created equal. When it comes down to it, you need someone who has your best interests in mind and is suitable for your specific needs. You might be thinking, "Well, John, that's obvious, but you have to tell me more!" I've put together ten commandments for selecting a wealth investment advisor.

Picking your advisor and advisors will help you achieve your goals more quickly without the headache of figuring it out yourself. Again, it is not necessary to be a master at everything. You just need to know how to hire the right people. To properly manage your money, you need to build a network of investment advisors but be careful about selecting investment advisors.

THE ENDLESS HARVEST RULE:

To acquire wealth, you need someone working with you
to help organize your finances.

Choosing the right investment advisor is critical to your long-term investment success. This person can advise you on current tax, investment, and economic factors affecting your financial picture. Remember, even though you rely on an investment advisor, you need to continue participating in decisions. Don't turn over complete control of your investments.

Throughout your lifetime, you should rely on the expertise of a good accountant, lawyer, banker, life insurance agent, and investment advisor. You remember those definitions from the previous chapter on your financial network. Simplify your life by delegating tasks to trained professionals who need the knowledge to succeed. Use investment professionals for your investments and accountants to assist with your taxes. Don't try to save a few dollars and do your tax return yourself. Use professionals to advise you of upcoming changes in the tax laws.

There are 10 commandments you should follow when hiring your team:

Commandment 1: Like a good doctor, the broker must have a caring attitude.

To do well, you want a broker interested in you doing well and achieving your goals—someone who cares whether you are happy and satisfied with your investment strategy.

Commandment 2: Hire a broker who has the proper credentials.

Be careful about hiring a broker just because their card shows they are a president or have the title "center of the financial universe" or "financial expert." There is much leeway in small firms concerning titles. Many of the largest firms have stricter requirements regarding titles. For my title of Vice President, I had to achieve several requirements such as writing and passing the Partners Exam from the Canadian Securities Institute, certain numbers of years in the firm, and specific sales targets.

A designation is a good indicator of the broker's commitment to improving their knowledge base. It is also an objective and standardized measurement of investment knowledge.

Make sure to ask for the advisor's educational and training background? Some excellent designations are:

MBA - Masters of Business Administration
CFP - Certified Financial Planner
CFA- Chartered Financial Analyst
CIM - Canadian Investment Manager
FCSI - Fellow of the Canadian Securities Institute
CLU - Chartered Life Underwriter
BCom/BBA - Bachelor of Commerce
CA - Chartered Accountant

CMA - Certified Management Accountant
CGA - Certified General Accountant

Commandment 3: Have a broker who manages your money with periodic reviews of your investments and investment strategy.

A good broker conducts an annual or semi-annual financial checkup. Asset allocation or adjusting your portfolio periodically will maintain a healthy asset mix and keep your portfolio on track. The broker should work out a simplified investment plan that you agree with and ensure you are aware of where your finances are at all times. Having a broker allows you to make investment transactions over the telephone.

Commandment 4: Use a broker who has a reputable firm that has a good research department and up-to-date information technology.

Your broker should save you the headache of tracking and searching for up-to-date financial information. Brokers have extensive training and are backed by firms with millions of dollars invested in market analysts and databases. With one database, I have access to all the news events pertaining to many stocks on Toronto Stock Exchange and New York Stock Exchange, plus day-to-day recommendations.

Without access to extensive databases, you could spend hours looking through newspapers and newsletters. I know a very successful dentist who will spend eight hours reading about the market and doing a stock analysis to save $35 on a trade. This is fine for a hobby, but "your time is money," so use professionals whenever possible.

Commandment 5: Find a broker who matches your needs.

There are different investment companies and brokers; your task is to find the one(s) that are right for you and your investment portfolio.

I recommend that most people use a full-service brokerage firm and work with an advisor whose skills match your needs. These firms provide greater access and guidance to investment ideas. Costs are comparable to discount brokerage houses for bonds, term deposits, and mutual funds. (stock trading may be a slightly higher cost)

THE ENDLESS HARVEST RULE:

A mistake people make is to look at financial advisors as being
interchangeable. Not all advisors are the same. Take time
to find the right advisor for you.

There are five different types of brokers. Your objective is to find the broker that best matches your investment portfolio requirements.

Type 1: General practitioners are jack-of-all-trades who handle everything from stocks to options.

Type 2: Penny stock traders specialize in speculative investments, usually penny stocks valued under $5. Speculative investments include penny mining, junior oil, gas, and technology shares.

Type 3: Mutual fund brokers strive to find a mutual fund to meet the needs of each client.

Type 4: Options and futures brokers focus on future and option traders, often using particular charting services and computer programs for futures trading.

Type 5: Specialized financial planning brokers seeking to build portfolios around clients' risk tolerance levels and goals.

Commandment 6: Choose the types of Investment companies to match your specific investment needs.

The main types of investment accounts are:

- Discount brokerage firms offer a full spectrum of products but no advice to individuals who want to pay low fees for stock trading.
- Independent mutual fund firms sell mutual funds for other firms. (Sometimes, they offer life insurance but don't offer any other stocks or bonds.)
- Mutual fund firms sell their own family of mutual funds.
- Life insurance firms sell life insurance, disability products, and mutual funds but don't offer stocks or other bonds.
- Fee-for-service financial planners prepare financial plans and assessments for people.

- Banks and trust companies offer term deposits, Guaranteed Investment Certificates (GICs), retirement savings plans, and mutual funds.
(They can provide referrals to full-service brokerage and discounts.)
- Full-service brokerage firms offer a full spectrum of products and advice.

Commandment 7: Never choose an investment advisor because they are friends or relatives.

You would not choose an eye surgeon or heart surgeon because they are a relative. You would select that surgeon based on experience, education, and because they are a specialist.

Some good questions to ask yourself when you are choosing an investment advisor:

- Are you comfortable dealing with the individual?
- Is the advisor's knowledge suitable for your investment goals?
- What is the advisor's specialty area, and is it compatible with your interests?
- Will the advisor develop a customized plan for you or randomly suggest investments?
- Is the advisor concerned with controlling risk or making gains?
- Will the advisor regularly follow up on your portfolio?
- Will the advisor try to minimize your taxes?
- Who will take care of your account if the advisor leaves the industry?
- Are you familiar with the investment firm's reputation?
  - How long ago was it established?
  - Does it have branches in other cities?
  - Does it offer all financial products such as bonds, stocks, and mutual funds?

Commandment 8: Hire a broker who has had sufficient experience on the job. At least three to four years of experience is a minimum target as a rule of thumb.

A graduating lawyer spends years after graduation as an Articling Student, and then they have to pass a bar exam. A graduating accountant needs to fulfill minimum standards plus qualifying exams. A graduating engineer needs to spend years to earn their professional status. A graduating doctor needs to spend years as an Intern and Residency.

Although no such restrictions exist in the brokerage and investment industry, it is crucial to ask for the years that the broker has been in the industry. You want someone with sufficient experience in the industry to manage your money.

Commandment 9: You want a broker concerned with managing investment risks.

It is dangerous if you have an advisor solely concerned with gains. This strategy can get you in trouble since the entire portfolio will be in high-risk investments. You want to ensure that your investment advisor is aware of investment risks.

Strategies to reduce taxes, market risk, and other risks should be part of your investment strategy.

Commandment 10: A good broker should take time to get to know your goals, and then they should tailor the investments and portfolio strategy to achieve these goals. A poor investment advisor is a glorified salesperson who wants to sell you investments with no system or customization.

A major tip is to come prepared for your meetings with your advisor. This will help you identify and avoid advisors who are just looking for a new customer or don't have your best interests in mind.

Before you meet with any investment advisor, you need to provide them with the following information:

- Your knowledge Level
  I would describe my investment knowledge as:
  None ___ A little ___ Fair ___ Good ___ Very Good ___ Excellent

- My main investment goal is: (1 most important, 4 least Important)
  Growth ___
  Income ___
  Safety of Principal ___
  Tax Savings ___

- From my financial advisor, I expect:
  No advice ___ Some advice ___ A lot of advice ___

- I have had experience in the past with:
  Mutual Funds ___   Term Deposits ___
  Canada Savings Bonds ___   Provincial Bonds ___
  Strip Coupons ___   Stocks ___
  Penny Stocks (under $2) ___ Retirement Savings Plans ___
  Options ___   Commodities ___
  Preferred Shares ___   U.S. Dollar Accounts ___

- I prefer to call my broker rather than have them call me. ___
- I prefer to have my broker call me rather than I call them. ___
- I expect the following things from my investment advisor ___

Some Other Tips:

It's time to consider switching brokers when:

- You start to question your broker's integrity.
- Your investment objectives and risk tolerance level are constantly incompatible with the broker's recommendations.
- There is poor communication between you and your broker.

Don't consider changing brokers just because:

- The market goes on a downswing.
- One of your investments decreases in value.
- Someone promises to get you a higher rate of return. (Promises are cheap.)

When you are opening up a brokerage account, there are several forms you will probably complete, such as:

- A "Know Your Client" information application.
- A standard account form is used to purchase investments.
- A Power of Attorney form transfers authority to act from one person to another.
  (You might grant power of attorney to your broker to make investment decisions for you to sell specific securities. A spouse with little investment experience may grant power of attorney to a more experienced spouse to make investment decisions on behalf of the first spouse.)
- Married couples often use a Joint Account with Rights of Survivorship form to easily transfer all assets to the remaining spouse should one spouse pass away.

251

- A Corporate Resolution Form that allows a company to trade in bonds, money market, mutual funds, and stocks.
- A Shareholder Communication form permits mutual funds and stock market annual reports to be sent to you.
- A form that allows the broker to take verbal orders over the phone.
- A margin form allows you to borrow against your non-retirement savings plan assets in a revolving credit format.

Today's financial world is very complicated and time-consuming. Tax law and investment climates change constantly and will continue to do so. To avoid procrastination, you must build a network of suitable financial professionals. A good accountant, banker, lawyer, and investment advisor is critical to helping you properly manage your investments.

USING PROFESSIONAL MANAGERS WITH MANAGED ACCOUNTS

There is another option I want to present to you, as well. If you do not like managing your money, do not want to make asset allocation decisions, or decide what stock or mutual fund to buy, you should consider using a managed account.

A managed account is an account set up by your broker who can use one or many investment managers to manage your money. You get good reporting and good taxation reports. You do not have to make any decisions except at the initial meeting when setting up your investment objectives and risk tolerance level.

A managed money account is a pool of money from investors who give control of the assets to a professional money manager. Managed money accounts are usually for large amounts of money managed money accounts that fall into four categories:

1. Mutual funds
   (They are the most common managed money accounts. Because they use a professional money manager to decide on daily investment decisions.)
2. Managed pooled accounts
3. Managed stock accounts
4. Self-managed stock accounts

Next, I will give you a list of definitions based on a dollar figure requirement. These definitions will help you better understand the options managed accounts present:

Private Portfolio Management Company (Minimum Often $100,000+)

There can be manual or computerized ways to manage your money with little or no input on the client's part. Managed money accounts manage the money on the client's behalf. For a fee, they provide the client with professional money management. This allows the busy, out-of-country, or uninterested investor with higher potential gains than simple bond or fixed income accounts. Mutual funds are the most common format for managed money accounts.

Pooled Managed Money Account (Minimum of $50,000)

These accounts use private money managers to create pooled accounts such as US Equity Pool, Canadian Equity Pool, Bond Pool, Money Market Pool, and Global Equity Pool. These pools are combined into different combination portfolios for clients. The most common three pools are:

1. Conservative Equity Pool - for conservative investors with a focus on safety.
2. Moderate Equity Pool - for a balance between growth and safety.
3. Growth Equity Pool - for an emphasis on growth and less on safety.

Personal Portfolio Managers (Minimum of $100,000 Registered Plans and $150,000 Non-Registered Plans)

This is an excellent way for investors who want a portfolio of stocks without having to do the work of buying and selling stocks. The fund managers are often elite managers who specialize in their particular area. (Examples include Canadian equity managers, Canadian balanced managers, US equity managers, US growth managers, Global equity managers, Global balanced managers with global stocks and bonds, and International managers with non-US stocks and bonds.) The management fees for non-registered plans can be tax-efficient, and in some cases, the management fees can be tax-deductible.

Asset Allocation Funds ($1500+) are Computer Managed Mutual Funds

Movement is between equity funds, bond funds, and money market funds. The weighting varies according to how the computer assesses which area will get the best returns. This generally needs a lower amount of money to enter into this plan.

Discretionary Accounts (Wrap) ($75,000+)

These are managed manually and usually trade in the stock markets. The customer is actively involved in buying and selling stocks in the portfolio. Your most significant advantage is getting a set fee (or percent cost), and you can trade many times without additional commission charges. A portfolio of stocks is the most common format. The user builds a stock portfolio instead of buying mutual funds.

I am experienced in the use of managed accounts and find them helpful for someone who does not enjoy managing their investments; or for those that are either too busy or have large sums of money, which would be difficult to manage on their own. Managed accounts offer a wide selection of fund managers and good diversification at reasonable costs. They are ideal for the retired, wealthy, or disinterested investor.

THERE ARE BERNIE MADOLFFS IN THE WORLD THEY ARE PREDATORY

I needed to add a part to this chapter to warn you against predatory investment advisors. Predatory people exist in all shapes and sizes in this world. Unfortunately, they can do considerable damage to you in the finance world, which is sometimes irreversible. The best example to describe Bernie Madoff. So, who Is Bernie Madoff?

Bernard Lawrence, "Bernie" Madoff, was an American financier who executed the largest Ponzi scheme in history. This scheme defrauded thousands of investors out of tens of billions of dollars over at least 17 years and possibly longer. He was also a pioneer in electronic trading and chair of the Nasdaq in the early 1990s. He died in prison on April 14, 2021, serving a 150-year sentence for money laundering, securities fraud, and several other felonies.

For simplicity, here are the key takeaways from this real-life story:

- Bernie Madoff was a money manager responsible for one of the largest financial frauds to date.
- Bernie Madoff's Ponzi scheme, which likely ran for decades, defrauded thousands of investors from tens of billions of dollars.
- Investors put their trust in Madoff because he created a front of respectability, his returns were high but not outlandish, and he claimed to use a legitimate strategy.
- In 2009 Madoff was sentenced to 150 years in prison and forced to forfeit $170 billion.
- As of December 2018, the Madoff Victims Fund had distributed more than $2.7 billion to 37,011 victimized investors in the U.S. and around the world.

There is a whole industry of scammers out there. It is an unfortunate truth of this industry. I needed to add this into the book because you need to be aware of it. I am not trying to scare you from this. I am only trying to educate you on the truth of the industry. A lousy investment advisor can be your worst nightmare, but a great investment advisor will become your best friend.

There was much information in this chapter, so I want to summarize it. Here are some criteria for picking an investment advisor. Make sure:

1. They make financial plans a part of their strategy.
   (Plans help to make the future clearer. A gap in your financial plans occurs when your desired future is not what you wish to happen. Without financial planning, the future may occur in a way you do not like.)

2. They provide you with financial reporting on what has happened in the past and present in dollars and percentages.
   (Being unaware of how you have done in the past will leave you unable to evaluate whether your performance is in line with your expectations.)

3. They do a portfolio mix.
   (What is your portfolio asset allocation plan?)
   (Where are you investing your money?)
   (What is the level of investment income?)

4. They have a risk strategy.
   (What is the investment advisor's risk strategy?)
   (How are risks managed?)

5. They offer investor education and updates.

6. They offer multiple investment products and services.

7. They offer other financial professional expertise.

8. (E.G., life insurance, wills and estates, banking, tax, and financial planning)

9. They personalize your plan to match your needs.

10. Plans are adjusted periodically when circumstances change.

11. They ask questions and provide you with meetings periodically.

There is a lot to think about when choosing the right investment advisor. Do your due diligence; I promise it will pay off. I've given you lots of information to think about. Please don't ignore any of it because it is necessary for your Endless Harvest and sustaining your future. Let's switch gears a little now and talk about simplifying things. (The goal of having a financial advisor is to make your life easier, or you can do this yourself.)

REDUCING THE HASSLE FACTOR
OF YOUR WEALTH PLAN

This formula is simple, Complexity = Stress. The great thing is that you can apply this to not only your finances but your entire life.

But let's talk about diversification for a moment. Most people have too many investments in too many places. And by doing that, they think they have diversified. They have a Guaranteed Investment Certificate (GIC) at a bank, a work Retirement Savings Plan (RSP), a discount stock account they are trading, a tax-free savings account, mutual funds at a life insurance agent, and more. When I ask them how they are doing, they honestly do not know. I ask them how much money they have accumulated, and they do not know. I ask them whether they have the right mix of investments, but they do not know. Diversification is necessary, but not at the cost of overcomplexity.

Because of this, one of the things I recommend is simplifying into self-directed investments. Self-directed investments allow you to access most mutual funds, stocks, and bonds in one place. Therefore, you can create a diversified portfolio and have it in one statement. Yes, just one. The one statement is the key. If you look at your investments and have one statement for your retirement plan and your investments, you can get a single report that shows you how well you are doing and how many fees you are paying.

I want my clients to know a couple of key questions:

- How much am I paying in fees?
- What is my return on income?
- What are my overall returns for the last year, two years, and the last five or six years?

You need to consolidate your investments into one or two statements, or it is just too complicated to stay on top of them. (even if you are an expert financial advisor)

The critical point is first to consolidate and then diversify your investments into a few well-run portfolios.

Typically they are:

1. Retirement Plan
2. TFSA
3. Non-registered Investment Plans
4. Professional Corporations and Corporate Assets
5. Registered Education Savings Plans
6. Bank Account for Savings and Checking Accounts

GETTING ORGANIZED
SIMPLIFYING YOUR INVESTMENT LIFE

"There is a misconception that an investment portfolio must be time-consuming and complicated. An effective portfolio should be simple, low-maintenance, and provide a good return with a low-risk level. If someone spends much time managing their investments, there is a lack of organization or a poor investment structure."

– John Yamamoto

THE ENDLESS HARVEST RULE:

It is difficult to make money from investing until you organize your portfolio. Plan, Plan, Plan

Are you controlling your investments, or are your investments controlling you? If your investments are in control and you lose sleep at night, you need to get organized. A healthy portfolio needs regular cleaning and maintenance. You can use basic time management skills to simplify your investments. Keep your work to a minimum by delegating work to a professional investment advisor. They will clean up your investments just as much for themselves as they will for you. It benefits both parties as a win/win.

Organizing your portfolio is the first step in building a successful and straightforward investment program. To become organized, you need to:

- Set financial goals.
- Assess your debt situation.
- Determine where you have your money.
- Reorganize where you invest your money.
- Find an investment advisor.
- Reorganize your savings plan.

SIMPLIFY, CONSOLIDATE, AND REDUCE THE NUMBER OF PLACES WHERE YOU INVEST YOUR MONEY

Does this sound like you? Retirement savings plans in seven different places, penny stocks in a safety deposit box, stocks and mutual funds at two brokerage firms, inadequate or too much life insurance, Canada Saving Bonds in a drawer, and an out-of-date will, or no will at all.

Physically putting your investment statements together is a great way to start. Get started consolidating your investment by finding all of your receipts and putting them into one folder or binder.

Consolidation of your portfolio

Why fight trying to keep track of your money in dozens of different institutions, statements & different people. Consider consolidating them in one place while still maintaining a diversified portfolio.

Bonds   Mutual Funds

Stocks   New Issues

GIC's & Term Deposits   Treasury Bills

Life Insurance   Guaranteed Mutual Funds

THE ENDLESS HARVEST RULE:

Don't keep your bonds and stocks at home in a drawer or a safety deposit box. This will lead to clutter.

Another important reason for not having securities at home or in a safety deposit box is estate planning. If you store your investments at home, you can misplace them, have them stolen, or even destroyed in a fire. Occasionally people pass away, and no one knows about the investment's existence or the location of a safety deposit box—the assets lay unclaimed.

You should store your investments in your account at a brokerage house for safekeeping. It also helps to facilitate the sale of any stocks if there is a sudden negative turn of events for that particular company's shares. Also, if you move, you don't have to inform every company you have stocks of your new address. This could also prevent you from missing a claim or exercise date.

THE ENDLESS HARVEST RULE:

Consolidate your retirement savings plans into one self-directed retirement savings plan. It makes tracking results relatively simple.

Let's look at an example where Jim goes to a major brokerage firm. He chooses to invest in 7 term deposits at seven different institutions:

$8,000 at National Bank
$10,000 at Sunlife Trust
$21,000 at Laurentian Bank
$5,500 at Royal Bank
$12,000 in three different term deposits for 1,2,5 years at Citibank
$15,000 at Alberta Treasury Branch

Imagine the difficulty Jim would have trying to control and evaluate his performance if he invested at those different locations. It would also be problematic for Jim to shop around. Jim eventually chose the best solution by consolidating his term deposits at a brokerage house that offers multiple firm term deposits.

To maintain control of your investments, you must consolidate your investments into as few places as possible. If you can reduce the number of sites you have investments, you can more easily adjust the asset mix, assess the areas of weakness, and calculate your rate of return and income taxes. It also avoids the headache of summarizing your net worth and total asset values.

LOCATE AND RECORD THE LOCATIONS WHERE YOU HAVE YOUR MONEY

THE ENDLESS HARVEST RULE:

Take time for a yearly financial tune-up.

You should evaluate all your investments yearly. You can then sell or weed out some securities and ensure that your investments meet your expectations. Just like your car, you should keep your portfolio tuned up. If you constantly miss oil changes and never rotate your tires, you'll notice your vehicle will have many issues.

Take a few minutes to complete the following questions about your investments during your annual financial tune-up:

Should I:

Update or create a will? _____
Increase or decrease my life insurance? _____
Look at disability insurance? _____
Reorganize my investments? _____
Start or learn to maximize my retirement savings plan
contributions? _____
Reorganize my investments to minimize tax? _____
Get a reliable accountant? _____
Get a reliable investment advisor? _____
Start a trust or education savings plan for my children
or grandchildren? _____
Other , _____

Do I have international investments in my portfolio? _____

Does my portfolio match my level of risk tolerance?   _____

Is my portfolio balanced between fixed income,
stocks, mutual funds, and cash?   _____

Does my investment portfolio match the market conditions?   _____

Am I over-diversified so that I have many small amounts
in my portfolio?   _____

Is my portfolio under control, or has it become too much work?   _____

Is my portfolio all in one basket?   _____

Do I have liquid reserves in my account to cover emergencies?   _____

Do I have a retirement savings plan?   _____

Do I have a Registered Education Savings Plan (RESP)
or pension plan?   _____

Do I have a balance between short and long-term bonds
and term deposits?   _____

Is too much of my money in short-term checking and saving
accounts?   _____

Do I invest to minimize taxes?   _____

BANK ACCOUNT INFORMATION

Name of Financial Institution _____

Address: _____

Account: Saving _____ Checking _____ Account Numbers _____

Name of Financial Institution _____

Address: _____

Account: Saving _____ Checking _____ Account Numbers _____

SAFETY DEPOSIT BOXES

BOX 1:   Location: _____

Key Location: _____

Contents: _____

BOX 2:   Location: _____

Key Location: _____

Contents: _____

Retirement Savings Plan INFORMATION (Attach copies of relevant statements)

NAME _____ LOCATION _____

ACCT NUMBER _____ PHONE NUMBER _____

NAME _____ LOCATION _____

ACCT NUMBER _____ PHONE NUMBER _____

NAME _____ LOCATION _____

ACCT NUMBER _____ PHONE NUMBER _____

NAME _____ LOCATION _____

ACCT NUMBER _____ PHONE NUMBER _____

INVESTMENT INFORMATION (Attach copies of relevant statements)

NAME _____ LOCATION _____

ACCT NUMBER _____ PHONE NUMBER _____

NAME _____ LOCATION _____

ACCT NUMBER _____ PHONE NUMBER _____

NAME _____ LOCATION _____

ACCT NUMBER _____ PHONE NUMBER _____

NAME _____ LOCATION _____

ACCT NUMBER _____ PHONE NUMBER _____

REAL ESTATE

PRINCIPAL RESIDENCE
ADDRESS _____
MORTGAGE HELD BY: _____

OTHER PROPERTY
ADDRESS _____
MORTGAGE HELD BY: _____

ADDRESS _____
MORTGAGE HELD BY: _____

INSURANCE COMPANY _____ POLICY NO. _____

WILLS
LOCATION _____ LAWYER _____ PH. NO. _____

This simple worksheet lets you stay organized and on top of your financial plan. When doing so, you will find that reaching your goals is much easier and very attainable. Organization leads to progress, progress leads to success, and success leads to peace of mind. That is what we all look for during retirement, isn't it?

Next, we will have a short chapter on the reality of your future. I don't know your specific situation, but I want to educate you on the truth you need to know.

HOW SECURE IS YOUR FUTURE?

When looking at your future, there are two things you need to be aware of. One is the reality of poverty in the world. The second is being realistic about your future goals. To start, let's talk briefly about the specter of poverty.

Government statistics show a large percentage of seniors living at the poverty level. Many people find themselves there due to unexpected job loss, out-of-control debts, a business failure, gambling, medical bills, or illnesses. It's not uncommon to see seniors living off the income from their children. It is great to see your children paying you back, but do you want to risk your future on their success? That sounds like a gamble to me.

The specter of poverty can arise to the financially unprepared. This book seeks to prepare for a wealthy future free from that fear. By applying these basic strategies, you will keep yourself free from the poverty line:

- Give yourself a defensive investment program
- Control debts and spending
- Create a systematic savings plan
- Control risks
- Build a solid portfolio

Build a rainy day or defensive fund by reducing your vulnerability to a sudden financial disaster. Once you have achieved this, you can move on to create a luxury fund, a big purchase account, and a debt reduction account. You remember those from our previous chapter on organizing your finances, right?

In addition to applying the above basic strategies, also be aware of your goals. Make sure they are not unrealistic or need to be set higher. Always remember to account for yearly inflation.

We spoke about the retirement gap at the very beginning of the book. The gap is the difference between where you want to be and where you are. Test the gap between where you are now and your future. So how secure is your future after testing?

One thing that will keep you safe is looking at the future today with conservative assumptions. I've found that this strategy keeps me calm, and I am often surprised at how much money I have left at the end of the year—looking back at your financial plan and smiling rather than worrying is always nice.

We have talked about a lot, and we are almost done. To wrap up this section, I want to give you some essential rules to follow and mistakes to avoid. These apply to asking yourself questions about your finances and asking financial advisors about your situation. Below I will explain the essential rules to follow and mistakes to avoid.

During my multiple decades of professional experience and a lifetime of interest in the finance world, there are some secrets I have learned. I would like to dedicate this chapter to passing along those secrets. These will help you avoid some of the significant pitfalls and landmines I have seen. Alternatively, it will guide you down the correct path and speed you to a much quicker financial Endless Harvest. In short, I will summarize some of the main topics discussed throughout this book.

To start, I have eight simple rules I want you to remember when building your Endless Harvest portfolio.

Rules For Building an Intelligent Portfolio

1. Keep most of your investments invested in global or sector equity mutual funds and top-quality stocks.
2. Set specific and written goals.
3. Get your investments organized and simplified.
4. Set up automatic savings plans.
5. Keep a written record of all your investment and personal financial documents.
6. Systematically structure your portfolio.
7. Adjust it regularly.
8. Choose professional financial advisors.

THE SECRETS TO BUILDING A WEALTHY PORTFOLIO

What is a portfolio?

A portfolio is a collection of tradable or sellable assets in a marketplace. It can be stocks, bonds, mutual funds, term deposits, saving accounts, and real estate. Remember that a portfolio consists of different forms of money. Stocks and bonds represent various forms of money. They act as money storage vehicles.

What is money?

Money is commonly mistaken to be a unit of exchange. Money is valuable because it represents a storage vehicle or tangible form of time. Once you have stored enough time in the form of money, you can retire.

What is the purpose of a successful investment?

A successful investment strategy is to create as much passive income as possible.

What is passive income?

Passive income is income you receive from your investments without effort from the owner. Interest income from bonds and term deposits, dividends from stocks and mutual funds, or revenue from investments are examples of passive income.

Active income comes directly from your efforts. Passive income comes from your investments. It happens without any action from the owner. While working, it is vital that you save as much active income and place it into passive income. This is because when you retire, you will rely solely on the income created from your passive income sources.

Let's take a look at your career in a timeline:

Early Career
100% Active Income   0% Passive Income

Middle Career
80% Active Income   20% Passive Income

Later Career
50% Active Income   50% Passive Income

Retired
0% Active Income   100% Passive Income

Why have professional portfolio management?

As we get older, our passive income becomes more and more important since we must live off of this passive income. We must better manage our portfolio to avoid losing our precious portfolio to risks at retirement. We also need to ensure our portfolio works to generate the maximum amount of passive income.

SIMPLIFY, SIMPLIFY, SIMPLIFY

Here is the main question. Do you control your money, or does your money control you? We live in a hectic world. Rush, rush, rush; we spend our lives in a hurry. This book is designed to help simplify your finances and money management. This program has been designed to help you become wealthy for life. That is why this book is titled, *The Endless Harvest*, not just Harvest.

Today we face two main problems. The first is that our lives are too complicated. Our lives are complex since we have too much information, too many tasks, and too many decisions to make. The second problem is that we have too little time to do the things we enjoy. We have to be in ten places at once and often feel unrested. Since we do not get to spend that time doing the things we enjoy, we often do things we do not like to do with our limited free time. This book is designed to teach you how to take on the burden of managing your money and reduce the amount of time you need to spend on your investments.

People's biggest mistake is that they think money management must be complex and difficult. They either avoid it altogether or create extra work by checking their stocks and mutual fund prices daily, having money all over town, and making money management a hassle. This book will help you simplify the money management process.

The Endless Harvest is designed using practical experience with technical and academic research. It is not a system to have no down days. It is not a perfect portfolio that periodically goes up and down. It is a way to create permanent wealth for the long term.

Money management is more of a philosophy than a science. This book uses data and research, but in the end, prosperity and wealth are philosophical beliefs. You can earn millions of dollars and still have not accumulated any permanent wealth. You must set up a program to keep, accumulate, and build your wealth long-term. Earning money is not the same as keeping the money.

COMMON RETIREMENT MISTAKES TO AVOID

Critical Mistake 1: Underestimating the Number of Years in Retirement

When you plan, I always recommend that you make sure the plan extends to age 90. People tell me, "Well, my parents never lived to age 90, and neither did my grandparents." That does not mean you will not live through 90. The big mistake people make is, "I want to retire at 65, and then I am going to throw all my investments in a term deposit earning 2% and be super conservative." Then, they live to be 90 years old and run out of money at age 75.

Part of what I always tell people is to set the timeline long. Set it to age 90, even if your parents died at 65. I do that because the biggest danger we face is longevity risk. Longevity risk is the risk of outliving your money. Most people worry about stock market crashes and terrorism, but the reality is the issue of living longer than your money. Make sure that longevity risk is in your plan.

Critical Mistake 2: Assuming an Unrealistic Rate of Return

The second mistake people make in financial planning is setting the return too high. Many people set their plans at 10% or even 12%. My idea of planning is to have no higher than a 5% return in your plan. If you set aside a 5% return and achieve a 7% return, that is fine—actually, it is excellent. You have more money than you planned.

However, If you plan for 8% and get 5%, you are now short of the money you need for retirement. The biggest mistake financial planning books make is setting the return at 10%. 5% is more realistic. Set your expectation to live to 90 and have a return of 5%. By being conservative, you will have more money than you think.

Critical Mistake 3: Not Updating Your Plan

The other mistake people make is preparing a financial plan once and never looking at it again. They go to a planner, they get a plan done, and 20 years later, that plan did not turn out to be very accurate, and they do not have another plan. My recommendation would be that every two years, at minimum, you should work out a new plan. The plan will show whether the gap is starting to appear or not.

As you keep the plan current, the plan is more accurate. It's kind of like a road map. As the world changes, your map should change a little bit as time goes on; the world changes faster and faster. If your goals were too high and your returns were terrible the last two years, it will show up in the new plan. A plan every two years is the way to go.

If your advisor does not believe in planning, you may want to consider another advisor because planning is the most critical investment element. I'm not talking about which stocks or bonds you own. It is more important to have the right plan for your unique goals.

The plan also allows you to do "course corrections" or "rebalancing." If you are missing your plan goal, you may need to adjust the plan. Maybe you have to save more money, or perhaps you have to work longer. Revise your financial map every two years.

Critical Mistake 4: Not Considering the Impact of Financial Headwinds in Your Retirement Planning

Financial headwinds are adverse events or circumstances that can derail your retirement plan.

Next, we will wrap up *The Endless Harvest* by taking a 10,000-foot view of this material, revising your plan, and putting it into action. This is where you may say, "the rubber meets the road." We've learned much through-out this book, leading to this point.

Here, I invite you to take my hand and take a 360-degree view of *The Endless Harvest* together. Here we get you set up and pointed in the right direction.

HOW TO USE THIS INFORMATION

Today we live in a world of abundance. There are an infinite number of things to buy. Here is the problem. We earn finite or limited amounts of money and limitless ways to spend our money. The formula is simple. Finite or limited ways to make money and infinite places to spend our money. Supply and demand favor spending over earning.

The rule of "Pay Yourself First" must be followed! You must spend less than you make. To have an Endless Harvest, you must find ways to generate the income you need to live the lifestyle you desire.

Debt can be a curse if it controls you. When you are working solely to pay your debts, it can be very depressing. When you spend more than you make, you are moving backward financially. When you spend less than you earn, you move forward by investing even a few dollars a month into permanent wealth.

Stop wasting your money on possessions. Possessions are tangible or physical items that do not generate any income. Often buying that extra lamp, couch, extra set of china, and other consumer items do not make you any happier. They waste your money and clutter up your home. Next time you have a garage sale, it should remind you how worthless most possessions are. With the last garage sale I had, I earned about 5 cents on the dollar for many of the items we sold. This was done simply to reduce the clutter in our home and not for the money. I donated the remaining items to local charities.

Also, poor investors buy liabilities using debt. That is a double negative; no, it does not equal a positive like in multiples with mathematics. They waste their money by borrowing to buy liabilities such as boats, cars, clothes, cigarettes, and alcohol. These are liabilities that decline to zero over time. These items also generate no cash flow of interest, capital gains, or dividends.

Pay yourself first before your bills may seem like a simple rule. Why do so many people not do it if it is so simple? To acquire permanent wealth with your Endless Harvest, you must spend less than you make. Take some of the surplus wealth and invest it into long-term capital.

273

THE 12 STRATEGIES FOR GETTING INCOME FOR LIFE

That being said, let's go into 12 strategies for getting income for life. These are all strategies that have been discussed throughout the book, but I would like to list them here to make things easy. I'll include some numerical data to keep things concrete and "down to earth."

Many retirees are what I call asset-rich and cash-poor. In other words, they have a big house they renovated three times and no money in investments. How will they live on the income generated from their portfolios when they retire? What I try to do is have them restructure. They run their investment portfolios, so we try to maximize the return or the guaranteed yield off every dollar. Every dollar becomes a cash cow that will generate income for them.

If you look at 5% as a target income, which is probably realistic today, anything above that is a gain I would be happy to get. With stock markets crashing up and down for many years now, you must have something you can count on to pay your income and expenses when you retire. That's typically income from four sources.

1. The first source of income is dividends from stocks.
2. The second source is interest from bonds, GICs, and term deposits.
3. The third one is being paid rental income from real estate investment trusts.
4. Finally, the fourth source of income is typically government and private pension plans.

If you add those, they should be ample enough for most people to retire.

Now let me share the 12 Rules for Becoming and Staying Rich. I've been providing financial advice since 1988 and found things that work consistently over those years. Here they are:

Stay Rich #1: Run your investment portfolio like a business.

First, I tell clients, "Run your investment portfolio like a business." A business is run to generate income. Most people run their investment portfolio like a casino. They are trying to gamble and make money by buying this and switching to that. When you retire, you want to run your portfolio like a business. You want to get positive cash flow from the business.

In other words, if I have $1,000,000, I'm trying to get 5% per year out of that portfolio. On $1 million, I made $50,000 a year running that account like a business. I'm getting rid of the stuff that isn't performing. If it isn't generating positive cash flow, it gets replaced with things that have cash flow.

Run your investment portfolio like a business. Most businesses are run on pretty accurate reporting, so one of the things we insist on is giving clients precise reporting.

- How well have you done in the last year?
- How well have you done since we have been together?
- How well have you done in the last seven years?
- What is your income generating on your portfolio each year?
- How much have you put in?
- What is it costing you?

These are the reports we give clients, and we also do a financial plan showing you where you are now and where you will be if you keep doing what you're doing.

It's always good to know how you are doing. In bad times it's good to know how bad you're doing as well as in the good times. "What were you up or down in last year?" We think you know that because if you know it, it's better than not knowing it. Many say, "I don't want to know how bad I'm doing or how well I'm doing." Part of running your investment portfolio like a business is good reporting. Bad news doesn't go away if you ignore it.

On an annual basis, we take out the investments that are not producing any results. In other words, we have an investment that we thought would generate 5% yielding 1%. So we replace that at some point with something generating 5% again. Like a business, if you have a bunch of machines or employees that aren't working out, you change them. So we do change those portfolios actively.

We don't believe you buy and hold something. We believe you buy and hold it unless it's not producing what you want. We're continually improving the result. It is also important to keep costs competitive. Not the lowest necessarily, but competitive in that we don't want costs to be an impediment. We try to make costs part of our formula, like a business.

Stay Rich #2: Change the focus from capital gains to income.

My number two strategy for retirement is to change the focus from capital gains to income. When you focus on capital gains, you are trying to buy something for $10 and sell it for $20. When you get to retirement, that is a risky proposition.

Income is something where you get a check every month for owning something. Let's say you have a rental property and get $1,000 a month from tenants. That's income. Make sure you get that income every month or every year. When you approach your retirement, focus on income. Everything you own must generate some income—ideally 4% to 5%.

Stay Rich #3: Know the difference between assets and capital.

The number three strategy is to know the difference between assets and capital. Many retirees, especially baby boomers, are asset-rich and capital-poor. Assets are things like your home, car, boat, and cabin at the lake. The problem with those is that they don't generate any income.

Capital generates positive capital in dollars and cents. Capital is anything that pays you for owning it; assets are things you own. If you retire with a $1 million home, a $1 million cabin, and $200,000 in cars and other toys but no capital, you are asset-rich and capital-poor. We want to focus on selling or converting things over to generate a 5% minimum return. Capital is the key.

Stay Rich #4: Know the true cost of negative capital.

Number four is to know the true cost of negative capital. Negative capital are the things you own that cost you money. An example of negative capital would be a mortgage. It would be property taxes. It would be interest on your credit card debt or line of credit debt. Negative capital is costly.

Most people aren't aware of negative capital. For example, they buy a house for $400,000, pay it off in 15 years, and pay $200,000 in interest. That is negative capital. We want to reduce negative capital and increase positive capital when approaching retirement. You want to get as much money from your investments as possible and pay as little as possible in interest since you will be living off passive income and not active income.

Stay Rich #5: Stop buying "stuff."

Number five isn't super popular. My number five strategy is to stop buying 'stuff.' In the book The Millionaire Next Door, they talk about the stuff factor. We're drowning in clutter. We have no space in our overfilled homes. Our basements are full of stuff. We can't park our cars in our garages because they are filled with stuff.

Stuff are things you buy that you don't need to buy. Typically, we have too many clothes. We buy too many toys. And what happens when we retire is we don't have enough money saved because we bought too much stuff along the way.

Stay Rich #6: Everything must pay you above the inflation rate.

Number six states that everything must pay you above the rate of inflation. Inflation of about 1% to 2% a year means things will get more expensive yearly by about 1.5%. If you go to your grocery store and buy your meat and bread, it's 1.5% higher than the previous year. So your investments also have to generate a positive return and a return above inflation.

When you project the income you will need at retirement; you must increase it by 1% to 2% a year. Many people think, "I need $4,000 a month to live," but when they retire 20 years from now, they need $5,000. If they don't calculate for inflation, they will struggle to make ends meet. Inflation is a huge and real number, especially if you retire at 60 and live to be 85. Twenty-five years of inflation is a big deal.

Stay Rich #7: Stop or reduce taxes on your investments using retirement savings plans and TFSAs.

My number seven strategy is to reduce taxes on your investments. In Canada, we have RSPs and tax-free savings accounts. These are great vehicles to reduce taxation. Everything in those accounts grows tax-free until you withdraw at some point. So stop paying 10% or 20% taxation on your investments. Put them in those two accounts first.

Once those are maxed out, put them in investments, but try to use the tax shelters first. I think many people are looking for ways to reduce their taxes. Of course, we want to do that, but you have to plan for taxes at the end of the day. If you follow my earlier strategy of running your investments like a business, you will be paying taxes on the income. Think about 20% or more in taxation when you retire.

One thing to consider is paying for a lot of the stuff—house, rent-to-own cars, etc.—while working. Pay for things now so that when you retire, your car is paid for, and you have the house renovated. This way, you aren't taking as much out of your retirement plans at that point.

Stay Rich #8: Do an annual financial plan for gaps between what you desire and what will happen in your retirement.

My number eight strategy for retirement is to do an annual financial plan. You want to know if there is a gap between what you want in retirement and what will happen. If someone says to me, "I want to retire in five years, and I want $4,000 a month," then I do the math and show them whether they can retire or not. More often than not, there's a gap when I do the math for them.

In other words, the person retiring wants to retire at 60 but can't retire at 60 without running out of money. As a result, they need to do a couple of things. They need to either work longer or save more.

Stay Rich #9: Manage risks scientifically.

Strategy number nine is that risks must be scientifically managed as potential losses. In other words, losing money and managing risks scientifically is a key to retiring effectively. Most risks are things people don't know are risks. Not knowing about risk doesn't mean it doesn't exist.

Consider the analogy of gravity. Not believing or understanding how gravity works doesn't reduce the effect of gravity if you walk off a building. The risk is there whether you know it or not. Not understanding financial risks is one of the biggest mistakes most investors make. The most common mistake is underestimating or being unaware of the risks of various investment solutions.

For example, let's take people who have thousands of dollars in a checking account earning zero return, yet they are withdrawing 5% a year. That's a risk. They run out of money, and they don't know why. It's because they had no viable return on their investments.

Stay Rich #10: Maximize the four primary sources of income in retirement.

The number ten strategy is to maximize the four primary sources of income in retirement. Most people work 20, 30, or 40 years in a job or their business, and they are used to earning money every other week. Then the business gets sold, or they retire. They are saying, "I'm used to a paycheck every two weeks. Now I have no paycheck. How do I live now?"

The sources of income shift in retirement from active employment to passive investment income. Two sources of income are government and private pension plans. Those are very helpful; you should always apply for government and private pension income.

Once you receive those, you want to maximize the income from stock dividends. The shares will pay you an income every month or every quarter. You may also want to get bonds that pay interest income.

The last one to look at is real estate investment trusts. It is important only to buy real estate investment trusts that are high quality—with dependable income. They should be paying you rental income 4% to 6%. That will top off your income.

1. You're getting checks from my government pension or private pension.
2. You're getting checks from my stocks.
3. You're getting checks from my bonds.
4. You're getting checks from my real estate investment trust.

That is how you maximize the different income sources. Get rid of anything not paying you at least 3% to 5% in your account. Get rid of anything just sitting there, like a pound of gold sitting in your safety deposit box.

Stay Rich #11: Compound Interest: the 8th wonder of the world.

My number eleven strategy is all about the power of compound interest. Albert Einstein mentioned that the most powerful formula is compound interest. Compound interest is when you get interest from interest. Compound interest is going to provide you with income for life.

If you spend the last compound interest you received in December, starting in January, you get your new checks coming. When those are spent the following January, you get them again. You want to get what is called residual or reoccurring income. That could go on for a sustainable lifetime. You get there by utilizing compound interest.

The negative side of compound interest is if you owe money. So keep the debt low. Especially at retirement, try to have little to no debt because if you're paying out the compound interest on loans, a mortgage, and more, it will dampen your overall lifestyle.

Stay Rich #12: Applying the chicken and the egg principle.

I call retirement strategy number twelve, the chicken and egg principle. If you live off the eggs and don't kill the chickens, you have a sustainable income source for life. The trick is how to access your money without killing the chickens. Your income declines when you start killing your chickens and eating them.

You want to try and take out about 5% a year of your capital. Avoid taking out any more than that. When the stock market is good, the bond market is good, and you can make 10%, but try to keep your income at 5%. That's a very safe number long term. On $500,000, that's $2,000 a month. On $1,000,000, $4,000 a month. These are the strategies to create a sustainable income for life. If you don't touch the principal capital, you never have to worry about running out of money.

In my 30+year career as an investment advisor, I have seen excellent role models of what to do and what not to do. The biggest mistake is to overestimate your ability and knowledge and to underestimate the amount of knowledge and what is then needed to turn cash into income.

Many people without any formal education are now managing their life savings in their basement. That is the most prominent example of what NOT to do. A fraction of people can manage their portfolios correctly. If you are learning how to manage your portfolio in your basement and you find out that you weren't very good, a lot of your life savings will be gone. The big lesson is not to take big investment risks without realizing their risks.

Most people trading their accounts don't understand how much risk they are taking. They don't know how risky their trading strategy is. On the flip side, I had a lady with a disability that stopped her from working, and she handed over her life savings and said to me, "I'd like you to manage this. I need about $3,000 a month, but I don't want to run out. And I will need money once in a while for a wheelchair here and there plus some other drugs and pharmaceutical things."

Over 25 years, living on the income we generated, she had more money than she gave me initially when she died. Plus, she lived all those years off the funds. The thing about income-generating strategies is that it's the only real way. I have seen in 30+ years now where people have built wealth. They have only built wealth through income generation from the portfolio. That is the only way.

When they compounded it rather than spent it, they accumulated a huge portfolio in a relatively short period—short being five to 10 years. That's the key. That's the case study I use to show how it can be done. I've created wealth for dozens and dozens of people and recreated it over and over using the same methodology.

That is going through the main income strategies I talked about. You can call it return on capital or return on the rate of return, but a lot of it is like a snowball rolling down the hill. As the snowball rolls down the hill, it gathers snow and gets bigger and bigger. At the bottom of the hill, it's a gigantic mountain of snow. It's very similar in wealth. Einstein said, "The law of compound interest is the most powerful formula in the universe." Using the power of compound interest has led to many successful retirements in my lifetime.

CONCLUSION

It is crucial to think of money as life energy or life force. Money is valuable because it represents time and the effort needed to earn it. Since we have a finite amount of life and a limited amount of time, money is valuable because of the amount of time in our life that we spend to earn it. Suppose a person makes $40,000 yearly for an after-tax income of $28,000. It would take one year of that person's life to earn money to purchase a $28,000 car.

Money is a storage vehicle for time. Suppose Karen needs $3,000 a month for living expenses. If she saves $3,000, she can take a month off work since she could live off this money for the month. If she has saved $6,000, she can be off work for two months. The primary value of money is as an easy and universally acceptable storage vehicle for time or human labor. If Karen saves $3,000 a year for long enough and invests it correctly, she can eventually retire or not work permanently.

You can also think of it this way. If you earn $36,000 per year ($3,000 per month) and save $6,000 a year, you are banking two months for your retirement—you can retire two months earlier. The more money you save, the more time you are banking and the earlier you can retire.

Even inheritances are storage vehicles for money. A parent or relative spent part of their life working hard to earn this money. (Even though we did not personally have to spend our life energy or time to earn it.) Be careful to invest this money wisely because if you spend this money foolishly, you are spending years of your life earning this money.

For example, a high-earning medical professional earned $150,000 a year for the last five years. She has not saved any money. Since she has not saved anything, she is no closer to retirement than five years ago. It is important to understand that financial independence results only from having some money to cover your living expenses. You cannot take any time off without any money to cover your living expenses. It is not important how much money you earn. It is the amount you save and invest into permanent wealth that matters. Once you do this, it becomes Endless Wealth.

Focus on maximizing, compounding, and reinvesting the cash flow from your investments. Also, invest in income-generating investments.

From all the content in this book, I want you to take away ten ways to get your money to work for you, rather than you working for your money:

1. Separate your temporary wealth from your permanent wealth.
2. Use risk management techniques to reduce unnecessary dangers to your money.
3. Learn to create gardens of wealth to provide income now or in the future.
4. Learn to see your investments as seeds that need to be planted into income-producing assets. (capital)
5. Do not be discouraged if you do not see massive results right away. The results will multiply over time.
6. Sell off non-paying or low-performing assets.
7. Close down all unnecessary bank accounts.
8. Build a network of investment specialists to help you organize and manage your money.
9. Set up an automatic savings account to invest and build your portfolio into multiple diversified investments.
10. Globalize your portfolio.

There are many myths about financial planning. One of the biggest is that you will retire rich if you earn a considerable salary. You can separate your money into two categories by creating a series of accounts. The first category is permanent wealth. This money has to generate your retirement income in the form of dividends, interest, and capital gains. The second category is temporary wealth. This is money that you spend on food and other daily living expenses.

The Endless Harvest is a method vital to properly convert your money into income streams, gardens of wealth, or the money tree concept. These are the same ways of labeling the maximum income portfolios necessary for an endless wealth-income stream at retirement. Many high-income people, such as hockey players, actors, business owners, doctors, dentists, lawyers, etc., have had to work into their old age because they did not understand the importance of an endless wealth system. You will be different.

Your level of wealth is limited only by the level of your knowledge. After reading and understanding this book, you are undoubtedly way ahead of the pack. Investments will evolve, and we have given you a baseline that will never change but does not stop learning. Time keeps going, and trends evolve.

Continuous improvement is one of the core principles of the Toyota Production System. If you can take 1 to 2 hours per week and learn from your mistakes by not making them again, your system will constantly improve. I am encouraging you not to stop your momentum here. Keep pushing forward!

This leads us to the very end of this book. My job is not to make you the most money. My job is to make you the returns you need to live the life you want. By following The Endless Harvest method, you will work towards and live a financially free life.

If you are interested in getting some help, you can always contact me. Connect and message me on LinkedIn:
https://www.linkedin.com/in/johnyamamotoplanning/

I do want to warn you. I am not your guy if you want to make 1000% in the next 30 days. But if you are looking for a successful advisor to follow that has not only walked the road but has guided others towards success, then I would love to talk.

Whether pursuing your Endless Harvest alone, with another advisor, or myself, please take action. Use this book as a compass for your successful future by growing, protecting, and maintaining wealth.

Do not take the basic simplicity of The Endless Harvest for granted. These principles result from years of experience and studying why ordinary people with average income became millionaires at retirement. Conversely, it also explains why some people with huge incomes and salaries retire bankrupt in their later years. Reread these principles until they become part of your money management system.

Lastly, I want to thank you for reading The Endless Harvest humbly. If you enjoyed this book, please share your experience on Amazon. My goal is to help as many people achieve financial freedom as possible. There is no value to you from this book if you don't take action. Start working on your Endless Harvest now.

Sincerely yours, John Yamamoto

ABOUT THE AUTHOR

John believes in training people to become more successful in controlling their financial lives. His mission in life is to help people have better futures. John is not here to help manage your money, and he is here to help manage your future. He is currently writing a series of investment books.

John Yamamoto specializes in creating a risk-adjusted cash flow base with investment strategies. And John has pursued formal business education and earned both a Bachelor of Commerce and a Master's Degree in Business Administration from the University of Alberta in Canada. *2086*

Due to his continued studies, he has earned one of The Canadian Securities Institute's highest levels of education. The Institute has granted him the designation of Canadian Investment Manager (CIM) for his investment, commodities, and options training. John is also a believer in networking. At this time, John is an active member of The Genius Network, The Strategic Coach, Abundance 360, and The Rotary Club.

Personally, John strives to leave the world more prosperous and abundant. He has a strong drive to make the world a healthier place for the lives of future generations. Donating to the Rotary Club, 4 Ocean, and scientific research centers focused on curing polio and cancer are only a few of his charitable contributions. John lives happily in Canada with his wife and daughter.

John believes in the need for investment in education for children in school and adults. My primary short-term goal is to bring the power of cash flow to all investors. Focusing on maximizing positive cash flow and minimizing negative cash flow is critical to your financial success.

Connect with John on LinkedIn:
https://www.linkedin.com/in/johnyamamotoplanning/

Best Age 60
2021

THE ENDLESS HARVEST RULES

Investing Basics

THE ENDLESS HARVEST RULE: To become wealthy for life, you need to create a permanent pool of capital. The capital must generate enough cash flow to fund your lifestyle.

THE ENDLESS HARVEST RULE: Assets are improperly defined as physical possessions such as your car, house, or stamp collection. These are possessions, not assets. The Wealthy know that true assets are anything that generates a return on investment or cash flow.

THE ENDLESS HARVEST RULE: It is dangerous to your financial future to put off saving and investing until some later date. The best time is now. You will always have bills to pay. Start investing. Even pocket change is a great place to start.

ENDLESS HARVEST RULE: Start by setting up a reserve fund of three months to one year of expenses. This will provide you with financial freedom from short-term stresses or financial disasters such as a job loss or unexpected financial expenses.

Become a Cash Flow Millionaire

THE ENDLESS HARVEST RULE: Most portfolios suffer from malnutrition. They are not fed enough cash to grow and provide for retirement.

THE ENDLESS HARVEST RULE: Buy stocks of companies that you admire.

THE ENDLESS HARVEST RULE: «Interest rates reflect the health of the economy—the higher the interest rate, the unhealthier the economy.» John Yamamoto

THE ENDLESS HARVEST RULE: It is important to buy bonds from quality issuers. This helps minimize the risk that the bondholder will not honor their interest payments or go bankrupt before maturity.

THE ENDLESS HARVEST RULE: The best time to buy bonds is during recessions because interest rates are at their highest.

THE ENDLESS HARVEST RULE: Equity mutual funds are generally less risky than individual stocks because they do not have unsystematic risk. This is the risk of losing your money in a stock that goes bankrupt. Mutual funds do not have any insurance or guarantees by the government. The value of mutual funds will fluctuate with the investment held by the fund. Although they fluctuate in value and are not guaranteed, mutual funds cannot go to zero value. To go to zero, all of the assets held by the funds would all have to have zero value. (Extremely unlikely)

THE ENDLESS HARVEST RULE: Never keep all your money in one asset. Especially having your home as your only asset.

THE ENDLESS HARVEST RULE: Investors waste time researching the wrong decisions.

THE ENDLESS HARVEST RULE: Tend your money but make decisions based on reason, not emotions or fear and greed.

How to Stay Rich

THE ENDLESS HARVEST RULE: Avoid surprises by determining how much money you need for your retirement lifestyle.

THE ENDLESS HARVEST RULE: To become financially independent, you must focus on putting your money into assets that appreciate over time. Learn not to confuse depreciating with appreciating assets.

ENDLESS HARVEST RULE: You will never be Permanently wealthy until you:

1. Control your spending
2. Eliminate consumer debts
3. Invest in assets, not possessions

ENDLESS HARVEST RULE: Learn the habit of shopping for capital investments in stocks, ETFs, and mutual funds rather than possessions or stuff.

ENDLESS HARVEST RULE: Since you are less secure after buying that extra item on credit, you are borrowing against the future. By paying off those loans, you are buying back your future earnings.

ENDLESS HARVEST RULE: Pay cash for everything. Think about paying cash as paying for something now. Think about a credit card as borrowing from and hurting your future.

ENDLESS HARVEST RULE: Permanent Wealth =

Conversion of Money to Capital

ENDLESS HARVEST RULE: Permanent Wealth =

Conversion of Temporary Capital to Permanent Capital

How to Manage Millions

THE ENDLESS HARVEST RULE: Be realistic about the amount of money you will need at retirement. It is typically much larger than people expect.

THE ENDLESS HARVEST RULE: You don›t have to be old and rich to do estate planning. Everyone needs an estate plan to benefit their loved ones, not just themselves. Wills, enduring powers of attorney, and personal directives are vital for everyone 18 and over.

THE ENDLESS HARVEST RULE: Have a lawyer write up your will.

THE ENDLESS HARVEST RULE: Buy cars and depreciating items with cash and borrow to buy your investments if you are an aggressive investor.

THE ENDLESS HARVEST RULE: Ask yourself, *Are you making efficient use of your resources? Is there cash in your clutter?*

THE ENDLESS HARVEST RULE: Outliving your money will be the biggest risk to people in the future.

Ask the Right Questions

THE ENDLESS HARVEST RULE: To acquire wealth, you need someone working with you to help keep your finances organized.

THE ENDLESS HARVEST RULE: A mistake people make is to look at financial advisors as being interchangeable. Not all advisors are the same. Take time to find the right advisor for you.

THE ENDLESS HARVEST RULE: It is very difficult to make any money from investing until you get your portfolio organized. Plan, Plan, Plan

THE ENDLESS HARVEST RULE: Don't keep your bonds and stocks at home in a drawer or a safety deposit box. This will lead to clutter.

THE ENDLESS HARVEST RULE: Consolidate your retirement savings plans into one self-directed retirement savings plan. It makes tracking results relatively simple.

THE ENDLESS HARVEST RULE: Take time for a yearly financial tune-up.

THE ENDLESS HARVEST RULE: Hire the right people. No one financial expert can do it all. Have a team: A financial advisor, tax accountant, will and estate lawyer, and banker

GLOSSARY

Averaging Down: Buying more of a security at a lower price than the original investment, thus reducing the average cost per share. E.g., 100 shares at 10 = average share price of $10. If the price drops to $4 and you purchase another 100 shares, the average price of each share is only $7 a share.

Bank Rate: The minimum rate that the Bank of Canada makes for short-term advances to the members of the Canadian Payments Associate, Investment Dealers, and most commonly the chartered banks.

Blue Chip: A stock with a record of continuous dividend payments, is well known nationally, and is active with strong investment qualities.

Bond: A certificate where assets are pledged as security against default. It is a debt where the issuer promises to pay the holder a certain amount of interest over a specific length of time.

Capital Loss or Gain: Loss or profit resulting from a sale of a capital asset with tax consequences.

Cash Flow: The net income of a company for a period of time and any deductions that are not paid out in actual cash, such as depreciation.

Certificate: A document as evidence of ownership of a stock, bond, or other security.

Commission: A fee charged for buying or selling securities or mutual funds on behalf of a client.

Common Stock or Shares: Securities representing ownership in a company that carries voting privileges.

Corporation/Company: A business form with a legal identity separate from its owners created under federal or provincial statutes, usually where the owners have no liability for its debts.

Coupon Bond: A part of a bond certificate that entitles the holder to an interest payment of a specified amount that is clipped and presented upon its due date.

Cyclical Stock: A stock in an industry that is sensitive to swings in economic business cycles.

Debt or Debt Securities: Where the borrower pays interest for the use of the money it borrows off lenders and is obligated to repay it at a set date.

Depreciation: Charges against earnings that write off the cost of an asset over its estimated useful life due to wear and tear etc.

Discount: Amount by which a preferred stock or bond sells below its par value. E.g., a treasury bill is bought at a discount. It matures to be worth $10,000, but the purchaser buys it at $8,800.

Discretionary Account: An account where the client has given specific written authorization to a partner, director, etc., to select securities on his or her behalf.

Diversification: Spreading risk by buying different types of securities and investment products. For example, 50% bonds and 50% stocks.

Dividend: Money distributed to shareholders out of company profits in proportion to the number of shares they own.

Fundamental Analysis: A form of security analysis that is based on fundamental facts on a company like sales, earnings, level of debt, and other tangible, measurable facts.

Guaranteed Investment Certificate (Term Deposit): Available from trust companies that requires a minimum deposit at a predetermined rate of interest for a stated term. Usually not redeemable before maturity.

Interest: Money paid to a lender by the borrower for the use of his or her money.

Liquidity: From the investment point of view, it means the ease of selling an asset. It depends on the ability of the market to absorb the market. In non-investment terms, it means the corporation's current assets to current liabilities.

Margin: Credit offered by a broker based on the securities in the account as collateral on the loan. The exact percentage of money loaned depends on the firm and the quality of the investment. Penny stocks are sometimes not marginable.

Maturity: Date at which the bond or debenture is due and becomes cash.

Money Market: Short-term debt instruments like Treasury bill, Term Deposits, etc., with a year or less to mature.

Mutual Fund: Money pooled by individuals to be invested on their behalf, usually in a specific kind of investment such as common shares, mortgages, or money market instruments. well-run

Net Worth: Is the difference between assets and liabilities.

Offer: The lowest price that a person will be willing to sell. A bid is the highest price that one is willing to buy.

Penny Stock: These are low-priced, usually under $3, which are speculative issues. Usually do not pay dividends.

Portfolio: Different holdings of securities such as bonds and stocks.

Premium: The amount by which a stock or bond may sell above its par value.

Price Earnings (Price-Earnings Ratio) Ratio: A common stocks market price divided by the annual earnings per share.

Prospectus: A legal document that describes the details surrounding the security being offered to the public.

Real Rate of Return: The stated or nominal rate of interest less inflation and taxation.

Registered Retirement Income Plan (RRIF): Used when a retirement savings plan is to be converted by the owner for the purpose of earning income.

Registered Retirement Savings Plan (RRSP): It is a government-approved tax-sheltered plan to help you save for retirement. All growth is tax-free within the plan. Any money up to set limits is tax-deductible directly against income.

Short Sale: An aggressive strategy where the security is sold by a seller who does not own the security. You must always declare a short sale at the time of placing the order.

Strip Bonds: High-quality federal or provincial government bonds where some or all of the interest coupons have been detached. The remainder is traded separately from the strip coupons.

T-bill or Treasury Bill: Are short-term, usually a year and under in maturity. Available in 30, 60, 90, six-months, and one-year terms. Minimum denominations vary but are usually $5000 to $1,000,000 in size. They are sold at a discount, which is when you buy them at a discount, and with interest accumulating mature at par. For example, you might pay 8,200 for a 10,000 dollar 1-year T-bill.

APPENDIX

Building Wealth in the '90s, Gordon Pape, Prentice Hall Canada, 1992.

Wealth without Risk, Charles J. Givens, Stoddart Publishing Ltd., 1991.

The Canadian Securities Course, Published By the Canadian Securities Institute, Toronto, 1993 Edition.

Canadian Securities Institute, Canadian Insurance Course Textbook, Toronto, Ontario, 2002.

The Money Coach, Riley Moynes, Copp, Clark, Pitman Ltd., 1992.

The Canadian Securities Course, Published by the Canadian Securities Institute, Toronto, 1987/88 Edition.

Boom, Bust and Echo, David Foot and Daniel Stoffman, Macfarlane, Walter and Ross, Toronto, 1996.

Tax Planning For You And Your Family 1997, KPMG, Carswell Thomson Professional Publishing, Scarsdale, Ontario, 1997.

The K-wave, David Knox Barker, Profiting from the cyclical booms and busts in the general economy. Irwin Publishing, 1995.

Riding the Business cycle, William Houston, How six climatic and economic cycles are changing our lives, Little, Brown and Company, 1995.

The Craft of Investing, John Train, HarperCollins Books, 1994.

Investment Psychology Explained, Martin J. Pring, John Wiley & Sons Inc., 1993.

The Money Masters, John Train, HarperCollins Books, 1980.

Understanding Wall Street, J. Little, Lucien Rhodes, Liberty Publishing Company, Maryland, U.S.A., 1980.

The Complete Idiots Guide to Personal Finance For Canadians, B. McDougall, M. Reardon, Prentice Hall, Canada, 1997.

Fundamentals of Investing, RBC Dominion Securities, Private Clients Service, 1998.

25 Myths you've got to avoid if you want to manage your money right, Jon Clements, Simon and Shuster, N.Y., 1998.

Introducing Chaos, Z. Sardar, I. Abrams, Icon Books, Cambridge, UK, 1999.

The Great Boom Ahead, Harry S. Dent Jr., Hyperion, New York, New York, 1993.

Roaring 2000's, Building the wealth and lifestyle you desire in the greatest boom in history, Harry S. Dent Jr., Simon and Schuster, New York, NY, 1998.

The Strategic Coach Tools, Can Sullivan, Toronto, Ontario, 2000.

Investing Secrets of the Masters, Babin and Donovan, McGraw Hill, New York, 2000.

Contrarian Investment Strategies: The Next Generation by David Dreman, 1998, Simon and Schuster Performance of the Dow Jones Industrial Average through 11 major post-war crises.

Microsoft® Encarta® Reference Library 2004. © 1993-2003 Microsoft Corporation.